EARTH CAPITALISM

EARTH CAPITALISM

Creating a New Civilization through a Responsible Market Economy

Compiled by the
Goi Peace Foundation

Patrick U. Petit, editor

With a foreword by **Bill Gates**

Routledge
Taylor & Francis Group
LONDON AND NEW YORK

First published 2009 by Transaction Publishers

Published 2017 by Routledge
2 Park Square, Milton Park, Abingdon, Oxon OX14 4RN
711 Third Avenue, New York, NY 10017, USA

Routledge is an imprint of the Taylor & Francis Group, an informa business

Library of Congress Catalog Number: 2010024623

Library of Congress Cataloging-in-Publication Data

Earth capitalism / [edited by] Patrick U. Petit.
p. cm.
Includes bibliographical references and index.
ISBN 978-1-4128-1106-4 (alk. paper) -- ISBN 978-0-202-36355-4 (alk. paper)
1. Environmental economics. 2. Capitalism--Environmental aspects. 3. Social entrepreneurship. 4. Social responsibility of business. 5. Sustainability. I. Petit, Patrick Uwe.

HC79.E5E15 2010
330.12'2--dc22

2010024623

ISBN 13: 978-1-4128-1106-4 (pbk)

Companies are meant to serve society, not the other way around; and companies that do not—and are not seen to—serve society will fail.

Stephan Schmidheiny
Businessman and Philanthropist

CONTENTS

B. Towards a Responsible Market Economy

PART II: INNOVATING NEW ECONOMIC PRACTICES FOR SUSTAINABILITY

A. The Role of Business in Sustainable Development and Peace-Building

Foreword

Innovating for a Better World

Bill Gates

When some people look at the world today, they see disease, poverty, and ignorance. It is not hard to understand why. There is too much suffering. There is too little peace. Modern communication including the Internet makes it easier to see the suffering that still exists. But I believe that these observers are missing the key trend.

The fact is, any way you look at it—in terms of millennia, centuries, or decades—the world is getting better. Healthier. Wealthier. More educated. More peaceful.

Archaeologists have shown that in ancient societies where tribal warfare was the norm, the chances that a man would die at the hand of another man were often above 25 percent, and sometimes as high as 50 percent. In the 20th century in Europe and the United States, however, the chances are somewhere close to one percent. And that's despite two World Wars.

Not quite 50 years ago, in 1960, 70 million babies were born, and 20 million children died. In 2007, 130 million babies were born, and 10 million children died. In short, even though the number of births has almost doubled, the number of children's deaths has been cut in half.

That is surely humanity's greatest achievement in the past 50 years. Saving lives needs no justification, of course. It justifies itself. But better health has a multiplier effect. As health improves, life improves in every way. Income goes up. Literacy goes up. Ultimately, good health is the cornerstone of a peaceful society.

Now, 10 million children dying is still 10 million too many. The goal is zero. But if the world already saved 10 million children, it can save 10 million more.

I think it's important to recognize the progress that we've made, because it puts the future in a slightly different perspective. The context for the work we must do is not a string of failures. It is a long-term trend of success. And innovation is the main reason for that success. As the world contends with an economic crisis, innovation will continue to spur success, as long as we don't forget the people whose lives are difficult even in the best of times.

Innovations in communications technology have shrunk the world dramatically. Computers connect us all in an ever-tightening network. We can now text message, e-mail, and videoconference with people in an instant, and all over the world. On the Internet, we can see photos and video minutes after they're taken.

The old saying that we are all in this together has never seemed so real. People have always believed in bonds of mutual responsibility. That's just human nature, to help others. But now we can see how far those bonds extend. They tie us not just to the people on our block or in our city, but also to people in countries we'll never set foot in.

So technology has brought new people and new problems to our attention. And it is also helping us solve those very problems. Every day, advances in science and technology are making it possible to save lives in entirely new ways. To diagnose and cure disease. To prevent disease in the first place.

Innovation doesn't have to be high-tech. It can be a better way to deliver medicine to hard-to-reach places. A smarter way to help small farmers get their crops to market. A more strategic way to encourage financial institutions to work with poor clients.

All these innovations are ongoing. We will continue to learn more about what needs to be done. We will continue to be able to do more.

Our task is to see to it that innovation is pointed in the right direction. To make sure that the best minds apply themselves to solving the most important problems. Because it doesn't happen automatically.

Let's take the example of malaria, which we all know is one of the world's worst diseases, especially for small children.

Yet the world spends substantially more on curing baldness than on curing malaria. That's a market failure. Nobody dies from baldness, but a lot of people are both willing and able to pay for any improvement there. There are hundreds of millions of people who would be willing to pay for life-saving malaria treatments, if only they could afford to. I am certain that we all agree that malaria should be far, far ahead of baldness on the world's list of priorities.

So what can we do to make sure that we're innovating on challenges like malaria in proportion to the need? Philanthropy has an important role to play, and at the Gates Foundation we're working with many partners on solutions. But we realize that we can only be part of the answer.

First, governments must lead the effort. They are the primary source of the world's money to face the challenges of the developing world. Japan has made a good start through the G8 process. In 2000, it helped create the Global Fund for AIDS, Tuberculosis, and Malaria. The Global Fund is a major innovation in global health financing. It is already the biggest funder of malaria programs in the world.

Second, research institutions must encourage their smartest scientists to focus on the most important problems. These institutions are the primary source of the world's ideas. At the Gates Foundation, we started an initiative called Grand Challenges Explorations, which gives small grants to help scientists test radical new ideas with the potential to revolutionize global health. We're placing bets on untested but provocative theories because real progress comes from path-breaking thinking. We announced our first round of winners in October 2008, and three of them are Japanese scientists.

One of the grantees is Hiroyuki Matsuoka of Jichi Medical University. Professor Matsuoka's idea is simply breathtaking. The way people get malaria is from a mosquito bite. But Professor Matsuoka envisions a mosquito that, when it bites you, delivers a vaccine against malaria, instead of the disease itself. Essentially, he hopes to turn the mosquito into a flying syringe.

Another winner is Hiroshi Kiyono of the University of Tokyo. Professor Kiyono is trying to create a new kind of vaccine that people can administer all by themselves. All you have to do is swallow a dose. It doesn't have to be refrigerated. It doesn't have to be injected by a health professional with a syringe. These breakthrough innovations are still in the very earliest stages of discovery, but they have the potential to change the lives of hundreds of millions of people.

Third, businesses must provide the entrepreneurial talent to get things done. Businesses are the primary source of the world's expertise. And that expertise can be used to develop and deliver products for global health. For example, one of the best tools we have for preventing malaria is insecticide treated bed nets. And experts at Sumitomo Chemical are building a better bed net.

Sumitomo's net has insecticide infused in its fibers. Nobody has to spray insecticide on the net, and the insecticide can't wash off. That means the net can last for five years, which is much longer than most other nets. Sumitomo has licensed its technology to a local manufacturer in Tanzania, and it's working closely with African governments to make sure that these nets are delivered to the families that need them.

These are just a few examples of the important work that researchers and companies are doing. We all need to do more.

I know that, as I ask for more, the world is in the midst of an economic crisis. It may be tempting for governments to concentrate exclusively on domestic concerns. It may seem appealing to businesses to limit expenses that aren't deemed essential.

But this is a global economic crisis, and the fact that it's global ought to reinforce the message that it is not wise to turn inward.

In our world, governments, businesses, and philanthropists in every country are inextricably tied to each other. The only long-term strategy for economic health is more cooperation and more innovation. Indeed, the combination of cooperation and innovation is the path to peace.

Governments, especially rich governments, must be more generous. Universities must devote more resources to cutting-edge research, not less. Philanthropists need to provide more for the needs of the poorest. Business must be more creative. Especially now.

If everybody plays their part, then the world will keep getting better. And we will be able to look back in 50 years and say that we saved hundreds of millions of lives. We will be able to say that ours was truly a century of peace.

Preface

Patrick U. Petit

The world faces the gravest financial and economic crisis since the Great Depression. The deepening global recession is dragging down all kinds of businesses with no bottom in sight. Inappropriate macroeconomic policies and excessive expansion of financial institutions in the blind pursuit of profit, the lack of self-discipline among financial institutions and the failure of supervision and regulation to keep up with financial innovations—these are some factors cited as the main causes of the current global economic malaise. However, they are rather the symptoms. The root causes lie within capitalism itself—its dogma and ideology incorporated into societies by its various players such as producers and consumers, entrepreneurs and managers, investors and shareholders, debtors and creditors.

Trying to regulate capitalism and its institutions or turning to national protectionism are superficial policies and inefficient attempts to fix the global financial and economic slump.

This crisis should rather be considered an invitation to reassess our role in upholding capitalism, and a chance to recreate the global market economy, which we have lost control of. What is the state of our personal greed and insatiability for wealth, money, goods and power? How deep are we identifying ourselves with them as the source of our self-esteem and self-love? How much more are we still yearning for to compensate a feeling of emptiness within ourselves? And how far are those values the core of our happiness? Isn't the 'pursuit of happiness' more than the accumulation of wealth and power? Or perhaps the state of happiness has nothing to do with money and power.... These are very pertinent questions we should sincerely ask ourselves in these times of economic instability.

I truly believe that greed and insatiability are a human malady and the true source of disparities around the world. They have created violent conflicts and poverty over more than a century. Greed is the reason why we are depleting the Earth's natural resources and destroying its ecosystems. By doing so, we have lost the awareness that we sacrifice human relationships and threaten the survival of the Earth's living species and systems, not to mention our own species. We are so much consumed to satisfy our hunger for more with the hope of finding happiness and peace of mind.

However, happiness does not cost the Earth. People can live happy lives without consuming large amounts of the Earth's resources. The New Economics Foundation in London has released a 178-nations "Happy Planet Index" (HPI) study that shows that "we should not sacrifice human relationships, which are the main source of happiness, for the sake of economic growth." The index is based on consumption levels, life expectancy and happiness, rather than national economic wealth measurements such as GDP, which is "outdated, destructive and doesn't deliver a better quality of life." According to this study, nations which score well show that it is possible to produce high levels of well-being without excessive consumption of the planet's resources. It is interesting to note that, while many small island nations perform very well, the G8 countries perform badly on the HPI.

The Happy Planet Index suggests to us that we have to readjust our lifestyles. A good life is based on a balanced give-and-take principle. When we take something from society or the Earth, we have to maintain a balance by giving something equivalent back to them. Happiness is founded on gratitude and an overall appraisal of life. Giving back is an expression of gratitude and respect for life. It is legitimate to make profits and accumulate wealth through economic activities, but in order to create balance and harmony we have to give a share of those profits and wealth for the benefit of society. Important is that we do it on a voluntary basis. The same principle applies for the management of the Earth's natural resources and goods. Indigenous peoples have always upheld this wisdom and basic principle, which keep all life in balance and harmony. They know well how to manage the Earth's economy and wisely harmonize with the Earth's ecological systems. Unfortunately, most of us have separated ourselves from our natural environment and from our true nature. The way we deal with our environment is indeed the reflection of how we perceive ourselves.

The current global crisis urges us to create a responsible capitalism, which benefits all living beings on this planet. It reminds us to live a simpler life based on true well-being and life-satisfaction. Simple living is not about living in poverty or self-inflicted deprivation. It is about—in the words of Duane Elgin, author of *Voluntary Simplicity*—"living in a way that is outwardly simple and inwardly rich."

This book, *Earth Capitalism: Creating a New Civilization through a Responsible Market Economy,* presents some of the leading edge economic concepts, business models and best practices toward the creation of responsible capitalism—a viable scenario to emerge from the current severe global economic and financial crisis.

The Goi Peace Foundation would like to extend its heartfelt gratitude to the distinguished authors and organizations, which have contributed to this book. These exemplary leaders are but a few of the hundreds of business organizations and networks around the world that are contributing to the evolution of our economic system and civilization at large. Their innovative ideas and creative initiatives are an invaluable source of inspiration and motivation for humanity as it seeks to find a way forward and achieve a sustainable and prosperous world for all. Now is the time for the global community to come together as one and co-create an all inclusive, dynamic Earth Capitalism.

Munich
Summer 2009

Introduction

Hiroo Saionji

The Goi Peace Foundation is pleased to present this publication as a part of its Initiative for Creating a New Civilization.

The Creating a New Civilization Initiative, which our foundation launched together with our partners in 2005, brings together organizations and individuals who see the pressing need to respond to the environmental, social and economic crises confronting us today. Our aim is to network various innovative activities and people creating positive impact on the world, and build a critical mass of humans that could facilitate the transformation of our cultures and co-create a sustainable and harmonious planetary civilization based on reverence for all life, respect for our diversity, gratitude for nature, and emphasis on spiritual values.

As a way to synthesize fresh approaches toward creating a new civilization, the Goi Peace Foundation proposes the "4-S Concept"—an integrated platform with four foundational pillars: Sustainability, Systems, Science and Spirituality.

The first "S"—Sustainability—concerns the survival of the Earth itself, with its nature and ecological systems. Environmental, social and economic problems—such as global warming, resource depletion, wealth disparity and cross-cultural conflicts—are all interconnected global issues caused by human activities that are threatening our very survival. We are at a bifurcation point where we either continue on the present path toward destruction or choose the path to a sustainable future.

The second "S"—Systems—refers to the various systems we human beings have established, including our economic and political systems. Humanity is a part of the larger natural living systems of Earth. How can we harmonize our human systems with the principles of nature and the ecosystems? Our current institutions and various sociocultural systems are unsustainable and need to be transformed to operate as a whole system on a planetary scale.

The third "S"—Science—is an important component in creating a new civilization. At the cutting edge of the sciences—including physics, cosmology, the life sciences, and consciousness research—new world-views are emerging together with a deeper understanding of life. These new sciences could bring about a paradigm shift that could be the key inspiration and foundation for building a new civilization.

The forth and final "S"—Spirituality—includes personal experience, but also has a more universal implication. The inner awakening and the empowered creativity of individuals are the real forces that will shape our collective future. Our behaviors and priorities will drastically change if we evolve our consciousness to a higher level and experience the interconnectedness of all life. We must ensure that all human activities in our future global society, whether politics, economics or business, are founded on spiritual values.

These four components are obviously interdependent. Our immediate task is to transform our systems in order to move beyond the imminent crises and ensure sustainability of our planet. At the same time, we must broaden our perspective to see the larger story of who we are and where the next stage of human evolution will lead us.

In 2008, The Goi Peace Foundation published a book entitled *Earthrise: The Dawning of a New Civilization in the 21st Century,* highlighting pioneer organizations in diverse fields that are paving the path for the emerging new civilization.

To further the initiative, we present our latest publications under the following titles:

- *Earth Capitalism: Creating a New Civilization through a Responsible Market Economy*
- *Creating a New Civilization through Social Entrepreneurship*

These volumes offer some concrete strategies and practices for creating a new civilization. They come out at a particularly appropriate time, when the current global financial and economic crises are causing widespread anxiety, and at the same time affirming our conviction that this is the unprecedented opportunity for change.

Earth Capitalism compiles articles by forward-thinking scientists, economists, business leaders and social activists with strategic visions for a more just and sustainable world. It introduces concepts for a new economic paradigm supported by concrete ideas for alternative models of economy and innovative ways in which future business may be conducted.

Creating a New Civilization through Social Entrepreneurship highlights the global movement of social entrepreneurship and some of the leading organizations that are advancing this citizen sector movement. While looking at this social trend in the context of a larger global transition we are currently going through, the volume also presents examples of innovative individuals that are tackling major social problems and triggering systemic change.

The core message repeated throughout both books is that in order to solve the complex global problems of today, it is not enough to simply patch up the existing civilization founded on an old paradigm. If we are to construct a better and promising future for all, we need to change our thinking and acting, adopting new values, priorities and deep wisdom.

Throughout the past century, we human beings mostly valued material things, and strove to create materially affluent lives for ourselves. We focused our efforts and energy into development and production, promoting lifestyles governed by speed, greed, and consumerism. While this materially oriented preoccupation fostered a great expansion of material civilization, we now know we can no longer continue on this way. We must shift our focus on the outer and material world to the development of our inner spiritual world. It is time we stop and rethink what is truly valuable and what real happiness is for humanity.

The articles you will read in these two volumes tell us that there are a growing number of people around the world who have awakened to altruistic values and planetary consciousness and are actively carrying out their mission as a responsible member of the global community. As social entrepreneurs and business leaders, they are optimizing their innovative minds and creative power to serve society, giving new meaning to capitalism and democracy.

We hope that the reading will ignite the love, courage and compassion and the entrepreneurial spirit in you, so that you may play your unique role in creating a new civilization. Now more than ever, each one of us is called upon to become an agent for positive change.

Tokyo
Summer 2009

PART I

THE ECONOMIC PARADIGM FOR AN EARTH IN BALANCE

A. THE FUTURE OF CAPITALISM

Reforming Markets Globally and the Role of Social Innovation for Sustainability

Hazel Henderson

The Roots of Economic Globalization

Since the economic globalization, deregulation and privatization of the 1980s, much has been made of the idea of market reforms. The World Bank, the IMF, the WTO and countless business and political leaders have advocated such market reforms—meaning opening borders to "free trade," deregulation, privatizations of publicly owned companies and natural resources, floating currencies and opening capital accounts known as "the Washington Consensus."

After the Asian financial meltdowns of 1997–98, and the misapplication of these "market reforms" by the IMF, these conventional economic textbook recipes for economic development became widely discredited—most evidently in Latin America. Many developing countries, particularly in Africa, look to China as a model, which survived the Asian crises unscathed by pursuing policies diametrically opposite to the Washington Consensus. Latin Americans look to the European Union as a model as they seek to integrate their countries' economies, trade, resources and stock markets. Meanwhile, most countries North, South, East and West still search for more sustainable forms of human development that can bring greater peace, social justice and wisdom in stewarding the Earth's living ecosystems—the basis of all wealth (see my *21st Century Strategies for Sustainability,* Foresight, UK, Feb. 2006).

The evolution of our human species and our successive innovations from nomadic tribes to agriculture to industrialization was founded on our genius for bonding, trust and cooperation, as many re-evaluations of Charles Darwin's *Origin of Species* (1859) and *The Descent of Man* (1871) have now revealed. This cooperation led humans to congregate in villages, towns, cities, corporations and labor unions. Cooperation led humans to regional compacts like the European Union and MERCOSUR and the international order of today. Our preeminent social innovation is the United Nations and all its ancillary organizations and their ethical and altruistic mandates: universal health, education, human rights, environmental stewardship and peace. Neuroscientists, endocrinologists and psychologists now have found that the biological basis for this cooperation includes the function of mirror cells in human brains which allow imagination, innovation and empathy and other modes of social learning as well as the hormone oxytocin, which increases in mothers to facilitate the nurture of their young.

Charles Darwin would not have been surprised at these later discoveries since he held that human survival mandated cooperation. He expected that altruism among humans would extend beyond family and tribe to a wider ethic among peoples. Adam Smith also expected the evolution of moral behavior among humans in both his *Theory of Moral Sentiments* (1759) and the better-known *The Wealth of Nations* (1776). Both Charles Darwin and Adam Smith also recognized the evolutionary importance of competition for fostering robust species and to spur creativity and innovation. Yet, both realized that competition occurred within broader contexts of human cooperation. We see this clearly with the world's major corporations, with their intricate global supply chains of smaller companies orchestrating the production of everything from airplanes to fashions, furniture and toys.

So, where did the discipline of economics go astray, departing from these understandings, with its over-emphasis on competition? Whence came economics' general ignoring of cooperation, sharing and trust to which Charles Darwin attributed our success as a species?

The phrase which became the dominant meme in economic texts was "the survival of the fittest." Often attributed to Darwin, the phrase was actually coined by Herbert Spencer in his *Principles of Biology* in 1864. Seized on by the English elites in that Victorian era, "the survival of the fittest" became their rallying cry and justification for their privilege and led to the pervasive spread of "Social Darwinism." This pernicious, selfish philosophy was thus attributed to Darwin and permeates neoclassical economics. Only recently have scholars set the record straight, for example, social scientist David Loye in his Darwin's *Lost Theory of Love* (2000) and others.

Not until 2005 did *The Economist* take editorial responsibility for "that poisoned phrase, 'survival of the fittest'" and their over-promotion of competition in economic theories while underplaying the equally important role of cooperation in human affairs (*The Economist,* lead editorial, Dec. 20, 2005). As one who has delved deeply and written much about how economics went astray, I came to pinpoint how this faulty discipline of economics also downplayed the social and environmental consequences of its focusing on self-interest and competition. This "externalizing" of such costs to society and future generations was key in steering societies off course toward un-sustainability. I began to see economics, never a science, as a dysfunctional strand of cultural DNA which kept replicating and reinforcing regressive human behavior: from mistrust and selfishness to competition, greed, envy and acquisitiveness—almost all the deadly sins warned against in religious traditions. Societies guided by such economics were leading our small planet to conflict over resources and even global economic warfare ("Building a Win-Win World," Henderson, 1996).

Civic Society Rises to Defend Higher Values and Ethics

As I wrote, traveled and lectured around the world, sharing these views, I earned scorn, anger and ridicule from most of the economics profession and many business leaders. A corporate public relations journal in the 1970s called me the most dangerous woman in America. Yet, I came to believe that conventional economics, still taught in thousands of business schools and universities, promoted by think tanks, business associations and their political allies, was indeed the ubiquitous, malfunctioning source-code inserted into the hard-drives of most institutions and human minds. Increasingly, this narrow economic ideology, devoid of ecological wisdom and lacking human compassion, was spreading around the world in the policies of the Washington Consensus. I feared that, if not challenged by other more inclusive values and ethics, globalization driven by such "neo-liberal" economic ideology would undermine other vital human values and over-exploit every local social system and ecosystem on the planet.

Thus, my years of environmental and social activism informed my books, from co-founding Citizens for Clean Air in New York in 1964 and the Friends of Channel 13 Public Broadcasting Station and serving on the National Committee for Public Broadcasting, chaired by Norman Cousins; starting Environmentalists for Full Employment in 1970; to my appointment to the Technology Assessment Advisory Council to the US

Congress and the National Science Foundation from 1974 to 1980. In 1982 I accepted the invitation of the Calvert Group to join the Advisory Council of their socially responsible mutual fund. Beyond civic activism, I believe that economics should be challenged at its core by market actors who espoused social and environmental values beyond the single bottom line of maximizing financial returns to investors.

The birth of the socially responsible investment movement in the 1970s, with the launch of Pax World Fund, challenged the "market reforms" touted by the Washington Consensus and, instead, began the task of reforming markets themselves. The broader values of society were expressed in socially responsible investing as the "triple bottom line" (economic, social and environmental), developed by the Global Reporting Initiative consortium and spread worldwide. Our movement now embraces many trillions of dollars in dozens of countries, hundreds of unit trusts, pension funds, private equity and even hedge funds, as well as millions of individual investors. This growing movement has swept aside the "single bottom line" economics best described by the late Milton Friedman, winner of the first Bank of Sweden Prize in Economics, in the 1960s, lobbied onto the Nobel Awards to legitimize economics as a science.

Socially responsible investors, organized in coalitions including the Global Reporting Initiative, the Carbon Disclosure Project (representing $57 trillion of assets), the CERES Principles, the UN Principles of Responsible Investing ($15 trillion), the Social Investment Forum, the Equator Principles, the UN Global Compact, Brazil's Instituto Ethos, as well as consulting firms including SustainAbility, AccountAbility and Social Accountability International, now confront traditional thinking, company management and investment practices in all the world's stock markets. Some stock exchanges have made new listings, such as London's FTSE4Good, Dow Jones' Sustainability Group and New York's Domini Social 400 Index, now followed by many new indexes of cleaner, greener companies, solar, wind and renewable energy stocks.

Brazil's main stock exchange, BOVESPA, has produced a major social innovation: their Social Stock Market with a special electronic board, listing all of Brazil's most worthwhile charitable organizations and inviting market traders and investors to make social investments in addressing Brazil's social concerns. The fact that they do, and that these charities receive generous funding from such "social investments," attests to the broader human values and ethics of market players. Ethical Markets Media, LLC, my company, together with our Brazilian partners, are designing a Green Brazil Index to steer socially responsible investors toward helping build sustainable development in that country.

Challenging Mainstream Media

We are beginning to see the transition worldwide from fossil-fueled industrialism to the cleaner, renewable, sustainable economies of the future which I forecast in my *The Politics of the Solar Age* (1981, 1988). Yet, today all countries, whether democracies or dictatorships, have become "mediocracies," where media trumps all other groups, even governments in shaping public opinion. Meanwhile, mainstream mass media were also becoming market movers with 24-hour daily financial TV shows which helped transmit both stock market movements, bubbles and contagious financial crises around the world in real time. They were all funded and firmly entrenched in the fossil-fueled sectors and their advertising, while their paradigm was rooted in the "single bottom line" of obsolete economic texts. These media, even public broadcasters, could not see the shoots of the green economy sprouting up everywhere and dismissed the new "green" technologies and entrepreneurs as unrealistic "hippies" or "tree huggers." Meanwhile, fossil fuel and nuclear industry groups spent millions on advertising campaigns to deny the science of global climate change and promote more nuclear power and "clean" coal.

By 1997, I was convinced that mainstream media would be incapable of reporting accurately on the emerging trends in the global economy. Firstly, they were blinded by the conventional economic paradigm; secondly, due to the entrenched interest groups that controlled their advertising; and thirdly, because mainstream media had become a vast echo-chamber, moving markets and re-enforcing the past. I began creating the TV series "Ethical Markets" with topics, treatments and scripts for 45 initial half-hour programs to present the widest picture of the emerging cleaner, greener technologies, companies and NGOs, building this coming Solar Age. At first, I hoped to have a new Canadian TV channel air the series, but in spite of their enthusiasm, they were unable to operationalize their vision for a TV channel for "We the Peoples of the Earth."

So, with some TV experience from producing my series "Creating Alternative Futures" with the Public Broadcasting System's affiliate WUFT-TV at the University of Florida in 1983, I decided to launch "Ethical Markets" as a TV series for the PBS network in the USA. Ethical Markets Media, LLC, was incorporated as a hopefully for-profit, social enterprise in 2003, with expectations of finding some like-minded social investors to join me and my partner, Alan F Kay, the internet pioneer and mathematician who developed the methods of public interest polling (see *Locating Consensus for Democracy* in 1998 and *Militarist, Millionaire, Peacenik* in 2008). I and my co-producer Ellyne Lonergan, president of Glass Onion Productions, had hoped to find some socially responsible mutual funds and a few similar companies to sponsor the "Ethical Markets" TV series, but it was not to be. Our policy of screening all companies who might be sponsors or featured on "Ethical Markets" by all the most rigorous social, environmental and ethical auditing standards was simply unheard of. The clean, green companies that qualified were too small to afford advertising.

Adding to our difficulties, the PBS network was coming under the spell of the Bush administration with independent voices and programs such as those of Bill Moyers, being hounded as "left-leaning." Our essential mission statement was a challenge: "to reform markets by showcasing companies, entrepreneurs and asset managers embodying the highest social, environmental and ethical standards and by broadcasting their best practices globally on TV, to keep raising the bar on standard-setting worldwide." We knew we would not pass the Administration's "economic thought police" or the watchdogs at PBS headquarters. The only PBS series on business were the traditional "Wall Street Week" and "Nightly Business News," neither of which covered socially responsible investing or cleaner, greener companies.

We went ahead, producing the first thirteen shows with our own funds and small contributions from two friends, after an initial $100,000 grant from the Ford Foundation for our pilot, with the assistance of famed TV producer Alvin Perlmutter. We hired Executive Program Services, an independent firm of former PBS program managers who help independent producers find airtime on progressive PBS-affiliated stations—bypassing the Corporation for Public Broadcasting bureaucracy. Amazingly, these first 13 TV shows delivered by satellite free to PBS stations were picked up and reached some 44% of the PBS audience nationwide. Our 2007 TV special, "Growing the Green Economy" reached 49% of all US TV households. Yet, we were unable to air on New York's Channel 13 or Boston's WGBH, neither of which care for independent productions.

By 2006, I realized that the internet was the future for independent media. Our EthicalMarkets.com website began reaching its own audience of socially responsible investors and concerned citizens. In the same year, we produced and I moderated another five TV shows on "International Financial Reform" with my friends John Perkins, author of *Confessions of an Economic Hitman* (2004), Sakiko Fukudu-Parr, lead author of the United Nations Human Development Report, and with Kenneth A. Rogoff, then chief economist of the IMF, on this panel debate on how to reform the "global casino," the World Bank, the IMF and how to achieve the UN Millennium Development Goals.

By now, we had found the perfect partners in Brazil, Christina Carvalho Pinto, president of Full Jazz Advertising Agency, and Rosa Alegria, Brazil's foremost futurist, both members of our Research Advisory Board, along with Oscar Motomura, president of the famous executive institute Amana-Key. They launched a sister TV series from Sao Paulo, "Mercado Etico," and today they produce a widely watched TV show on Brazil's second largest cable channel, a weekly radio program on Globo as well as their website www.mercadoetico.com.br. We have other partners in Britain and Australia who license our programs. In North America, our TV series reaches colleges, libraries, government and business training programs via 10 million catalogs, licensed to Films Media Group, also at www.films.com. We also licensed our programs to LIME TV, founded by AOL founder Steve Case, and to Better Life Media, serving over 1 million hotel rooms.

In 2007, we launched our internet TV channel www.EthicalMarkets.tv where you can watch all our programs and others we think maintain our standards, on PCs, laptops and using any browser. Thus, Ethical Markets Media, LLC, shifted its basic strategy to the internet, as so many other independent news, TV and radio media have—bypassing the dysfunctional, ratings-driven, trivia-obsessed, traditional media businesses and their bloated costs. We have avoided the commercial censorship that became the sad fate of most mainstream news media. Their business model is broken. Driven by Wall Street's demand for greater profits, they closed news bureaus, fired journalists and conglomerated in death spirals of cost-cutting—while journalistic standards suffered and the public's distrust grew.

Ethical Markets Media, LLC, has yet to make a profit, but our social performance has been stellar. We expect to break even in the timeframe customary for media start-ups of 10 years, without the far greater investments new media often have. Our revenue model is unlikely to ever include much advertising (because our ethical standards still preclude most corporate advertisers and their tendency to "green wash" themselves). However, we are still licensing our programs, and I regularly give my usual lectures and presentations from my home using live, interactive videocasting as well as regular radio broadcasts. Thus, I no longer fly thousands of miles to give my lectures, reducing my fees, costs and carbon footprint by some 95% by using such videocasting over the internet via WebEx technology.

As our website grows to cover more aspects of the rapid growth of the green economy worldwide, our EthicalMarkets.tv is now on an energy efficient platform. We have become very concerned about digital efficiency as more video floods the internet, gobbling up so much bandwidth that an estimated up to 50 percent of all electricity generated on the planet may end up powering trivial video, wasteful chips, PCs, laptops, mobile devices, servers and data centers, as documented by one of our partners, the Uptime Institute of Santa Fe, New Mexico. Ethical Markets servers are powered by alternative energy, and our TV site is managed by Design Extensions, LLC here in Florida.

In 2008, we began experimenting with pure internet-based TV production, produced by our communications director Kemila Velan, a financial journalist and former editor of The Angel Journal for venture investors, who is based in Miami. Ethical Markets Media, LLC, continues its strategy of growing via partnerships, sharing resources and bartering content. Our 3-person office, like many internet companies, is still run out of our garage, with myself (still taking no salary) and Executive Director Rosalinda Lidh, with a masters in Environmental and Resource Policy from George Washington University, keeping everything running smoothly along with our business manager and accountant John Sundeman, CPA. We spearheaded the EthicMark® Award for advertising that uplifts the human spirit and society which I founded and funded in 2003. This EthicMark® now has a distinguished board of advisors and gave its first award in 2007 to the advertising campaign on tolerance and forgiveness by the Fund for Global Awakening. The EthicMark® is now a project of the World Business Academy, one of the closest of our over fifty partners.

Lastly, Ethical Markets Media, LLC, is one of the new breed of social enterprises in another aspect: our product is our set of ethical standards and our brand remains the integrity of our mission. Our strategy is based on global networking with all our partners and the intellectual and business leaders who serve pro bono on our Research Advisory Board. Rather than the banalities of social networking on such sites as Facebook and MySpace, our networking is focused on shared values, ethics and advancing our mission to reform markets globally. Thus, standards are crucial and raising them is vital to encourage higher ethical performance—particularly in finance.

Reforming Global Financial Markets

Ever since the 1980s when Britain's Margaret Thatcher and US President Ronald Reagan spurred deregulation of global finance and privatization, market fundamentalism became the main game. At last, the world is seeing the difference between money and real wealth, between "demand" in markets and the real needs of people without money. We cringe at the tragic pictures of poor people eyeing abundant, tempting supplies of food in the local markets around the world but who are forced to go away hungry or make their children patties made of mud, spices and whatever scraps of vegetation they can find. The games of traders, speculators, hedge funds, private equity and even pension funds and charitable foundation and university portfolio managers, driving up prices of oil and food, invoke increasing outrage and demands for reform. The June 2008 FAO Summit in Rome called for $10 billion more to pay these higher food prices. Yet, without financial reforms, this money will fatten players in the global casino.

The flaws of laissez-faire economics are again evident in the latest set of financial debacles, with $100 billion written down from faulty risk models and collapsed hedge funds to speculation in oil and commodities. Despite the efforts of socially responsible investors and asset managers to impose transparency, better corporate governance and true-cost pricing, little progress has been made to internalize social and environmental costs into risk-analyses, company balance sheets and national GDP accounting. These huge, mounting costs: from pollution to global climate change, ignored for decades by financiers, accountants and most official statistics, now feed the suspicions of millions that global finance is indeed a casino with rules rigged by the insiders.

In the ceaseless, now computerized, trading between all market players (recently measured in London's exchanges by the elevated testosterone levels of the mostly male traders), the games of money, power and ego are changing again—for the worse.

- Market players unwilling to submit to enhanced scrutiny of shareholders, analysts and the rigors of public stock ownership retreat into private equity deals—buy companies, saddle them with debt and often strip their assets and re-sell them.
- Companies try to boost their stock prices with share buy-backs—limiting the supply, e.g., oil companies banking huge oil price increases rather than investing in new supplies or facilities.
- Hedge funds (630 speculating in energy) total $2.9 trillion with their top ten managers earning $14 billion in 2007. They still proliferate

even after their many risk-analyses failures, as greedier investors seek ever-higher returns. The game, as with private equity, is also to buy companies with borrowed money. Speculating in commodities ($8 trillion of futures contracts in oil by June 2008) drives up the prices of other necessities.

- The game of "enhancing shareholder value" (versus other stakeholders' interests), played by private equity and hedge fund players, has led many asset managers of employee pension funds, foundations and university endowments to join these new greed sweepstakes. Many employees are shocked to find their pension fund managers investing their retirement funds in all these efforts to try to beat each others' market performance—contributing to the problems of plant closures, rising gas and food prices and carbon emissions.
- The newest game is the rise of sovereign wealth funds, swelled with oil revenues and trade surpluses. Norway has the oldest and most responsibly managed of these funds. Others are in Singapore, China, Qatar, Kuwait and the United Arab Emirates. Here the game is not just money but power and influence as well as buying real assets instead of holding slumping US dollars. The USA, the world's largest debtor, must court these funds, sending Treasure Secretary Henry Paulson, hat in hand, while President Bush pled with Saudi Arabia's King Abdullah for more oil.
- Banks, hurt by reckless investments in the alphabet soup of esoteric derivatives: CDOs, SIVs, CDSs (at $62 trillion), also look to sovereign wealth funds to bail them out, joining hedge funds and private equity supplicants. Taxpayers baulk at the bail out of Wall Street investment bank Bear Stearns, while central banks are exhausting their reserves, tools and remedies. US Fed interest rate cuts have weakened the dollar, feeding inflation and speculative bubbles in oil and commodities.

What are the likely outcomes of all these new games in the global casino—still unregulated since the Asian meltdowns of the late 1990s? Firstly, we are seeing the effects of the massive credit creation by central banks which fed the dot.com bubble, the housing bubble, the oil, food and commodities bubbles—a worldwide expansion of fiat currencies. The globalization of unregulated financial markets led to the rapid contagion—accelerated by computerized and algorithm-based automated trading. The "rocket-scientist" academic mathematicians, lured by the hedge funds, turned out faulty models which failed to see risks from these new conditions and how their own trading strategies were creating new systemic risks to their own financial markets.

Financial sectors of the US, UK and other market economies metastasized—just as they had done prior to the Wall Street Crash of 1929. In Britain, finance represents 25% of GDP and over 20% in the USA. Too many people are employed in trading, borrowing and financial engineering—rather than in producing real goods and services.

Money was an important invention in human societies, but it only retains its value if it is a good tracking and scoring system of the products and exchanges of the real economy. Pyramiding of paper and now electronic assets inevitably leads to write-downs, dislocating both the speculating players and the rest of the economy. We see now how the changing theories of central bankers distort real economies, from Alan Greenspan's belief that the dot.coms had created a New Economy to his urging US borrowers to try adjustable rate mortgages and hailing all the new derivatives as "financial innovations" that spread risk to those able to bear it.

Thus I wrote in my syndicated column for InterPress Service in June 2008 of needed reforms of these excesses in the global financial casino which include:

- taxing the 90% of speculation in today's $2 trillion of daily currency trading;
- curbing the $260 billion in index funds tied to oil and other commodities;
- reducing the 16 to 1 leverage allowed in oil and commodity trading by raising margin requirements;
- repealing the "ENRON loophole" passed in 2001 that de-regulated energy trading;
- repealing of US and EU subsidies and mandates for ethanol;
- greater transparency and oversight of hedge funds, private equity and sovereign wealth funds.

Many more fundamental reforms are necessary: requiring central banks to use their more targeted tools beyond manipulating interest rates, e.g., increasing the capital reserves banks must hold and raising margin requirements on stock purchases. Reforming tax policies is urgent: taxing carbon emissions, pollution, waste, planned obsolescence and resource-depletion while reducing income and payroll taxes. Shifting the still-massive subsidies showered on the oil, coal, gas and nuclear industries to production tax credits to accelerate the growth of renewable energy. Solar, wind, geothermal, tidal, fuel cells, hydrogen, mass transit, smart DC electric grids as well as capturing the 40% of energy currently wasted in the US fossil fuel economy can shift human societies to the Solar Age as described in my *Ethical Markets: Growing the Green Economy* (2007) and in our TV series.

As we at Ethical Markets Media, LLC, help change the financial games and fix accounting errors in the global casino, I helped co-organize the European Parliament's Beyond GDP Conference in 2007. I created with Calvert Group the Calvert-Henderson Quality of Life Indicators (updated regularly at www.calvert-henderson.com) to show how we can also change the obsolete scorecards. There is widespread public recognition in the survey we funded by Globscan of London, in ten countries of the need to fix the errors of money-measured GDP growth, and correcting its omissions of social and environmental costs has begun (www.beyond-gdp.eu). Including all these factors and indicators of health, education, poverty gaps, environment and quality of life can help shrink the global casino and restore finance to its proper function.

We move forward, now, into 2008 with a vision of providing depth to the layers of social innovation for sustainability. Ethical Markets Media, LLC, is collaborating to provide mentoring and research opportunities to sustainability consultants and students from graduate programs in sustainability from around the world. The Ethical Markets Sustainability Research Group will facilitate interactions between current and future leaders, making accessible to these global players resources gathered from all over the world. By gathering in a centralized location people, schools, businesses and output such as reports, books, articles and databases, we facilitate collaboration and raise awareness that social innovation for reforming markets is at last going mainstream.

Because Ethical Markets Media, LLC, is a global network organization, I have added herewith names of our key partners, as well as those of our world-class Research Advisory Board. Together, we hope to keep expanding into other countries, licensing our programs to other TV partners, so as to keep raising global standards and reforming markets to serve humanity and sustain our planet for our common future. We continue to believe that just, peaceful, humane economies within sustainable ecosystems are built through cooperation and sharing of information and resources.

Ethical Markets Media, LLC, Partners from around the World

Ashoka Fellowship; Business Alliance for Local Living Economies; Calvert-Henderson Quality of Life Indicators; Ethical Corporation—London, UK; Global Reporting Initiative—Amsterdam, The Netherlands; Green For All; InterPress Service—Rome, Italy; Kosmos; Cleantech; Markkula Center for Applied Ethics; MaximsNews Network; Mercado Etico—Sao Paolo, Brazil; NewEnergyNews; E. F. Schumacher Society; Skoll Foundation; SustainCommWorld; UN Principles of Responsible Investing; Uptime

Institute; World Business Academy; American Monetary Institute; Brooklyn Bridge/TBLI—Amsterdam, The Netherlands; Center for Social Markets—London, UK and Kolkata and Delhi, India; Covalence—Geneva, Switzerland; Centre for Sustainability and Excellence—Athens, Greece; CSR Wire; Earth Advertising; Earth Policy; Ethics World; Future 500; Globescan—Toronto, Canada; Green Micro Finance; Green Money Journal; GreenAwards—London, UK; Inside Wealth; Positive News—Shropshire, UK; Progressive Asset Management; Rachel's Network; Radical Middle; REN21—Paris, France; Rudolf Steiner Foundation; Institute of Noetic Sciences; Simple Living; Simplicity Forum; Simultaneous Policy—London, UK; Solar Living Institute; Story of Stuff; Womenable and World Changing.

Ethical Markets Media, LLC, Research Advisory Board (by areas of expertise):

Socially Responsible Investing

Joan Bavaria, President and Co-founder, Trillium Asset Management; Hal Brill, President, Natural Investment Services, Inc.; Susan Davis, President, Capital Missions Co.; Dr. Judy Henderson, Chair, Global Reporting Initiative—Canberra, Australia; Barbara Krumsiek, President and CEO, The Calvert Group; Marcello Palazzi, President, Progressio Foundation—The Netherlands; Robert Rubinstein, CEO, Brooklyn Bridge/TBLI Group—Amsterdam, The Netherlands; Steve Schueth, President, First Affirmative Financial Network; Timothy Smith, President, Social Investment Forum; Rodger Spiller, Money Matters Inc.—Auckland, New Zealand; Tessa Tennant, Director, ASRIA—Hong Kong; Eva Willmann de Donlea, Director, Conscious Investments, Pty, Ltd.—Sydney, Australia.

Corporate and Government Accountability Research

Susan Aaronson, Author of "Taking Trade to the Streets;" Verna Allee, Author of "Increasing Prosperity through Value Networks;" Gary Brouse, Director, Interfaith Center on Corporate Responsibility; Kim Cranston, President, Institute for Organizational Evolution; Linda Crompton, President, BoardSource; Susan Davis, Chair, Grameen Foundation—Geneva, Switzerland; Cliff Feigenbaum, Publisher, Green Money Journal; Prof. Michael Hoffman, Executive Director, Center for Business Ethics, Bentley College; Matthew Kiernan, Managing Director, Innovest Inc.—Toronto, Canada; Mindy Lubber, Executive Director, CERES; Ed Mayo, Chief Executive, National Consumer Council—London, UK; Nell Minow, Co-founder, The Corporate Library; Robert A.G. Monks, Author of Corpocracy; Professor S. Prakash Sethi, President, International Center for Corporate Accountability, Inc., Baruch College; Deirdre Taylor, Vibrance Media and Productions; Alice Tepper Marlin, President, Social Accountability International; Shann Turnbull, Ph.D., Principal, International Institute for Self-governance—Sydney, Australia; Toby Webb, Editor, Ethical Corporation Magazine—London, UK.

Sustainability/Renewable Resource Sectors

Ralph Abraham, Ph.D, Professor of Mathematics, University of California-Santa Cruz; Christine Austin, Teal Onstad Productions; Tariq Banuri, Stockholm Environment Institute—Pathumthani, Thailand; Jacqueline Cambata, President, Triad Co. Ltd.; Rena David, Founder of GREEN AUDIT, Inc.; Peter Davies, OBE, Business in the Community—London, UK; Prof. Michael Dorsey, Department of Environmental Studies, Dartmouth College; Riane Eisler, President, Center for Partnership Studies; Duane Elgin, Author and Co-founder of Our Media Voice; Carl Frankel, Senior Editor, Green@Work; Lori Grace, Sunrise Center; Alisa Gravitz, President, Co-op America; Julian Gresser, Chairman, Alliances for Discovery; Denis Hayes, President, Bullitt Foundation; Francis P. Koster, Ed.D., Innovation Consultant; Tachi Kiuchi, Chairman, FUTURE 500—Tokyo, Japan; Walter Link, Chair, Global Leadership Network; Richard Lippin, MD, President, The Lippin Group; Elsie Maio, President, Maio & Co.; Dr. Paul E. Metz, European Business Council for a Sustainable Energy Future—Brussels, Belgium; Prof. Bedrich Moldan, Director, Environment Center, Charles Univ.—Prague, Czech Republic; James Motavalli, Editor, E—The Environmental Magazine; Prof. Robert Nadeau, Author of The Wealth of Nature, George Mason Univ.; F. Byron Nahser, Provost, Presidio School of Business; Richard Ottinger, Dean Emeritus, Pace University Law School; Nancy Roof, Editor, KOSMOS; Claudine Schneider, President, Solar Alliance; Carol S. Spalding, Ph.D., President, Rowan-Cabarrus Community College; Stephen Viederman, Past President, Jessie Smith Noyes Foundation; Richard Wilson, UK Business Council for Sustainable Energy—London, UK; Zhang Hong, CEO, Shanghai Wallstreet Strategies Advisors—Shanghai, China; Zhouying Jin, Professor, Innovation & Strategies, Chinese Acad. Soc. Sciences—China.

Social Venture Capital

Mark Donohue, Expansion Capital Partners; Elizabeth Harris, UNC Partners, Inc.; Nicholas Parker, Co-founder and Chairman, CLEANTECH Venture Network LLC—Toronto, Canada; D. Wayne Silby, Esq., President of Calvert Ventures, LLC, and Founder of Calvert Social Investment Funds; Radames Soto, President, Kinina Ventures; Edward B. (Woody) Tasch, Chair, Investors Circle; Stuart Valentine, President, Iowa Progressive Asset Management; Steve Waddell, Executive Director, GAN-NET.

Globalization/North-South Equity, Justice

Rosa Alegria, President, Perspektiva Co.—Sao Paulo, Brazil; Prof. Walden Bello, Co-Director, Focus on the Global South, Chulalongkorn University—Bangkok, Thailand; Frank Bracho, Former Ambassador of Venezuela to India—Caracas, Venezuela; Rinaldo Brutoco, President, World Business Academy; Fritjof Capra, Author of The Web of Life; Christina Carvalho Pinto, President, Full Jazz Advertising Agency—Sao Paulo, Brazil; Thais Corral, Director General, REDEH—Rio de Janeiro, Brazil; Prof. Michael Hopkins, Ph.D., Author of The Planetary Bargain—Geneva, Switzerland; Paul Freundlich, President, The Fair Trade Foundation; Devaki Jain, Author of Women Development and the UN—Bangalore, India; Rushworth M. Kidder, President, Institute for Global Ethics;

Ashok Khosla, CEO, Development Alternatives—New Delhi, India; Annabel McGoldrick, Peace Journalism—Oxford, UK; Oscar Motomura, CEO. Amana-Key Desenvolvimento & Educacao Ltda.—Sao Paulo, Brazil; Jane Nelson, Harvard University; David Roodman, Center for Global Development; Elisabet Sahtouris, Evolution biologist—Barcelona, Spain; Ziauddin Sardar, Editor, FUTURES Elsevier, Ltd.—London, UK; Miklos Sukosd, Ph.D., Department of Political Science, Central European University—Budapest, Hungary; Wouter Van Dieren, President, Institute for Environment & Systems Analysis—Amsterdam, The Netherlands; Judith Woodard, Christopher Street Financial Co.; Norio Yamamoto, PhD., Executive Vice-president, Global Infrastructure Fund Research Foundation—Tokyo, Japan; Susana Oseguera Yturbide, Communications Internacionales—Mexico City, Mexico.

Small, Medium-size Enterprise, Micro-finance /Community Development

Rebecca Adamson, President, First Nations Development Institute; Rosalind Copisarow, Founder, Fundusz Mikro—Warsaw, Poland and UK; Lynne Franks, CEO, Seed Fusion—London, UK; Sharon Hadary, Executive Director, Center for Women's Business Research; Robert MacGregor, President Emeritus, Center for Ethical Business Cultures; Terrence Mollner, Trustee, Calvert Social Investment Fund; Pam Solo, President, Institute for Civil Society; Michaela Walsh, Founding President, Women's World Banking; Julie Weeks, President, Womenable.

What Will Happen in Capitalist Societies in the Future? A Dialogue on the Future of Modern Civilization

Hiroshi Tasaka

Human Society Is Developing Dialectically

* *What Will Happen in Capitalist Societies in the Future?*

This question is an extremely important one today at a moment when global capitalism is being confronted by some extremely serious obstacles. But because the question is historical in its dimensions, simply relying on a "technology to predict the future" will not provide the answers. What we need, instead, is to understand a "philosophy to foresee the future." In other words, we need to understand a philosophy that talks about the laws that underlie change, development, and evolution in our world.

* *What Kind of Philosophy Is the Philosophy to Foresee the Future?*

Dialectic. In Western philosophy, dialectic began in Greece with Socrates and was systematized by Georg Hegel, the German Idealist philosopher. Also, Karl Marx used this philosophy in his theory of social change and Jean-Paul Sartre discussed its tenets in the context of Existentialism. In Eastern philosophy as well, dialectic has been dealt with at a profound level by Buddhist, Taoist, Esoteric Buddhist, Zen and other thinkers. Dialectic offers two laws in particular that are extremely helpful when foreseeing the future of capitalist societies: the "law of development through spiral process" and the "law of development through interpenetration of opposing objects."

** What Is the Law of Development through Spiral Process?*

This is the law which says that the world develops as if it were climbing a spiral staircase. In other words, if you look from the side at people ascending a spiral staircase, they appear to be progressing and developing because they are heading upward. However, if you look at them from above, they complete one revolution and return to their original positions. Therefore it appears that the revival and restoration of old things occur. But on a spiral staircase, people do not merely return to their original positions; they always move to a higher level. Similarly, in "spiral development," there is not simply revival and restoration. Rather, something develops to a new stage and this enables old things to add new value as they are revived and restored.

** What Are Specific Examples of the Law of Development through Spiral Process?*

For example, two leading-edge business models which have emerged from the Internet revolution: the "Net auction" and the "reverse auction." These models are, in fact, revivals of old nostalgic business models. Previously, before the development of capitalism, trading methods such as "bidding" and "limit pricing" existed in every market. Having once been eclipsed by the development of capitalism demanding rationalization, they have gained new life as a result of the Net revolution. But there is a difference: while one could bid or limit prices with only several hundreds of people in the past, the Net auctions and reverse auctions can involve millions of participants. These methods have indeed revived at a higher level of the spiral staircase. Likewise, e-mail represents a revival of the nostalgic culture of "letter writing" within the context of a new system. And e-learning is certainly the revival of "private tutoring" and other forms of individualized learning in a more advanced and sophisticated form.

** What Then Is the Law of Development through Interpenetration of Opposing Objects?*

It is the law which says that things which oppose and compete with each other come to resemble each other through interpenetration. For example, the policies of opposing political parties, such as those of the Conservative and Labor Parties in the UK, end up becoming alike. The way in which capitalism and socialism have learned from each other's policies, adopting approaches to social welfare on the one hand and the principles of market competition on the other, is another case in point.

The Voluntary Economy Will Revive through Spiral Development

** Then, Based on These Two Laws of Dialectic, What Will Happen in Capitalist Societies in the Future?*

Capitalism will evolve into an entirely different form of capitalism in the future. This is because such spiral development and interpenetration will occur in the "economic principles" on which capitalism has traditionally been premised.

** Specifically, What Affect Will the Law of Spiral Development Have on These Economic Principles?*

In capitalist societies today, the economic principle that so clearly predominates is the "monetary economy." However, the oldest economic principle in human society, the "voluntary economy," will revive and begin to have a major impact on society.

** What Kind of Economic Principle Is the Voluntary Economy?*

The capitalism of today is premised on an economic principle called the monetary economy. The monetary economy is an economic activity in which people act with the aim of "acquiring money." By contrast, the voluntary economy is an economic activity in which people act with the aim not of "acquiring money" but of "satisfying mind." In other words, in a voluntary economy people cooperate out of goodwill and kindness, share their knowledge and wisdom, and work together in a spontaneous way.

** Is the Voluntary Economy an Old Economic Principle?*

Yes. The voluntary economy is actually the oldest economic principle in human history. This is because before "money" was invented and the monetary economy came into being, humankind carried out its economic activity in the "barter economy" (the exchange economy), in which things were exchanged directly for other things. But in the primitive communities that existed before barter arose, the "gift economy" prevailed, in which people gave things of value to other people out of goodwill and kindness. In such communities, in other words, the voluntary economy was front and center.

**Did the Voluntary Economy Disappear Because of the Development of Society?*

No, that is not what happened. The "voluntary economy" has consistently remained an important economic principle throughout human history. It is because that even today certain kinds of economic activity, such as housework, child care, education in the home, caring for the elderly, community service, and so on, are occurring without an exchange of money in every corner of society, based on goodwill and kindness and on friendship and affection among people. Therefore, if the voluntary economy ceased to exist, the monetary economy would also, at that very moment, be forced to halt its activities. Let us say, for example, that families no longer provided any education to children on matters of discipline or manners. In this case, with only school education to rely on, society would no longer produce any talented people capable of working cooperatively.

The Internet Revolution Will Accelerate Spiral Development and Interpenetration of Opposing Objects in the Economy

** Despite Such Obvious Importance, Why Has the Voluntary Economy Not Been Valued Very Highly Until Now?*

There are two reasons why the voluntary economy was relegated to the position of a "shadow economy" in the long course of human history. The first is that its activities were limited to the "narrow domains" of the household or the community. The second is that the true picture of this economy remained "invisible" because it could not be evaluated in terms of the objective measure of "money."

** If That Is So, Why Will This Voluntary Economy Now Revive and Begin Increasing Its Impact in Coming Society?*

It is because the Internet revolution has occurred. As a result of this revolution, conditions have changed. Firstly, the Net revolution has liberated the voluntary economy from the bonds of these "narrow domains." In the Internet community today, people from around the world can gather, share their knowledge and wisdom, and cooperate with one another. Their activities can then have a global impact through the Internet. Secondly, the Net revolution has made the voluntary economy "visible." Although its activities still cannot be evaluated quantitatively in terms of "money," these activities can now be seen by large numbers of people through the "Net." The Linux Community, in which engineers from around the world gather without compensation and continue to develop and improve this operating system, is a representative case.

A Hybrid Economy Will Emerge through Interpenetration of Opposing Objects

** As the Voluntary Economy Continues to Exert a Greater Impact, What Else Will Occur as a Result?*

The second law of dialectic will come into play, which is the "law of development through interpenetration of opposing objects." Consequently, economic principles will take a major evolutionary step forward.

** What Affect Will the Law of Interpenetration of Opposing Objects Have on Economic Principles?*

The two principles that now stand in opposition, the monetary economy and the voluntary economy, will begin to interpenetrate and merge. This will give rise to a "new economic principle" which we should call the "hybrid economy."

**Is This a Theoretical Forecast Based on Dialectic?*

No, this principle is already a reality. Take, for example, Amazon.com, the Internet bookseller. In the context of the monetary economy, Amazon.com has created an extremely profitable business model. But, the most popular service on its site is the grassroots reviews, which owes its existence to the voluntary economy. In other words, Amazon.com's business model arises out of a hybrid economy and is not merely a "business model" but rather something that should be called a new "social system." Another example is the rapidly expanding method of "prosumer-based product development." In this method, "companies that make products" (producers) gather in the Net community with "people who use them" (consumers); both sides share knowledge and wisdom, and cooperate in the task of developing new products and services. This business model, too, is supported by the voluntary activity of consumers. It should thus also be referred to as a social system that has emerged from a hybrid economy.

** Do These Activities Occur Only in the World of the Internet?*

No, these kinds of activities also occur frequently in the real world. But there is one major reason why so many examples of spiral development and interpenetration of dialectical laws can be found in the Internet world. This is because, as indicated by the terms "dog year" and "mouse year," the changes to things in this world are accelerating; and what once took place over a period of seven or eighteen years now happens in a single year. As a result, whereas we human beings once ascended the spiral staircase leisurely over several hundred years, we are "running up" the stairs in several decades. That is why today the theme of the dialectical development of society, which was once the purview of historians and philosophers, is now an everyday concern for politicians, administrators and managers.

** What Then Are Some Examples of the Hybrid Economy Occurring in the Real World?*

In fact, the most emblematic examples of the hybrid economy are the trends toward "corporate social responsibility" (CSR) and "social entrepreneurship."

Alliance between Companies and Social Entrepreneurs Will Prompt an Evolution of Capitalism

** Why Does CSR Reflect a Movement toward a Hybrid Economy?*

The CSR movement has become a major global trend, as evidenced by the ISO's formulation of international standards with respect to CSR. And, in recent years, this movement has extended beyond the narrow scope of simply compliance or corporate ethics and has moved toward a more broadly encompassing approach of how to contribute to society as a company. These movements by companies whose essential aim is to earn "business profits" represent an increasing recognition of the value of "social contributions," and can be seen, so to speak, as interpenetration from the monetary economy toward the voluntary economy.

* *Why Does Social Entrepreneurship Reflect a Movement toward a Hybrid Economy?*

On the other hand, social entrepreneurship has also become a major global trend. Social entrepreneurship arose in response to the increasingly severe difficulties that traditional non-profit organizations are having in sustaining their undertakings as government supports and benefactors contribution are discontinued. To overcome these problems, social entrepreneurs attempt to generate profits from their own undertakings and to use these profits to achieve organizational independence and sustainability. These movements by organizations whose essential aim is "social contributions" represent an increasing recognition of the value of "business profits," and can be seen, so to speak, as interpenetration from the voluntary economy toward the monetary economy.

* *What Will Be the Movements of CSR and Social Entrepreneurship from Now?*

Based on the law of interpenetration of dialectic, the movements of CSR and social entrepreneurship will inevitably converge over the long term. In other words, what have traditionally been referred to as "for-profit companies" and "non-profit organizations" will evolve and interpenetrate each other, resulting in all companies and organizations eventually becoming what are called "social enterprises." To put it another way, whether the organization is a large corporation or a small venture start-up, a NPO or a social venture, the age will come when all organizations whatever their form will be compelled to respond simultaneously to two challenges, posed in the following two questions. The first question is "Through businesses, what is the organization doing to contribute to society or to bring about social change?" The second question is "How will the organization earn profits from its undertakings in order to sustain the organization's undertakings?" In a fundamental sense, all companies and organizations will have to succeed in establishing the viability of both social contributions and business profits.

** Specifically, What Should Be Done to Promote a Paradigm Shift towards the Hybrid Economy and to Encourage Many Companies to Evolve into Social Enterprises?*

We can do this by pursuing a "social alliance," which can be described as a situation where for-profit companies and social entrepreneurs ally each other and seek to evolve into social enterprises through an exchange of knowledge and wisdom and mutual learning. This kind of alliance differs from the ordinary "business alliances" in that both parties aim to co-evolve into a social enterprise. Specifically, it is considered that for-profit companies would provide social entrepreneurs with brands, marketing channels, and business know-how, while social entrepreneurs would provide for-profit companies with grassroots consumer networks, grassroots consumers' voice, know-how about operating voluntary communities, and other input. Already, a coffee-shop-chain company is providing access to its network of stores to a social entrepreneur who is engaged in efforts to establish fair trade in the coffee business. In return, the social entrepreneur is providing the company with an opportunity to contribute to society. In the coming age, companies are likely to pursue "social alliances" as one vital aspect of their CSR.

** What Kind of Enterprises Will Such Social Enterprises Evolve Into?*

They will evolve into "earth enterprises." In this era of the global environmental problems, social enterprises that recognize their responsibilities toward "society" and seek to contribute to society will invariably become aware of their responsibilities toward "the Earth" as a whole, and then aim to become companies that contribute to the sustainability of the living system that is the Earth. The hybrid economy in which these "earth enterprises" are rooted will, in fact, go on to play an extremely important role in solving the global environmental problems.

** In What Way Will the Hybrid Economy Play an Important Role in Solving the Global Environmental Problems?*

Until now, a method from economics known as the "internalization of external cost" has primarily been relied on to solve the environmental problems. This is a method to bring "external costs," which arise outside the market economy, such as the damage caused by environmental destruction, into the market through environmental regulation and have them reflected in company costs. This can be considered a method to pay for the cost of environmental destruction by bringing these costs within themonetary economy. Emissions trading which deals with the problem of global warming is a concrete example of this approach. In addition, however, to solve the global environmental problems, the methods that link the monetary economy and the voluntary economy, that is, methods that utilize the hybrid economy will become extremely important hereafter.

** Specifically, What Are Some of These Methods?*

For example, there are "carbon offset products." These can be described as follows: When a company sells a certain product, it promises to use a part of the selling price of the product to capture the identical amount of CO_2 that is emitted during the manufacturing of that product. These carbon offset products tie the "business models" of companies to the "voluntary minds" of consumers and can be considered a new system of the hybrid economy. On the other hand, the use of what is called "corporate currency," which includes such things as airline mileage and credit card membership rewards programs, is expanding today. A system in which consumers donate this corporate currency to NPOs or social entrepreneurs of their choice has emerged. This, too, can be considered a new system of the hybrid economy.

A Paradigm Shift toward Participatory Innovation Will Occur

** Then, When a Paradigm Shift in "Economic Principles" Occurs, What Will Happen Next in Capitalist Societies?*

A paradigm shift in "innovation" will occur. That is to say, we see a paradigm shift from traditional "beneficiary innovation" toward "participatory innovation."

** What Kind of Innovation Is "Participatory Innovation?"*

Until now, in capitalist societies, something called "beneficiary innovation" has prevailed. In this innovation, a small number of exceptionally talented experts drive innovation in technologies and products, in services and businesses, and in systems and institutions, while a large number of people are placed in the position of merely receiving the benefits of such innovation. However, in societies in the near future, a large number of people will begin participating directly in the process of innovation. Examples of such participation include prosumer-based product development and open-source policy making. These are illustrations of what we might call "participatory innovation."

** What Does the Paradigm Shift toward Participatory Innovation Mean for Social Entrepreneurs?*

The role of social entrepreneurs is to drive "social innovation." When social innovation and participatory innovation become linked together, social innovation becomes an even larger and more powerful trend.

Direct Democracy Will Also Revive in the Fields of Economy and Culture

** When this Kind of Paradigm Shift In "Innovation" Occurs, What Will Happen Next in Capitalist Societies?*

A major paradigm shift will occur in "democracy." It is because direct democracy expands not only in the domain of politics but also in the domains of economy and culture.

**What Does "Direct Democracy in Economy and Culture" Mean?*

Firstly, as a result of the Internet revolution, a large number of people are finding it easy to express their own opinions and ideas. So, rather than traditional "indirect democracy," where people choose decision makers and delegate their decision making to them, this revolution has facilitated the establishment of "direct democracy," where people participate directly in decision making. Therefore, a paradigm shift to "direct democracy" will occur in various fields from now. This kind of direct democracy will then become a reality not only in the domain of politics but also in the domains of economy and culture. Traditionally, it was generally thought that democracy was a political problem. In fact, however, it has been an economic and cultural problem as well. And, the traditional economy and culture have long been placed in a condition of indirect democracy.

* *What Constitutes Direct Democracy in the Domain of Economy?*

In the world of economy, although a large number of consumers had different and diverse needs, companies comprehended these needs through the broad-brush approach of the "market research." Almost as if, as a consequence, they had adopted the "representative system," companies have developed products to meet the largest common denominator and supplied these products to the market. However, in the coming age, because of the expanding use of the following three methods, prosumer-based development, Long Tail marketing, and high-mix low-volume production, consumers will say what they truly want in a product and actually be able to obtain these products. In other words, direct democracy in product development will become a reality. Similarly, today rapidly expanding "affiliate programs," in which consumers recommend products that they like and encourage others to purchase them on their personal websites and blogs, can be viewed, in one sense, as the realization of direct democracy in marketing.

* *What Then Constitutes Direct Democracy in the Domain of Culture?*

Until now, in capitalist societies, as in economy, culture has also been created through the representative system and indirect democracy. For example, in the world of music, artists have been discovered by a few major labels or large production companies, which then have engineered booms and have created musical culture. However, in the coming age, a large number of people will easily be able to compose and perform their own music and release it to the rest of the world over the Internet. They will also be able freely to review and recommend the music of their favorite artists. For a large number of people, this will signify the realization of direct democracy in the creation of culture and the beginning of "an era in which culture is personally created" instead of "an era in which culture is unilaterally provided."

* *Then, Why Is Direct Democracy in Economy and Culture Important?*

It is because it will change people's consciousness of democracy. Until now, democracy has been understood as participation in the "decision making" process of society. However, through the realization of direct democracy in economy and culture, the consciousness of a large number of people will begin to change. In other words, the meaning of democracy for many people will change. It will come to mean not merely participation in "decision making" but participation in "social innovation."

Knowledge Capitalism Will Deepen into "Empathy Capitalism"

** When a Paradigm Shift in "Democracy" Occurs, What Will Happen Next in Capitalist Societies?*

The paradigm of "knowledge capitalism" will change. "Knowledge capitalism" can be defined as capitalism in which the most important management resource is knowledge capital. In the society of the future, however, as participatory innovation takes center stage and direct democracy in economy and culture spreads, the meaning of the term "knowledge capital" will fundamentally change.

**Why Will the Meaning of Knowledge Capital Change?*

It is because we will enter an age of "collective intelligence." In other words, in the era of participatory innovation and direct democracy in economy and culture, it will become crucial to utilize the wisdom of many people at the grassroots as well as the knowledge of a small number of experts. In the context of the Internet revolution, this wisdom is referred to as "collective intelligence" or "wisdom of crowds." Companies in the coming age will be required to utilize such collective intelligence as knowledge capital.

**Then, What Is Important for Utilizing Collective Intelligence?*

One might venture to call it "empathy capital." In other words, the degree to which those companies obtain empathy from consumers becomes extremely important. This is because collective intelligence is not a management resource in the monetary economy which can be merchandised with "monetary capital"; rather, it is a management resource in the voluntary economy. To put it differently, collective intelligence is a management resource that can be exchanged for something that we should call "empathy capital," which includes empathy, trust and a good reputation from the consumer. And, for companies in the coming age, "empathy capital" will become especially important. Therefore, today's knowledge capitalism will deepen into something that we should call "empathy capitalism."

***What Then Should Companies Do to Obtain "Empathy Capital?"*

Above all, companies must evolve into "social enterprises" which highly value their contributions to society. They must then also evolve into "earth enterprises."

Capitalist Societies Will Evolve into Living Systems

** Then, What Kind of Societies Will Emerge When Capitalist Societies Become Characterized by Terms Such as the Internet Revolution, the Hybrid Economy, Participatory Innovation, Direct Democracy in Economy and Culture, Empathy Capitalism, and the Like?*

The capitalist societies of the future will become an extremely sophisticated and advanced "living system," in which "living phenomena" frequently occur. Such phenomena include self-organization and emergence, evolution and co-evolution, the formation of ecosystems and the butterfly effect, and so forth.

** Then, Why Will Capitalist Societies Evolve into "Living Systems?"*

It is because companies, markets and societies will increasingly take on the properties of "complex systems." In other words, the Internet revolution, the hybrid economy, participatory innovation, direct democracy in economy and culture, and empathy capitalism all enhance the inter-relationship of people within companies, markets and societies, causing them to heighten the "complexity" of such systems. The cultural anthropologist Gregory Bateson once said that "In complex things, life dwells." As Bateson pointed out, as the complexity of systems increases, they do indeed begin to display behaviors of living systems.

** Why Will the Terms Which Characterize the Future Capitalist Societies Mentioned Above Enhance the Inter-Relationship of People in Companies, Markets and Societies?*

There are three reasons for this. Firstly, the Internet revolution will amplify the informational connections among people in companies, markets and societies. Secondly, the hybrid economy and empathy capitalism will connect people closely together not only through financial relationships but also through relationships based on goodwill, kindness, empathy, and trust. Thirdly, participatory innovation and direct democracy will increase people's motivation to connect with each other.

** What Will Happen When Capitalist Societies Increasingly Take on the Properties of Living Systems?*

Of particular importance in this regard is the "butterfly effect." As expressed metaphorically, "when a butterfly flutters its wings in Beijing, it sets off a hurricane in New York," meaning that a slight fluctuation in a small part of a system will cause large changes in the system as a whole. This can sometimes appear in negative forms, such as when the economic failure of one industry in one country sparks a worldwide recession. On the other hand, it is also possible that a single social entrepreneur or a single social enterprise can change the direction of the world in a positive way. In other words, social entrepreneurs and social enterprises will be able to use the "evolution of capitalism" as a tailwind and "wisdom to cope with living systems" as a rudder in changing society in the coming age.

** Then, Where Can the Wisdom to Deal with Capitalist Societies as Living Systems Be Found?*

Unfortunately, much of this kind of wisdom cannot be found inside modern civilization, which has developed on the basis of the mechanical system paradigm. Such wisdom, in fact, exists in the "old civilizations" which are found in each country. The reason is that, without exception, old civilizations in each country formed the foundation to the kind of wisdom that emerged from the living system paradigm. Such wisdom includes knowing how to live in harmony with the environment, how to create empathy in society, and how to temper the insatiable desires of the human beings. Consequently, in the process of evolution, capitalist societies of the future will incorporate the wisdom which resides in old civilizations and give birth to a "new civilization." That evolution is also a process of spiral development and interpenetration, that is, exactly the dialectical development of human civilization.

Entrepreneurs Creating the Economic Paradigm for the Future

*Paola Babos[1] and Monica Sharma[2] **

> *"A human being is part of the whole called by us the universe, a part limited in time and space. He experiences himself, his thoughts and feelings as something separated from the rest, a kind of optical delusion of his consciousness. This delusion is a kind of prison for us, restricting us to our personal desires and to affection for a few persons nearest to us. Our task must be to free ourselves from this prison by widening our circle of compassion to embrace all living creatures and the whole of nature in its beauty."*
>
> —Albert Einstein

Today we are living in a time of deep interdependence and seemingly great paradoxes. Never before have we had more abundant opportunities to fulfill people's needs worldwide. Each day we seamlessly move massive amounts of capital and other financial instruments around the globe. More than 100 million human beings cross borders and another 100 million move from rural to urban areas in search of opportunities. Information is constantly being generated and moved through cyberspace, connecting people globally and revolutionizing our capacity to communicate and exchange across time and space. A new global culture is taking shape among the younger generation, often redefining the tastes, beliefs and values of local societies.

Yet in spite of the abundance of resources and technology available to us, the world economy teeters on the brink of a global economic breakdown. The deepening credit crisis in major developed market economies, triggered by the continuing housing slump, the declining value of the US dollar, persistent global imbalances and soaring commodity prices poses substantive threats to sustainable human development and well-being. Most shockingly, in a world economy that moves $2 trillion a day, we are witnessing the unfolding of a food crisis that is wholly man-made, with severe consequences for people across the world. Furthermore, we have been using the equivalent of 1.25 planets' worth of resources since 1997 resulting in the unsustainable use and degradation of nearly two thirds of ecosystem services[3].

The increasing instability of global markets and their reverberating effects on people across countries and continents underscore the limits of our current economic practices. The patterns underlying our current limits are mostly hidden from view. Even when we see them, we often do not know how to create an alternative. After each crisis we look back to identify its causes and identify ways to 'fix the mess' without ever really addressing the hidden underlying causes of their systemic nature and increasing frequency.

Why does our current economic model careen from crisis to crisis when we supposedly have the most advanced technology and resources ever to satisfy human needs worldwide? What new approaches can we take on to reconstruct and transform economic practices for human and planetary well-being? To answer these questions, we explore what is missing in current economic thinking and practices, shedding light on what becomes possible in an economic structure that puts people at the centre of its design. We present examples of emerging economic practices that integrate equity with effectiveness and efficiency. Finally we look at how full-spectrum[4] approaches sourced in people's transformational leadership and entrepreneurship can be applied at scale to see the emergence of a new entrepreneurship paradigm that maximises returns to society.

Seeing the Shared Context of Our Crises

"Insanity is doing the same thing over and over again and expecting different results."
—Rita Mae Brown

"You already know enough, so do I. It is not knowledge we lack. What is missing is the courage to understand what we know and to draw conclusions."
—Sven Lindquist

In the age of global complexity, it is a common fallacy to think that there is little we can do in relation to the economic and social systems that have so far shaped our mutual relationships and existence on this planet. Mostly we get bogged down in ideological debates over the tangled web of tensions and contradictions that characterize the interaction of social and economic forces. For example, the technological and material progress we have made over the past decade is unprecedented in the history of humanity. The development of market economies has benefited large numbers of people over the past century, generating technological innovations that enhance life and human well-being. Conversely, the benefits of economic growth are increasingly skewed in favour of a small minority, and the nature and scale of production and consumption patterns is jeopardizing our very existence on this planet.

While the global economy has grown seven-fold since 1950, disparity in per capita gross domestic product between the 20 richest and 20 poorest nations more than doubled between 1960 and 1995. Today, of the 100 largest economies in the world, 59 are global corporations. Some 85% of the world's GDP is controlled by one fifth of the population. Even in the United States, home to the world's largest corporations, economic growth is becoming less able to foster human development across different income groups. The "Measure of America" report commissioned by Oxfam and several foundations[5] points to the dramatic decline of American society relative to other advanced industrialized countries and the mounting social disparities within the US. Of the world's 30 richest nations, the US has the highest proportion of children living in poverty, 15%. Income inequality gaps are stark: the average income of the top fifth of US households in 2006 was almost 15 times that of the lowest fifth (or $168,170 versus $11,352). The top 1% of households possesses at least 33% of the national wealth, while the bottom 60% possess just 4% of the total.

To understand why rising social and economic inequalities are at the heart of our current crises, we need to acknowledge that the dynamics of economic and social development are no longer determined primarily at the national and local level: they are nested in and informed by complex global systems. Global finance, international trade regimes, patenting rules and governance systems shape policy choices and freedoms across every country and community on the planet. They represent interconnected 'software nodes' that inform and organize the 'hardware' of production and distribution. The way in which we organize these nodes has a profound impact on our capacities to create meaningful systems of production and consumption to provide for people's needs and well-being.

For example, in the domain of finance, Hazel Henderson[6] has eloquently explained over the years that while money has been an important invention in human societies, it only retains its value if it is a good tracking and scoring system of the products and exchanges of the real economy. Today we are witnessing the effects of massive credit creation in deregulated capital markets that fed the dot.com bubble of yesteryears, and the current housing, oil, and food crises. In essence, the deregulation of global finance has decoupled money from real wealth creation and 'market demand' from the actual needs of people.

Professor Michael Hudson at the Institute for the Study of Long Term Economic Trends traces the decoupling of money from real wealth to what he calls 'the magic of compound interest'[7]: that is, the tendency of debts to keep on doubling and redoubling through a complex set of market instruments in the finance, insurance and real estate sectors. Every rate of interest is a doubling time. No real economy's production and economic surplus can keep up with this tendency of debt to grow faster in a deregulated market.

The current strategy for wealth creation based on the global trading of complex financial products has unintended effects or costs. For example, leverage instruments such as complex derivatives use borrowed funds or debt to magnify or enhance the potential positive or negative outcome to increase the returns to equity. As the current financial crisis shows, after years of deregulation and inflated capital gains, leverage instruments have actually magnified systemic instability, mirroring the pitfalls of gambling strategies. Financial globalization has also fostered mergers and acquisitions on an unprecedented scale so that many of today's global corporations are larger than many governments. This has in turn hindered the financial viability of local small and medium size enterprises. As a result, deregulation of financial markets indirectly fosters polarization between those who live off the returns to wealth (that is, from the interest and rent extracted from finance and property and the capital gains derived from inflated asset prices) and those who live off what they can earn and who struggle to pay the taxes and debts they are encouraged to take on.

These unintended effects or costs are largely outside of our field of vision because national accounts—GNP and national income—do not distinguish how wealth is being created and distributed across the population. By the same token, our methods to track business performance have heretofore been limited to measuring return on investment and shareholder value. As a result, we fail to track the positive and negative externalities of productive systems on people and the planet.

In a brilliant 20-minute video titled 'Story of Stuff'[8], Annie Leonard maps what she calls the materials economy, showing the limits we are running up against, and some of the hidden social, economic and environmental externalities of a linear system in a finite planet that must be seen and urgently confronted.

- Extraction: Manufacturing is using up the planet's resources at an alarming rate. We have already consumed 33% of its resources. The US alone is using 30% of the world's resources despite having 5% of the world's population. If all countries were to consume at US rates, we would need 5 planets.
- Production: A 'profit above all' manufacturing strategy is wreaking havoc on our ecosystems and is responsible for climate change, water depletion, waste and toxic pollution. There are over 100,000 synthetic chemicals in use today, only a handful of which have been tested for individual, let alone synergistic impacts on health.
- Distribution: Once goods are produced, the main focus of distribution is to sell goods and services as quickly as possible, keeping prices down to increase sales volumes and keep the inventory moving. In a globalised world, price competition coupled with the drive to maximize profits means that manufacturers are externalizing production costs in a number of ways, including environmental pollution and exploitative labour practices, relocating factories and outsourcing jobs in order to pay the lowest wages.
- Consumption: The heartbeat of the entire system is a consumption culture that trains citizens to be avid consumers of goods and services by promising prestige, happiness, admiration, success and satisfaction. We see more advertisements in a year than our grandparents saw in their lifetime. We consume twice as much as 50 years ago, reversing values of thrift, resourcefulness and stewardship of the planet, in a paradigm where our consumption capacity defines our social status and value in society.
- Disposal: In the United States, 99% of purchased goods are disposed of within 6 months. In other words, American consumers have either used up or turned into garbage 30% of the world's resources. Recycling is therefore a necessary but not sufficient strategy for managing our resources and well-being.

In her vivid and succinct analysis, Annie Leonard examines how economic and social systems interact, pointing to the multiple limits we are facing. She shows that our patterns of production and consumption are unsustainable because they are not designed in the best interest of people and the planet. In fact we see that we live in a system in crisis, running a linear model on a finite planet, where people are the means of production and consumption, rather than the end of our economic engagement with each other and the world.

Figure 1 illustrates the logic of economic thinking and decision making today, where policies and regulatory environments in the domain of systems are geared to drive market efficiency and maximize returns in the inner domain of economic transactions.

Figure 1
Systems and Results

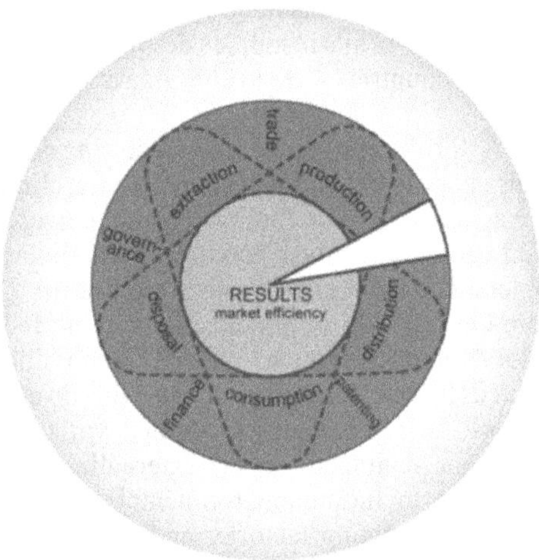

What is evident is that people's best interest does not necessarily inform decision making in this approach. Our responses are partial: we design policies and organize systems according to market efficiency and shareholder returns, with no built-in mechanisms to track the impact of productive and regulatory systems on the well-being of people and the planet. In this model, we fail to ask a fundamental question: for what and for whom are we designing effective policies and efficient markets?

Without addressing these questions, market efficiency as measured by profit making becomes both the means and end of decision making for institutions, corporations and society at large. Economic practices therefore emphasize the short term over the long term; they focus on shareholders' return and largely fail to account for the social and environmental costs born by other stakeholders, or for the generations to come. As we discuss in the next section, our current measurements for economic growth reflect the partial nature of this approach, where non-monetized dimensions of human well-being are unaccounted for and fail to inform the policy and investment choices we make.

Investing in Human Agency and Well-Being as a Pathway to a Different Future

> *"Wealth is evidently not the good we are seeking; for it is merely useful and for the sake of something else."*
>
> —Aristotle

Although we are apparently stuck in social, economic and political practices that are no longer working for the majority of people, cutting edge knowledge in the domains of physics and cognitive sciences, as well as real world social and economic applications, is showing us that innovation dynamics are fundamentally nested in human agency and expressed through social and interpersonal communication. Human agency is our capacity to make choices of our own, creating anew based on our deepest wisdom, insights and values, as distinct from the mere application of knowledge through 'either-or' constructs underpinning the scientific method.

Some economists are developing new frameworks focusing on a more holistic view of development that recognises the interaction between social and economic dimensions. Amartya Sen's work on the inter-relationship between development and freedom, Martha Nussbaum's work on ethics and human capabilities, and the applied research of the Oxford Poverty Human Development Initiative, led by Sabine Alkire, are some important contributions to this work. They see people as agents of development, "someone who acts and brings about change, and whose achievements can be judged in terms of her own values and objectives[9]."

Figure 2
Human Agency, Systems, and Results

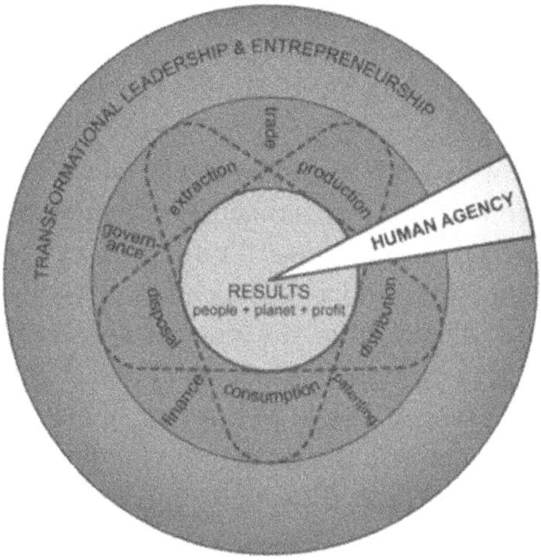

Figure 2 reflects the missing domain of human agency, sourced in people's leadership and entrepreneurial spirit and manifested in actions that reflect our interdependence and human values. It shows that our capacity to generate sustainable patterns for personal and planetary well-being is nested in the domain of human agency. Human agency is the capacity to make choices and lead change. It is given by a set of human capabilities or functionings—expressed as 'beings', 'doings' and 'havings'—that a person can choose from and accomplish. This view generates a new context to understand and positively transform current patterns of economic engagement, enabling results that simultaneously address the triple bottom line: people, planet and profit. It moves us away from linear methods towards more holistic approaches to address complex global challenges.

The hologram also shows that human freedoms—our individual and collective capacity to manifest human agency and expand our potential—are man made: they are partly determined and expressed through development policies, markets, and other social arrangements in the middle domain. We can therefore look at development as the extent to which social and economic arrangements expand human capabilities and freedoms.

Human well-being reflects a broader concept of development to include measures of life satisfaction, meaning and purpose[10], so that the material wealth we currently measure is complemented by dimensions of physical, mental and spiritual well-being (i.e. reflecting the range of human capabilities or functionings as 'beings', 'doings' and 'havings'). Some governments and institutions are exploring more holistic measures that reflect this approach in national accounting. Examples include Bhutan's Gross National Happiness[11] index; as well as efforts by the EU[12], Canada[13] and the OECD[14].

When policy making is guided by this broader concept of human well-being, our decision making processes reflect equity considerations necessary for expanding human capabilities. Equity refers to the distribution of economic and social benefits as they relate to universal principles of human dignity, respect for diversity/celebration of pluralism, non-discrimination, and interdependence. By including equity we acknowledge that the results of economic models and practices are not merely a function of market efficiency, but rest on ethical grounds related to the purposes we assign to markets, including distributional outcomes. When the purpose is articulated as human well-being, we can design effective policies and allocate resources efficiently in the best interest of people.

Nesting policy design in human agency allows us to generate alternatives in an iterative manner to shift economic institutions away from the injustices of stark inequalities, environmental destruction and debilitating boom and bust crises. With this as our aim, we can discover and institutionalise a new set of normative principles including social justice, equity, democracy, environmental sustainability and economic stability. This approach recognises the power of each of us to make choices that we value, engaging constructively with the world around us to reconstruct economic institutions in ways that are non-exploitative, non-destructive and stable.

Creating New Economic Practices

"Profit is not the explanation, cause or rationale of business behaviour and business decisions, but rather the test of their validity."
—Peter Drucker

A few thoughtful people from government, business and civil society are creating alternative economic practices recognising that people hold the experience, information and wisdom to generate sustainable solutions. They are asking piercing questions: "What forms of entrepreneurship foster human well-being across stakeholders? How can corporations truly perform on corporate social responsibility to deliver on the triple bottom line—people, planet and profit? If there are so many 'good' people with 'good' intentions, why don't we seem to make a dent in the world's problems?" Building on what is working in our practices, they integrate new strategies to maximise value to society.

Indeed, experience shows that we do not need to reinvent the wheel of economic institutions. For example, co-operatives[15] were developed to organise economic activities based on values of self-help, self-responsibility, democracy, equality, equity and solidarity starting in the 18th and 19th centuries. Today, modern co-operatives are business enterprises that extend ownership and control to stakeholders, including consumers, employees and members of the community in general. They serve purposes beyond profit maximisation: they openly and directly provide basic goods, financial services, education, housing and other goods and services to their members. By virtue of their governance principles[16] co-operatives are able to balance profit-making goals with other stakeholder needs. As the Mondragon Cooperative Corporation in Spain and the Federazione Trentina delle Cooperative in Italy show, it is possible to develop co-operative systems that are locally embedded to serve modern community needs and create value across stakeholders.

Today, co-operative enterprises and experiences have inspired the creation of new forms of business enterprises that combine social and economic goals. Some interesting examples include the development of Social Enterprises in Italy, of Community Interest Companies (CICs) in the UK and of B Corporations in the United States. These are innovative forms of for-profit companies that use new governance systems and strategies with the aim of generating profits while contributing to human well-being and social value. In the development arena, cooperative innovations include integrated models that combine fair trade, organic agriculture and microfinance.

And still this innovation remains partial. Cooperative movements around the world understand that—while these forms of economic and social innovation are important—their real strategic asset lays in the values and principles they stand for, not in the systemic innovations per se. As a result, they are looking for new methods and platforms that can empower people to understand the impact of global systems on local communities and generate new systemic expressions of cooperative values and principles.

Similarly, traditional businesses are learning from social enterprise models. Increasingly, they seek to maximise both economic and social returns serving all stakeholders. For example, Raj Sisodia, Jag Seth and David B. Woolfe define a new generation of companies[17] that are maximising value to society—across communities and generations. These humanistic companies—or Firms of Endearment (FoE)—are ultimate value creators: they create new types of capital through experiential value, social value, and of course, financial value. They find that publicly listed FoEs outperform the S&P 500 by significant margins over 10-, 5- and 3-year time horizons[18]. Similarly, in a 1992 study, Harvard Business School professors John Kotter and James Heskett studied the performance of 207 large U.S. companies in 22 different industries over a period of 11 years. They found that companies with strong business cultures that address all stakeholders and empower managers at all levels dramatically outperformed other companies by wide margins along three key indicators: revenue growth (682% versus 166%), stock-price increase (901% versus 74%) and net income increase (756% versus 1%)[19].

Innovations that focus on expanding human well-being are more than just sustainable: they respond to new market demands. Employees and consumers alike are looking for meaningful experiences. Businesses know talent is crucial to innovation. As a result they are creating new strategies to attract and retain the younger generation of workers. They look at the workplace as a way to constructively engage with the world:

a vehicle to express their full potential, including values of diversity and global interdependence[20]. Responding to this, new business practices focus on respect for individuals, transparency and empowerment. They create workplaces that are fun, balanced and flexible, offering creative quality-of-life benefits.

Similarly, businesses recognize that creating new ethical standards is a win-win strategy—for consumers, shareholders, stakeholders and the environment. Conscious consumers demand ethical products that nurture life and generate positive externalities for people. They are also increasingly disillusioned with current business practices focusing on profit alone and determined to expose companies that are exploitative through information and action campaigns[21]. For example, a 2004 Yankelovich poll found that 80% of respondents believe business is too concerned about making a profit and not enough about responsibility to workers, consumers and the environment.

Finally, today's technological revolution is generating new opportunities for alternative business paradigms. Open source systems that foster participation create innovation at scale in a way that was not possible in the post-industrial paradigm. Effective businesses are now learning to tap into the prosumer paradigm of the internet 2.0 revolution[22] and develop new forms of organizations that generate value through reciprocity between producers and consumers.

In essence this emerging paradigm recognizes that we can either continue with business as usual, never really addressing what is not working in our current paradigm; or we can learn to do things differently, transforming risks to generate new business practices that honour people's leadership, fostering human well-being and development worldwide. Business leaders are strategically placed to address the systemic patterns that create the context of our lives. They recognize that when we take ownership of our current reality, we discover new entry points for action and the power of each of us to innovate and create value—as professionals, employees and consumers alike.

Designing Policies and Strategies for Human Well-Being at Scale

> *"The world we have made as a result of the level of thinking we have done thus far creates problems that we cannot solve at the same level at which we have created them ... We shall require a substantially new manner of thinking if humankind is to survive."*
>
> —Albert Einstein

These new economic practices are encouraging, and yet they often stand out as isolated cases. Innovative co-operatives, social enterprises, 'humanistic companies' and their counterparts in government and civil society understand this. They recognize that their key challenges rests in how to systematically activate human agency so as to generate alignment and resonance on universal values among members, employees, consumers, management, public authorities and local communities.

Drawing on both development and business experience, we are working with business leaders who are seeking to break new ground in this direction. Through the UN Leadership and Capacity Development Initiative we design programmes that develop deep transformational practices to align value maximization with universal principles and integrate values with technologies, as well as equity with efficiency. Our own experience sourcing development programmes in human agency shows that it is possible to distinguish, design and deliver policies and strategies that expand human capabilities, transform dysfunctional systems, and create alternative patterns of engagement at scale.

We refer to this programmatic approach as 'full-spectrum' (Figure 1), where learning-in-action methodologies are used a) to activate human agency through transformational leadership and entrepreneurship, b) address systems manifesting in societal and planetary transformation, and c) use appropriate technology that works for everyone[23]. The 'full-spectrum' hologram is a cognitive response map for programmatic design at scale.

Figure 3
Full-Spectrum Design

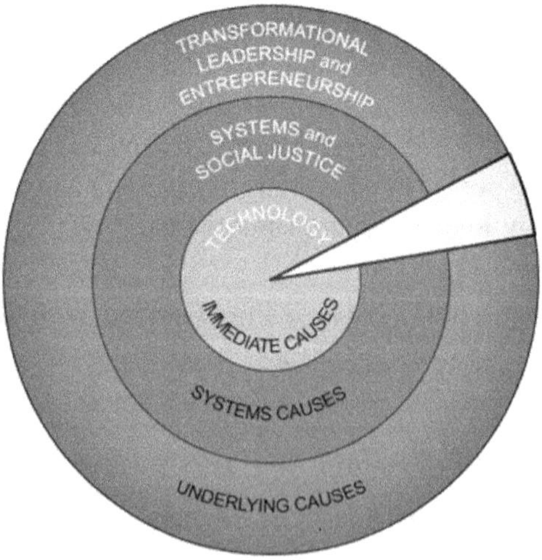

In this paradigm, we recognize that the source of all action—both individual and collective (including systems)—is human agency, the capacity of people to lead change. Knowledge, technology and skills are necessary but not sufficient for designing and delivering effective responses to complex global challenges. Rather, people's insights, information, experiences and resources are brought to bear in the design of responses, so that people everywhere are empowered to innovate and take action that systematically addresses complexity by understanding the underlying, intermediate and immediate causes of any given problem.

Just as we create strategies and policies to address systems issues, our experience shows that human agency and capabilities can be activated, nurtured and developed through leadership competencies, empowering people to be the change they want to see. Transformational leadership methods activate human agency by fostering Emotional Intelligence (EI) competencies[24] first researched and introduced into the business management lexicon by Daniel Goleman[25]. His research with more than 200 organisations around the world showed that EI matters twice as much as technical skills (IQ) in distinguishing high performance employees from mediocre-performing ones. In fact researchers have found that EI leads indirectly to competitive advantage because it is a prerequisite for the kind of leadership necessary to effect positive and sustainable strategic change[26].

Similarly, in *'Five Minds for the Future'*, Harvard professor Howard Gardner[27] builds on his pathbreaking research on multiple intelligences to elaborate the kind of cognitive abilities (or 'minds') that will be critical to success in a 21st century. Beyond the disciplined and synthesizing minds, corresponding to the inner and middle domains, Gardner introduces three other minds—the creating, respectful and ethical minds—which reflect the domain of transformational leadership and entrepreneurship. They equip individuals with the possibility to break new ground, pose unfamiliar questions and put forth new ideas and fresh ways of thinking. These three capacities remain one step ahead of even the most sophisticated computers and robots as they align action with human values and personal ethics. Gardner underscores the importance of cultivating all five minds not just for individual development, but for tangible success in a full range of human endeavors, including education, business, science, art, politics and engineering.

Transformational leadership methods that integrate personal transformation with social transformation can be used to generate new results sourced from people's deepest wisdom. In other words, by learning to use our full cognitive and leadership capacities we can think anew and create new patterns of economic and social engagement for human well-being at scale. Learning-in-action methodologies pioneered for development action through the Leadership for Results Programme on HIV/AIDS of the United Nations Development Programme (UNDP) generated extraordinary results, reaching 130 million people with over five thousand breakthroughs in 40 countries[28]. This work built on the successes of UNICEF's earlier maternal mortality reduction programme in six countries in South Asia[29].

The corporate world offers examples of innovations sourced from transformational leadership that have successfully addressed the triple bottom line—profit, people and planet. In South Africa, for example, Lonmin (a primary producer of Platinum Group Metals) has pioneered transformational processes and standards engaging all stakeholders—management, trade unions and stakeholder communities—to address the prospective closure of one of its mines. Using leadership competencies the strategy addressed critical issues of racial diversity and poverty, generating a new context and future for the mineworkers, their relationship with management and their communities. In India, iDiscoveri works with the education sector and has designed programmes and platforms that integrate leadership in education and management, serving both corporations and public schools[30]. There are a few examples in civil society organisations, such as Ashoka Foundation, where personal transformation manifests in significant transformation, and where interior deeper-rooted forces are addressed along with systems and technological approaches.

Moving to a New Organisational Paradigm: Enterprise 2021

Creating a new entrepreneurship paradigm that generates new patterns sourced in 'full-spectrum' design requires an evolution in organizational development to foster synergy and resonance across sectors, activities and communities. The focus is on taking a long-term perspective where revenue and value is generated not only for shareholders, but also for all stakeholders—integrating values and principles with new systemic patterns across employees, their communities, suppliers and distributors, and the world at large.

Enterprise 2021 is a learning-in-action organisation that displays emotionally intelligent leadership, commitment to exemplary citizenship and recognition that it is part of an economic ecosystem with many interdependent participants. It delivers full spectrum strategies and in-

Enterprise 2021

Inspiring Leadership

1. Led and managed by 'personally aware' individuals, who can distinguish systemic patterns and operate from 'ground of being'
2. Values human dignity, delivering high quality social and economic alternatives for all people, including the marginalized

Whole-System Organisation

3. Is sustainable as a whole system (across the value-chain and stakeholders)
   a. Managerially—as sourced in people's generative capacity
   b. Financially—combining wealth creation/profit while simultaneously contributing to humanity as a strategic choice
   c. Technologically—integrating technology with transformation and human dignity
   d. Environmentally—honouring the planet and all of life and nature in its beauty

Transformative Strategies for Effective Creation

4. Is able to distinguish, design and deliver full spectrum responses related to (i) people, (ii) products, and (iii) process
5. Is fully aware of global/national/local systems and capable of leveraging them to create full spectrum alternatives that empower others and generate 'win-win' solutions
6. Generates space of resonance—where other Enterprise 2021 seed and thrive
7. Actively pursues pathways of excellence to support, finance and sustain Enterprise 2021

Inside-Out Results For Sustainability And Equity

8. Is a 'stage 5' organization*:
   a. Healthy management: expanding human capabilities through personal transformation, participation, and mastery in a specific domain
   b. Principled leadership: the ability to influence without authority and generate results, with integrity/accountability/responsibility
   c. Embodies core principles and creates an enabling environment for human dignity, non discrimination, equity, and non violence
   d. Recognizes interdependence and values diversity: the ability to see different perspectives, providing a space for creating alternatives and innovation

* 'Stage 5' relates to the 'developmental stages of organizations' as they apply to managers, leaders, groups and organizations: Dennis Emberling (www.developmentalconsulting.com) and Allan Henderson, 'Commitment-in-action Programme', GHJ Consulting, 2005.

novations for systems transformation, generating spaces of resonance for principled action grounded in universal human values across people, processes and products. The examples detailed in the previous section represent organizations moving in this direction.

Enterprise 2021 is sustained by inside-out practices, where all actors and stakeholders are empowered to walk the talk and create change that works for everyone. The CEO is personally engaged in generating new strategies sourced in people's wisdom. Enterprise 2021 generates results along the triple bottom line by using transformational approaches that activate human agency and principled action among all players-governing boards, trade unions, shareholders, stakeholders, public authorities and communities. Learning-in-action platforms are designed to encourage innovations and breakthrough initiatives within and outside the company fostering personal engagement and commitment. Community service and corporate social responsibility is then transformed from a public relations instrument to the source of meaningful engagement by management, employees and stakeholders, where partnership is not simply 'technical support' for local civil society organisations, but the opportunity for one's own growth and contribution.

In this way, Enterprise 2021 creates urgency for positive action that generates social and personal value. It opens new pathways to address "systems issues" pioneering new standards within the industry and charting alternatives that impact the "triple bottom-line:" people-planet-profit.

Entrepreneurship that Works for Everyone

Global civil society and thousands of organizations and institutions worldwide have already committed to action sourced in our individual and collective wisdom through the creation of the Earth Charter[31]. Making that vision come alive for a sustainable future requires a paradigm shift in our current economic approaches, supported by new forms of organizations. Some of us are finding the courage to address difficult choices and find ways to harmonize diversity with unity, the exercise of freedom with the common good, short-term objectives with long-term goals. Are you a full-spectrum entrepreneur, a pattern maker of a different kind, bridging personal transformation manifests societal transformation? Every individual, family, organization, and community has a vital role to play:

- Are you a policymaker or elected representative who sees the power of human agency for generating sustainable wealth creation and human

well-being? How do you design policy frameworks and organize services to support the expansion of human freedoms and capabilities?
- Are you an economist, financial analyst or statistician, who seeks to urgently integrate equity with effectiveness and efficiency so that social and economic arrangements expand human capabilities? What new measures and indices are you using to track human agency and well-being?
- Are you a leader in your industry who can distinguish, design and deliver full-spectrum responses that generate innovation sourced from the creative space of the people you lead and the processes you change? What new standards are you generating to deliver along the triple bottom line and maximize value to society as a whole?
- Are you a consultant who addresses complex global, national and sub-national systems and their consequences for people and the planet? What tools are you using to empower people, organizations and institutions to generate social and economic alternatives that combine equity with efficiency and effectiveness?
- Are you an entrepreneur pioneering a new paradigm such as 'Enterprise 2021'? What platforms and approaches are you using to develop people's leadership and capabilities so that your organization delivers innovation across the triple bottom line?

Today we stand at a historical crossroad: we can continue to muddle through, from one crisis to the next, or we can chose to transform today's crises to seek a new beginning and a different trajectory for human evolution. In the face of global instability and insecurity, we have the opportunity to declare that this is enough—that we are more than mere means of development and exchange in a global marketplace. We can learn to trust the power of human agency and wisdom to create a different future, allowing new patterns to unfold so that we can embrace our essential oneness and realize our full potential. The choice is ours.

The authors gratefully acknowledge Ronald Critchlow for insightful comments and suggestions, and Uriel Ortega for designing the diagrams and asking thought provoking questions.

Note

* The opinions expressed in this article are those of the authors, and do not necessarily reflect the policies or views of the United Nations.

References

1. Paola Babos, Programme Officer, Leadership and Capacity Development, United Nations.

2. Monica Sharma, M.D., Director, Leadership and Capacity Development, United Nations.
3. www.millenniumassessment.org.
4. A response a) sourced in wisdom, b) recognizing patterns and creating alternatives, and c) generating concrete measurable results. See Monica Sharma, "From Personal to Planetary Transformation," in Kosmos, Fall/Winter 2007.
5. See http://measureofamerica.org.
6. See www.ethicalmarkets.com.
7. See http://www.michael-hudson.com.
8. www.storyofstuff.com.
9. Amartya K. Sen, op.cit., p. 19.
10. Gallup, State of Global Well-Being 2007.
11. See http://www.grossinternationalhappiness.org.
12. See http://www.beyond-gdp.eu.
13. See http://www.gpiatlantic.org.
14. For more information see OECD, The Global Project on Measuring the Progress of Societies, at http://www.oecd.org/pages/0,3417,en_40033426_40033828_1_1_1_1_1,00.html.
15. A co-operative is defined as an autonomous association of persons united voluntarily to meet their common economic, social and cultural needs and aspirations through a jointly-owned and democratically-controlled enterprise.
16. These include: voluntary and open membership; democratic member control; member economic participation; autonomy and independence; education training and information; co-operation among co-operatives; and concern for community.
17. Raj Sisodia, Jag Seth and Davide B. Wolfe, Firms of Endearment: The Pursuit of Purpose and Profit, Wharton School Publishing, 2007.
18. Over the 10 years ending June 30, 2006, public FoEs returned 1,026 percent for investors, compared to 122 percent for the S&P 500: more than an 8:1 ration. Ibid., p. 16
19. John Kotter and James Heskett, Corporate Culture and Performance, Free Press, 1992.
20. Edward E. Lawler III, "The Talent Lie," Strategy+Business Magazine, www.strategy-business.com/press/article/08204?gko=45947-1876-26908103&tid=230&pg=all.
21. Raj Sisodia, Jag Seth and Davide B. Wolfe, op.cit., p. 24.
22. Don Tapscott and Anthony D. Williams, Wikinomics: How Mass Collaboration Changes Everything, Portfolio, New York, 2006.
23. For a more detailed discussion of the 'full-spectrum' approach, see Monica Sharma, "From Personal to Planetary Transformation," in Kosmos, Fall/Winter 2007.
24. Emotional Intelligence (EI) competencies include four sets of leadership competencies: self-awareness, self-management, social awareness, and relationship skills.
25. Daniel Goleman, Emotional Intelligence, Bantam Books, 1995, New York; and Daniel Goleman., Richard Boyatzis, and Anne McKee, Primal Leadership: Realizing the Power of Emotional Intelligence, Harvard Business School Press, 2002, Cambridge, Mass.
26. Ranjit Voola, Jamie Carlson, and Andrew West (2004), "Emotional Intelligence and Competitive Advantage: Examining the Relationship for a Resource-based View," in Strategic Change, Mar/Apr, Volume 13, Issue 2, pp. 83-93.
27. Howard Gardner was named one of the top five influential business thinkers by the *Wall Street Journal* in a major feature titled "New Breed of Business Gurus Rises" on May 5th 2008.
28. Monica Sharma, 'Conscious Leadership at the Crossroads of Change,' *Shift Magazine,* n.12, September–November 2006.

29. See UNICEF, Saving Women's Lives: a call to rights-based action, UNICEF Regional Office for South Asia, 2000.
30. See http://www.idiscoveri.com.
31. See www.earthcharter.org.

Transformative Entrepreneurship from a Global and Integral Perspective

Nancy B. Roof

World in Transition: Endings and Beginnings

An entrepreneurial spirit of momentous proportions is exploding in every field of human endeavor. The world is ripe for change. Never before in our lifetimes have so many seen first hand the injustice and misery in the world, had the freedom to envision a new world, and been skilled enough to create a sustainable civilization worthy of the dignity of all Life. We are experiencing endings and new beginnings at the same time. In times of transformation the art of 'letting go' becomes as important as the entrepreneurship to create the new. Why is social and transformational entrepreneurship on the rise now?

There is widespread recognition that we are living in a time of transition between two eras. Some are calling it the Second Enlightenment as we begin to realize that the scale of accelerating change is of transformational proportions. As technology brings us closer to one global community the new science of interdependence confirms are interconnectedness. We are being pushed by the realization of the full impact of the damage we have done by exploiting the resources of the planet and our inability to live in harmony with each other threatening the survival of our species. Our inner lives are impoverished as well with growing alienation and fragmentation, the devaluing of feminine values of caring and concern and emotional connections. We are the first generation to know the extent of the world's injustices and misery through new technologies that bring this reality into our living rooms. It is within this context that a new spirit is rising.

When old ways do not work anymore, transformational entrepreneurs rise with new and creative ideas that can shape a new civilization. Their generative creativity solves the problems of the old and creates a whole new worldview and institutions that match.

Rise of Global Civil Society

In the past we relied on governments to solve our problems. We handed our power over to them believing that they represented our interests. We felt secure because we thought that the United Nations would solve our global problems. We looked to traditional sources of philanthropy to provide the financial backing for innovative projects we knew were important and would surely be sufficiently financed. These institutions no longer suffice to address the complexity of the global challenges we face today. Democratic global governance is lacking as nations continue to compete with each other rather than cooperate for the common good. Trust in governments and corporate power is at an all time low. In a world of accelerated change, central planning and decisions made now for future generations to fulfill are outdated before they become a reality. This kind of 'distance' decision-making loses its vitality and inhibits the kind of entrepreneurial spirit necessary for sustainable change.

Hierarchical systems are beginning to collapse in favor of decentralized power in the West and with it increased freedom to innovate. International civil society stepped into the vacuum in the 90s and began to coordinate efforts through major United Nations Conferences. We might say that collective global entrepreneurship emerged at that time. The founding of the International Criminal Court and the movement to outlaw landmines were two of the major accomplishments of the Collective working together. In the 21st century more integration occurred as the most successful global endeavors involve partnerships between governments, civil society, and business. A promising entrepreneurial effort by James Quilligan and Frithof Finkbeiner to coalesce global civil society into a major force for global change is called the Coalition for the Global Commons.

Rise of Global Philanthropists

We need a whole new relationship to philanthropy—and entrepreneurs are leading the way. My experience doing humanitarian work in the former Yugoslavia during the Balkans War was a real eye-opener. To my astonishment many groups designed their projects to meet the limiting requirements of grant-making foundations in order to be financed rather than meeting the needs of the desperate people. The result was numerous overlapping and repeated projects. Other groups flew into the war-zones in the morning—took photos of their landing and quickly took off. Mission accomplished! Fortunately some enlightened foundations, such as Kalliopeia are stepping into the vacuum where the importance of interior values and processes of change are recognized and quality is given precedence over quantity.

Bill Gates is one of several successful business entrepreneurs who is transitioning into global social entrepreneurship. Ted Turner and George Soros are early global philanthropic entrepreneurs who have had a worldwide impact through the United Nations and world economics.

Rise of New Consciousness and Values

Those who grasp the emerging future have expanded their values to global, universal, inclusive, evolutionary and transformational levels. Care and responsibility for all humanity is rapidly expanding beyond national boundaries. Studies of Western values indicate a steady movement away from materialism and status-seeking toward those for the common social good. A movement honoring Generosity of Spirit is beginning to arise spearheaded by such people as Michael Lerner, founder of the Spiritual Progressives, Nipun Mehta at CharityFocus and Pamela Hawley at UniversalGiving.

Entrepreneurs of the inner life and values that have had global impact include Barbara Marx Hubbard a pioneer in global consciousness; Jean Houston and Monica Sharma bringing inner and outer approaches to new global leadership; Ken Wilber, integral philosopher; Don Beck, founder of macro-psychology and Spiral Dynamics Integral; Ervin Laszlo, one of the first to merge science and consciousness towards a new civilization; the global humanitarian Prince El Hassan of Jordan marrying inner spirituality with global action for the global commons; Desmond Tutu, founder of successful forgiveness between nations; Kamran Mofid, founder of Globalization for the Common Good, expanding the understanding of globalization beyond transnational corporations; and many more. New spirituality arising with such groups as Global New Thought, marry the inner world of personal change with the outer world of service. In 1994 the foundational nature of values and spirituality was recognized at the United Nations and we co-founded the Values Caucus in 1994 with the help of Ambassador Somavia, now Director-General of the International Labor Organization, and in 2000 the Spiritual Caucus.

Rise of Global Social Entrepreneurs: The Hope of the World

Social entrepreneurs are a new and major force for global change. The term was coined in the mid 80s by Bill Drayton, one of America's top 25 leaders, according to *US News & World Report.* He founded Ashoka, the premier organization promoting Social Entrepreneurship worldwide. According to Drayton, "Social entrepreneurs are individuals with innovative solutions to society's most pressing social problems. They are ambitious and persistent, tackling major social issues and offering new ideas for wide-scale change."

Social entrepreneurs have the hope, vision and power to change the world, says David Bornstein, author of *How to Change the World.* They are "driven, creative individuals who question the status quo, exploit new opportunities, refuse to give up and remake the world for the better." Largely unreported by the media, the nonprofit sector is the fastest growing segment of society, he says. Millions of ordinary people are stepping in to solve many of the world's most intractable problems.

Jeff Skoll, founder and chairman of Skoll Foundation for social entrepreneurs says, "Human progress has always been led by visionary individuals who seek a better future and dedicate their lives to realizing that promise. These social entrepreneurs tackle some of the world's toughest challenges with grit and determination." As society's change agents, they are pioneers of "innovation that benefits humanity and has a positive impact on the world."

Exceptional people have always existed as beacons of hope. Social entrepreneurs like Mahatma Gandhi, Florence Nightingale, and Mother Theresa are known worldwide. We admire them because they are exceptional and rare. Today there is a massive emergence of individuals and groups with a global mission of world benefit. They are becoming a powerful third force, along with business and governments, with substantial potential influence to change the world.

Kosmos Journal tracks social entrepreneurs and identifies many of the outstanding individuals and groups who are transformational entrepreneurs, leading the way toward the emerging new civilization. They envision some new enterprise and accept full responsibility for its outcome. They shift perceptions, change mind-sets and values. They are self-aware and understand the gift they have to offer while recognizing right timing for its realization. Their passion leads them forward with strength. Courage and persistence overcome inner doubt and outer blockages. They are usually impelled with an inner sense of a mission they were born to serve ... and this mission becomes unstoppable.

They arise spontaneously in most cases, driven by an inner calling or out of outrage over gross injustices or the great suffering of a broken heart. Lack of time and funds are often overridden with determination and will. Because of their generous spirit and love they express constant and deep gratitude for the privilege of being able to serve—the gratitude that comes from living a life of consequence that makes a difference. Their goal is to give laser-like focus to the inner calling they must fulfill for the sake of humanity. They understand that they have only one piece of the whole puzzle and are a leader in that area only and a follower in others. Integrity, trustworthiness and transparency are their most important traits. They are free to go against the tide because they are not drive by the need for money and status.

The success of the enterprise has more to do with the strength of the inner intention of the leader than with the idea itself. When the entrenched interests of those who benefit from the status quo confront a new idea, it is clear that good ideas and being 'right' are not enough.

Many of the entrepreneurs I know who are making a global impact are driven by a strong spirituality and understand the need to change themselves in order to change the world. Little destructive habits of thought can diminish our resolve with doubts and fears and strong emotions can strain our capacity to be centered. We are most courageous when we know we are part of something much larger than ourselves. With spiritual development the urge to serve, to take responsibility and to make a difference becomes compelling.

An Integral Approach to Transformation Entrepreneurship

We at *Kosmos* Journal have discovered that a comprehensive or integral approach is necessary to realize sustainable global transformation in an increasingly complex world. The integral approach recognizes four interdependent dimensions involved with any transformation: the inner life of individuals, their outer behavior, collective worldviews or culture, and outer institutional systems. In the past we have tended to recognize one or two dimensions only, thus taking a partial approach to change. Most often in global circles we find an emphasis on the outer dimensions of politics, economics and law, and a lack of understanding about the importance of inner values, mindsets, attitudes and worldviews that are the foundation of any sustainable development.

The power of the interior dimension is unrecognized in many of the power elite of the world. Development and humanitarian aid often fails because of a lack of understanding that different mindsets and worldviews are the invisible cause of surface behavior. Time and again individuals and countries have exacerbated conflict thinking they were doing the 'right' thing for the other.

We have no trouble recognizing improvements and changes in developing countries where such groups are managing food, water, and life sustaining necessities as Ashoka so successfully illustrates. Unfortunately we tend to look at the outside of problems before recognizing the inner worldviews and mindsets that create many of the challenges the global community now faces.

In addition, the integral approach recognizes that all life is evolving and changing. All human life, cultures, nature, even the universe are processes rather than nouns or fixed things. Further, research indicates that the trajectory of evolution is towards larger wholes and the harmony and oneness of all life. Further, the integral approach recognizes the diverse deep structural value systems that underlie surface behavior.

Global Entrepreneur, Don Beck, founder of Spiral Dynamics Integral and Global Macro Psychology, is developing natural designs in many countries including Palestine with his talented assistant, Elza. His natural designs are based on discovering the emerging future based on deep listening to the needs of the people involved. Most important in his work is understanding the evolution of deeply ingrained value systems formed as a result of different life circumstances. Tracing the evolution of culture we find stages of development from survival, to tribal, to heroic, to traditional, to modern, to postmodern and integral. Without a consideration of these stages of development we can and have imposed our own experience and solutions on others. In developing countries we find tribal and heroic consciousness dominates. In Western society we find traditionalist, modern scientific materialism, and postmodern inclusive values—and sometimes integral with a global vision. These clashing worldviews account for many of the conflicts we experience today. Networks, partnerships, dialogues, listening skills and natural designs are needed to manage these differences as we move into the new civilization.

The Power of an Innovative Evolutionary Idea, Motivated by Love, Fulfilled with an Invincible Will

For me it all began with an amazing inner experience rather than an evolutionary idea. I was privy to early information about the genocide perpetrated in the former Yugoslavia of thousands of innocent people just like you and me. I was overcome with grief and felt helpless to change the situation. I then had an amazing inner experience, which I shall never forget. It was much bigger than compassion and caring. It was a huge inner explosion breaking my heart that had expanded to embrace the world-heart. I suffered for each innocent victim of the atrocity although I had never actually met any of them. I knew nothing about the former Yugoslavia except that a great injustice was happening. My inner world called me in the most powerful way to learn—and I did. Using my own finances I traveled to the war zone and interviewed dozens of people and organizations, asking the question. What do you need? The trauma and stress lived daily by the service providers proved unbearable and disabling. The innovative idea came directly from the people themselves who told me what they needed. The victims of war extended to families and caretakers—creating untold mental damage reaching way beyond the direct victims. We were in virgin territory. Attention had never been given to the secondary effects showered on families and service providers of direct victims. Despite all odds we found a way to set up the first training programs in a war-zone for service providers suffering from secondary traumatic stress.

My story is repeated over and over again by the newly arising social entrepreneurs for humanity.

Nancy Rivard was driven by compassion for orphaned children and unmet humanitarian needs she discovered while traveling worldwide as an airline hostess. She thought, "Why not utilize empty areas of airplanes to bring medicines and aid to those in need?" Moved by a broken heart and inspired by an innovative idea, she established the amazing Airline Ambassador program. She has received several awards in recognition of her entrepreneurial service that has hand-delivered $42 million in aid to 52 countries.

Another friend of *Kosmos*, Amber Chand, lived in a refugee camp for part of her childhood. She now runs a entrepreneurial business selling beautiful handicrafts made by women in refugee camps who have no other way of earning income.

John Marks had a powerful idea and he was skilled enough to put it into action. He asked, "What we related to each other through our commonalities rather than our differences?" Search for Common Ground was the result, now serving thousands in 17 countries with a $13 million budget.

It is inspiring to know that every single person has the potential to change the world for the better—and many already have. Peter Drucker says, "Whenever anything is being accomplished, it is being done by a monomaniacal with a mission." And that is what the social entrepreneur in each of us is.

Individuals and groups of people with an innovative idea, compassionate love of humanity and animated by an invincible will are the hope of the world. We are just beginning to see the immense power of this triple combination to effect worldwide change. The entrepreneurial spirit in each of us may well be what saves us all.

PART I

THE ECONOMIC PARADIGM FOR AN EARTH IN BALANCE

B. TOWARDS A RESPONSIBLE MARKET ECONOMY

Plan B 3.0: Mobilizing to Save Civilization

Lester R. Brown *

During the late summer of 2007, the news of accelerating ice melting arrived at a frenetic pace. In early September, the Guardian in London reported, "The Arctic ice cap has collapsed at an unprecedented rate this summer, and levels of sea ice in the region now stand at a record low." Experts were "stunned" by the loss of ice, as an area almost twice the size of Britain disappeared in a single week.

Mark Serreze, a veteran Arctic specialist with the U.S. National Snow and Ice Data Center, said: "It's amazing. If you asked me a couple of years ago when the Arctic could lose all of its ice, then I would have said 2100, or 2070 maybe. But now I think that 2030 is a reasonable estimate."

A few days later, the Guardian, reporting from a symposium in Ilulissat, Greenland, said that the Greenland ice cap is melting so fast that it is triggering minor earthquakes as pieces of ice weighing several billion tons each break off the ice sheet and slide into the sea. Robert Corell, chairman of the Arctic Climate Impact Assessment, reported that "we have seen a massive acceleration of the speed with which these glaciers are moving into the sea. The ice is moving at 2 meters an hour on a front 5 kilometers (3 miles) long and 1,500 meters deep."

Corell said that when flying over the Ilulissat glacier he had "seen gigantic holes (moulins) in it through which swirling masses of melt water were falling." This melt water lubricates the surface between the glacier and the land below, causing the glacier to flow faster into the sea. Veli Kallio, a Finnish scientist who had been analyzing the earthquakes, said they were new to northwest Greenland and showed the potential for the entire ice sheet to break up and collapse.

Corell noted that the projected rise in sea level during this century of 18–59 centimeters (7–23 inches) by the Intergovernmental Panel on Climate Change was based on data that were two years old. He said that some scientists now believe the increase could be as much as 2 meters.

In late August, a Reuters story began with "a thaw of Antarctic ice is outpacing predictions by the U.N. climate panel and could in the worst case drive up world sea levels by 2 meters (6 feet) by 2100," a leading expert said. Chris Rapley, head of the British Antarctic Survey said, "The ice is moving faster both in Greenland and in the Antarctic than the glaciologists had believed would happen."

Several months earlier, scientists had reported that the Gangotri glacier, the principal glacier that feeds the Ganges River, is melting at an accelerating rate and could disappear entirely in a matter of decades. The Ganges would become a seasonal river, flowing only during the monsoon season.

Glaciers on the Tibet-Qinghai Plateau that feed the Yellow and Yangtze rivers are melting at 7 percent a year. Yao Tandong, one of China's leading glaciologists, believes that at this rate, two thirds of these glaciers could disappear by 2060.

These glaciers in the Himalayas and on the Tibet-Qinghai Plateau feed all the major rivers of Asia, including the Indus, Ganges, Mekong, Yangtze, and Yellow Rivers. It is the water from these rivers that irrigates the rice and wheat fields in the region.

We are crossing natural thresholds that we cannot see and violating deadlines that we do not recognize. Nature is the time keeper, but we cannot see the clock. Among the other environmental trends undermining our future are shrinking forests, expanding deserts, falling water tables, collapsing fisheries, disappearing species, and rising temperatures. The temperature increases bring crop-withering heat waves, more-destructive storms, more-intense droughts, more forest fires, and, of course, ice melting.

We can see from ice melting alone that our civilization is in trouble. If the Greenland ice sheet melts, sea level rises 7 meters (23 feet). If the West Antarctic Ice Sheet breaks up, and many scientists think it could go before Greenland, it adds another 5 meters to the increase, for a total of 12 meters (39 feet).

The International Institute for Environment and Development has studied the likely effects of a 10-meter (33-foot) rise. Their 2007 study projected more than 600 million refugees from rising seas. More people than currently live in the United States and Western Europe combined would be forced to migrate inland to escape the rising waters.

Now that we are belatedly recognizing these trends and the need to reverse them, time is running out. We are in a race between tipping points in the earth's natural systems and those in the world's political systems. Which will tip first? Will we reach the point where the melting of the Greenland ice sheet is irreversible? Or will we decide to phase out coal-fired power plants fast enough to avoid this wholesale ice melting?

A rise in temperature to the point where the earth's ice sheets and glaciers melt is only one of many environmental tipping points needing our attention. While the earth's temperature is rising, water tables are falling on every continent. Here the challenge is to raise water use efficiency and stabilize population before water shortages become life-threatening.

Population growth, which contributes to all the problems discussed here, has its own tipping point. Scores of countries have developed enough economically to sharply reduce mortality but not yet enough to reduce fertility. As a result, they are caught in the demographic trap—a situation where rapid population growth begets poverty and poverty begets rapid population growth. In this situation, countries eventually tip one way or the other. They either break out of the cycle or they break down.

Over the last few decades, the world has accumulated a growing number of unresolved problems, including those just mentioned. As the stresses from these unresolved problems accumulate, weaker governments are beginning to break down, leading to what are now commonly referred to as failing states.

Failing states are an early sign of a failing civilization. The countries at the top of the lengthening list of failing states are not particularly surprising. They include, for example, Iraq, Sudan, Somalia, Chad, Afghanistan, the Democratic Republic of the Congo, and Haiti. And the list grows longer each year, raising a disturbing question: How many failing states will it take before civilization itself fails? No one knows the answer, but it is a question we must ask.

A Massive Market Failure

When Nicholas Stern, former chief economist at the World Bank, released his ground-breaking study in late 2006 on the future costs of climate change, he talked about a massive market failure. He was referring to the failure of the market to incorporate the climate change costs of burning fossil fuels. The costs, he said, would be measured in the trillions of dollars. The difference between the market prices for fossil fuels and the prices that also incorporate their environmental costs to society are huge.

The roots of our current dilemma lie in the enormous growth of the human enterprise over the last century. Since 1900, the world economy has expanded 20-fold and world population has increased fourfold. Although there were places in 1900 where local demand exceeded the capacity of natural systems, this was not a global issue. There was some deforestation, but overpumping of water was virtually unheard of, overfishing was rare, and carbon emissions were so low that there was no serious effect on climate. The indirect costs of these early excesses were negligible.

Now with the economy as large as it is, the indirect costs of burning coal—the costs of air pollution, acid rain, devastated ecosystems, and climate change—can exceed the direct costs, those of mining the coal and transporting it to the power plant. As a result of neglecting to account for these indirect costs, the market is undervaluing many goods and services, creating economic distortions.

As economic decisionmakers—whether consumers, corporate planners, government policymakers, or investment bankers—we all depend on the market for information to guide us. In order for markets to work and economic actors to make sound decisions, the markets must give us good information, including the full cost of the products we buy. But the market is giving us bad information, and as a result we are making bad decisions—so bad that they are threatening civilization.

The market is in many ways an incredible institution. It allocates resources with an efficiency that no central planning body can match and it easily balances supply and demand. The market has some fundamental weaknesses, however. It does not incorporate into prices the indirect costs of producing goods. It does not value nature's services properly. And it does not respect the sustainable yield thresholds of natural systems. It also favors the near term over the long term, showing little concern for future generations.

One of the best examples of this massive market failure can be seen in the United States, where the gasoline pump price in mid-2007 was $3 per gallon. But this price reflects only the cost of discovering the oil, pumping it to the surface, refining it into gasoline, and delivering the gas to service stations. It overlooks the costs of climate change as well as the costs of tax subsidies to the oil industry (such as the oil depletion allowance), the burgeoning military costs of protecting access to oil in the politically unstable Middle East, and the health care costs for treating respiratory illnesses from breathing polluted air.

Based on a study by the International Center for Technology Assessment, these costs now total nearly $12 per gallon ($3.17 per liter) of gasoline burned in the United States. If these were added to the $3 cost of the gasoline itself, motorists would pay $15 a gallon for gas at the pump. In reality, burning gasoline is very costly, but the market tells us it is cheap, thus grossly distorting the structure of the economy. The challenge facing governments is to restructure tax systems by systematically incorporating indirect costs as a tax to make sure the price of products reflects their full costs to society and by offsetting this with a reduction in income taxes.

Another market distortion became abundantly clear in the summer of 1998 when China's Yangtze River valley, home to nearly 400 million people, was wracked by some of the worst flooding in history. The resulting damages of $30 billion exceeded the value of the country's annual rice harvest.

After several weeks of flooding, the government in Beijing announced a ban on tree cutting in the Yangtze River basin. It justified this by noting that trees standing are worth three times as much as trees cut: the flood control services provided by forests were far more valuable than the lumber in the trees. In effect, the market price was off by a factor of three.

This situation has occasional parallels in the commercial world. In the late 1990s Enron, a Texas-based energy trading corporation, may have appeared on the cover of more business magazines than any other U.S. company. It was spectacularly successful. The darling of Wall Street, it was the seventh most valuable corporation in the United States in early 2001. Unfortunately, when independent auditors began looking closely at Enron in late 2001 they discovered that the company had been leaving certain costs off the books. When these were included, Enron was worthless. Its stock, which had traded as high as $90 a share, was suddenly trading for pennies a share. Enron was bankrupt. The collapse was complete. It no longer exists.

We are doing today exactly what Enron did. We are leaving costs off the books, but on a far larger scale. We focus on key economic indicators like economic growth and the increase in international trade and investment, and the situation looks good. But if we incorporate all the indirect costs that the market omits when setting prices, a very different picture emerges. If we persist in leaving these costs off the books, we will face the same fate as Enron.

Today, more than ever before, we need political leaders who can see the big picture, who understand the relationship between the economy and its environmental support systems. And since the principal advisors to government are economists, we need economists who can think like ecologists. Unfortunately they are rare. Ray Anderson, founder and chairman of Atlanta-based Interface, a leading world manufacturer of industrial carpet, is especially critical of economics as it is taught in many universities: "We continue to teach economics students to trust the 'invisible hand' of the market, when the invisible hand is clearly blind to the externalities and treats massive subsidies, such as a war to protect oil for the oil companies, as if the subsidies were deserved. Can we really trust a blind invisible hand to allocate resources rationally?"

Environment and Civilization

To understand our current environmental dilemma, it helps to look at earlier civilizations that also got into environmental trouble. Our early twenty-first century civilization is not the first to face the prospect of environmentally induced economic decline. The question is how we will respond.

As Jared Diamond points out in his book Collapse, some of the early societies that were in environmental trouble were able to change their ways in time to avoid decline and collapse. Six centuries ago, for example, Icelanders realized that overgrazing on their grass-covered highlands was leading to extensive soil loss from the inherently thin soils of the region. Rather than lose the grasslands and face economic decline, farmers joined together to determine how many sheep the highlands could sustain and then allocated quotas among themselves, thus preserving their grasslands. The Icelanders understood the consequences of overgrazing and reduced their sheep numbers to a level that could be sustained. Their wool production and woolen goods industry continue to thrive today.

Not all societies have fared as well as the Icelanders. The early Sumerian civilization of the fourth millennium BC had advanced far beyond any that had existed before. Its carefully engineered irrigation system gave rise to a highly productive agriculture, one that enabled farmers to produce a food surplus, supporting formation of the first cities. Managing Sumer's irrigation system required a sophisticated social organization. The Sumerians had the first cities and the first written language, the cuneiform script.

By any measure it was an extraordinary civilization, but there was an environmental flaw in the design of its irrigation system, one that would eventually undermine its food supply. The water that backed up behind dams built across the Euphrates was diverted onto the land through a network of gravity-fed canals. As with most irrigation systems, some irrigation water percolated downward. In this region, where underground drainage was weak, this slowly raised the water table. As the water climbed to within inches of the surface, it began to evaporate into the atmosphere, leaving behind salt. Over time, the accumulation of salt on the soil surface lowered the land's productivity.

As salt accumulated and wheat yields declined, the Sumerians shifted to barley, a more salt-tolerant plant. This postponed Sumer's decline, but it was treating the symptoms, not the cause, of their falling crop yields. As salt concentrations continued to build, the yields of barley eventually declined also. The resultant shrinkage of the food supply undermined this once-great civilization. As land productivity declined, so did the civilization.

Archeologist Robert McC. Adams has studied the site of ancient Sumer on the central floodplain of the Euphrates River, an empty, desolate area now outside the frontiers of cultivation. He describes how the "tangled dunes, long disused canal levees, and the rubble-strewn mounds of former settlement contribute only low, featureless relief. Vegetation is sparse, and in many areas it is almost wholly absent ... Yet at one time, here lay the core, the heartland, the oldest urban, literate civilization in the world."

The New World counterpart to Sumer is the Mayan civilization that developed in the lowlands of what is now Guatemala. It flourished from AD 250 until its collapse around AD 900. Like the Sumerians, the Mayans had developed a sophisticated, highly productive agriculture, this one based on raised plots of earth surrounded by canals that supplied water.

As with Sumer, the Mayan demise was apparently linked to a failing food supply. For this New World civilization, it was deforestation and soil erosion that undermined agriculture. Changes in climate may also have played a role. Food shortages apparently triggered civil conflict among the various Mayan cities as they competed for something to eat. Today this region is covered by jungle, reclaimed by nature.

The Icelanders crossed a political tipping point that enabled them to come together and limit grazing before grassland deterioration reached the point of no return. The Sumerians and Mayans failed to do so. Time ran out.

Today, our successes and problems flow from the extraordinary growth in the world economy over the last century. The economy's annual growth, once measured in billions of dollars, is now measured in the trillions. Indeed, just the growth in the output of goods and services in 2007 exceeded the total output of the world economy in 1900.

While the economy is growing exponentially, the earth's natural capacities, such as its ability to supply fresh water, forest products, and seafood, have not increased. A team of scientists led by Mathis Wackernagel concluded in a 2002 study published by the U.S. National Academy of Sciences that humanity's collective demands first surpassed the earth's regenerative capacity around 1980. Today, global demands on natural systems exceed their sustainable yield capacity by an estimated 25 percent. This means we are meeting current demands by consuming the earth's natural assets, setting the stage for decline and collapse.

In our modern high-tech civilization, it is easy to forget that the economy, indeed our existence, is wholly dependent on the earth's natural systems and resources. We depend, for example, on the earth's climate system for an environment hospitable to agriculture, on the hydrological cycle to provide us with fresh water, and on long-term geological processes to convert rocks into the soil that has made the earth such a biologically productive planet.

There are now so many of us placing such heavy demands on the earth that we are overwhelming its natural capacities to meet our needs. The earth's forests are shrinking. Each year overgrazing converts vast areas of grassland into desert. The pumping of underground water exceeds natural recharge in countries containing half the world's people, leaving many without adequate water as their wells go dry.

Each of us depends on the products and services provided by the earth's ecosystems, ranging from forest to wetlands, from coral reefs to grasslands. Among the services these ecosystems provide are water purification, pollination, carbon sequestration, flood control, and soil conservation. A four-year study of the world's ecosystems by 1,360 scientists, the Millennium Ecosystem Assessment, reported that 15 of 24 primary ecosystem services are being degraded or pushed beyond their limits. For example, three quarters of oceanic fisheries, a major source of protein in the human diet, are being fished at or beyond their limits, and many are headed toward collapse.

Tropical rainforests are another ecosystem under severe stress, including the vast Amazon rainforest. Thus far roughly 20 percent of the rainforest has been cleared either for cattle ranching or soybean farming.

Another 22 percent has been weakened by logging and road building, letting sunlight reach the forest floor, drying it out, and turning it into kindling. When it reaches this point, the rainforest loses its resistance to fire and begins to burn when ignited by lightning strikes.

Scientists believe that if half the Amazon is cleared or weakened, this may be the tipping point, the threshold beyond which the rainforest cannot be saved. We will have crossed the tipping point, with consequences that will reverberate around the world. Amazonian ecologist Philip Fearnside says "with every tree that falls, we increase the probability that the tipping point will arrive." Geoffrey Lean, summarizing the findings of a symposium on the Amazon in the Independent, says that the alternatives to a rainforest in the Amazon would be "dry savannah at best, desert at worst."

Daniel Nepstad, an Amazon-based senior scientist from the Woods Hole Research Center, sees a future of "megafires" sweeping through the drying jungle. He notes that the carbon stored in the Amazon's trees equals roughly 15 years of human-induced carbon emissions in the atmosphere. If we reach this tipping point we will have triggered yet another climate feedback, taken another step that could help seal our fate as a civilization.

The excessive pressures on a given resource typically begin in a few countries and then slowly spread to others. Nigeria and the Philippines, once net exporters of forest products, are now importers. Thailand, now largely deforested, has banned logging. So has China, which is turning to Siberia and to the few remaining forested countries in Southeast Asia, such as Myanmar and Papua New Guinea, for the logs it needs.

A similar situation exists with fisheries. At first only a few fisheries were under excessive pressure, mostly in the North Sea, off the east coast of North America, and off the coast of East Asia. Now with fishing fleets replete with factory processing ships and modern technologies, overfishing is the rule, not the exception. In the absence of intervention, the decline in scores of fisheries will culminate in collapse. Some, such as the cod fishery off the coast of Newfoundland and the Atlantic tuna fishery, may never recover. The Chilean sea bass fishery in the Southern Ocean and the sturgeon fishery in the Caspian Sea may also be approaching the point of no return.

As wells go dry, as grasslands are converted into desert, and as soils erode, people are forced to migrate elsewhere, either within their country or across national boundaries. As the earth's natural capacities at the local level are exceeded, the declining economic possibilities generate a flow of environmental refugees.

While the continuing erosion of the economy's environmental support systems has convinced environmentalists, natural scientists, and others of the need to restructure the global economy, many others are not yet convinced. What is happening in China may change their minds.

China: Why the Existing Economic Model Will Fail

For almost as long as I can remember we have been saying that the United States, with 5 percent of the world's people, consumes a third or more of the earth's resources. That was true. It is no longer true. Today China consumes more basic resources than the United States does.

Among the key commodities such as grain, meat, oil, coal, and steel, China consumes more of each than the United States except for oil, where the United States still has a wide (though narrowing) lead. China uses a third more grain than the United States. Its meat consumption is nearly double that of the United States. It uses three times as much steel.

These numbers reflect national consumption, but what would happen if consumption per person in China were to catch up to that of the United States? If we assume that China's economy slows from the 10 percent annual growth of recent years to 8 percent, then in 2030 income per person in China will reach the level it is in the United States today.

If we also assume that the Chinese will spend their income more or less as Americans do today, then we can translate their income into consumption. If, for example, each person in China consumes paper at the current American rate, then in 2030 China's 1.46 billion people will need twice as much paper as is produced worldwide today. There go the world's forests.

If we assume that in 2030 there are three cars for every four people in China, as there now are in the United States, China will have 1.1 billion cars. The world currently has 860 million cars. To provide the needed roads, highways, and parking lots, China would have to pave an area comparable to what it now plants in rice.

By 2030 China would need 98 million barrels of oil a day. The world is currently producing 85 million barrels a day and may never produce much more than that. There go the world's oil reserves.

What China is teaching us is that the western economic model—the fossil-fuel-based, automobile-centered, throwaway economy—is not going to work for China. If it does not work for China, it will not work for India, which by 2030 may have an even larger population than China.

Nor will it work for the other 3 billion people in developing countries who are also dreaming the "American dream." And in an increasingly integrated global economy, where we all depend on the same grain, oil, and steel, the western economic model will no longer work for the industrial countries either.

The overriding challenge for our generation is to build a new economy—one that is powered largely by renewable sources of energy, that has a much more diversified transport system, and that reuses and recycles everything. We have the technology to build this new economy, an economy that will allow us to sustain economic progress. Can we build it fast enough to avoid a breakdown of social systems?

Mounting Stresses, Failing States

States fail when national governments lose control of part or all of their territory and can no longer ensure the personal security of their people. When governments lose their monopoly on power, law and order begin to disintegrate. When they can no longer provide basic services such as education, health care, and food security, they lose their legitimacy. A government in this position may no longer be able to collect enough revenue to finance effective governance. Societies can become so fragmented that they lack the cohesion to make decisions.

Failing states often degenerate into civil war. As warring groups vie for power, they become a threat to neighboring countries when internal conflict spills over national borders. They provide possible training grounds for international terrorist groups, as in Afghanistan, Iraq, and Somalia, or they become sources of drugs, as in Myanmar (formerly Burma) or Afghanistan (with the latter accounting for 92 percent of the world's opium supply in 2006). Because they lack functioning health care services, weakened states can become a source of infectious disease, as Nigeria has for polio. In failed states, where governments are no longer in control, power is typically assumed by other elements in society. In Afghanistan, it is local warlords; in Somalia, tribal chiefs; in Haiti, street gangs. New governing groups may also include drug rings or organized crime.

In the past, governments have been concerned by the concentration of too much power in one state, as in Nazi Germany, Imperial Japan, and the Soviet Union. But today it is failing states that provide the greatest threat to global order and stability. As *Foreign Policy* magazine notes, "World leaders once worried about who was amassing power; now they worry about the absence of it."

The U.S. Central Intelligence Agency estimates the number of failing states at 20 or so. The British government's international development arm has identified 46 so-called fragile states. The World Bank focuses its attention on 35 low-income countries under stress, which it also describes as fragile states.

The most systematic ongoing effort to analyze failed and failing states is one undertaken jointly by the Fund for Peace and the Carnegie Endowment for International Peace, which is updated annually and published in each July/August issue of *Foreign Policy*. This invaluable service, which draws on thousands of information sources worldwide, is rich with insights into the changes that are under way in the world and, in a broad sense, where the world is heading.

In this analysis, countries are graded on 12 social, economic, political, and military indicators, with scores that range from 1 to 10. Scores for each indicator are aggregated into a single country indicator: the Failed States Index. A score of 120, the maximum, means that a society is failing totally by every measure.

In the first *Foreign Policy* listing, based on data for 2004 and published in 2005, 7 countries had scores of 100 or more. In 2005 this increased to 9 countries, and in 2006 it was 12—nearly doubling in two years. This short trend is far from definitive, but both the rise in country scores near the top and the near doubling of countries with scores of 100 or higher suggest that state failure is increasing.

Most of the top 10 countries in 2006 (see ranking Table on page 103) were near the top of the list in the two preceding years. In reviewing the data for 2006, Foreign Policy noted that "few encouraging signs emerged in 2006 to suggest the world is on a path to greater peace and stability." The one bright spot was the improvement in Liberia, which moved from ninth in 2004, on the verge of state failure, to twenty-seventh in 2006. When Liberia, after years of turmoil, held an election that brought Ellen Johnson-Sirleaf to the presidency in late 2005, it restored both a measure of political stability and hope for the country's future.

Ranking on the Failed States Index is closely linked with key demographic and environmental indicators. Of the top 20 failing states, 17 have rapid rates of population growth, many of them expanding at close to 3 percent a year or 20-fold per century. In 5 of these 17 countries, women have an average of nearly seven children each. Viewed in terms of the demographic transition, these 17 countries are caught in the demographic trap. They have progressed far enough economically to reduce mortality but not far enough to create the economic and social conditions for fertility decline.

In all but 6 of the top 20 failing states, at least 40 percent of the population is under 15. Such a large share of young people often signals future political instability. Young men, lacking employment opportunities, often become disaffected, making them ready recruits for insurgency movements.

Not surprisingly, there is also often a link between the degree of state failure and the destruction of environmental support systems. In a number of countries on the list—including Sudan, Somalia, and Haiti—deforestation, grassland deterioration, and soil erosion are widespread. The countries with fast-growing populations are also facing a steady shrinkage of both cropland and water per person. After a point, as rapid population growth, deteriorating environmental support systems, and poverty reinforce each other, the resulting instability makes it difficult to attract investment from abroad. Even public assistance programs from donor countries are often phased out as the security breakdown threatens the lives of aid workers, forcing their withdrawal.

State failure is not neatly contained by national boundaries. It often spreads to neighboring countries, much as the genocide in Rwanda spilled over into the Democratic Republic of the Congo, eventually drawing several other countries into the war that claimed some 3.9 million lives in the Congo over several years. More recently, the killings in Darfur have spread into Chad.

As the number of failing states grows, dealing with various international crises becomes more difficult. Actions that may be relatively simple in a healthy world order of functioning nation states, such as controlling the spread of infectious diseases, could become difficult or impossible in a world with many disintegrating states. Even maintaining international flows of raw materials could become a challenge. At some point, spreading political instability could disrupt global economic progress, suggesting that we need to address the causes of state failure with a heightened sense of urgency.

A Civilizational Tipping Point

In recent years there has been a growing concern over thresholds or tipping points in nature. For example, scientists worry about when the shrinking population of an endangered species will fall to a point from which it cannot recover. Marine biologists are concerned about the point where overfishing will trigger the collapse of a fishery.

We know there were social tipping points in earlier civilizations, points at which they were overwhelmed by the forces threatening them. For instance, at some point the irrigation-related salt buildup in their soil overwhelmed the capacity of the Sumerians to deal with it. With the Mayans, there came a time when the effects of cutting too many trees and the associated loss of topsoil were simply more than they could manage.

The social tipping points that lead to decline and collapse when societies are overwhelmed by a single threat or by simultaneous multiple threats are not always easily anticipated. As a general matter, more economically advanced countries can deal with new threats more effectively than developing countries can. For example, while governments of industrial countries have been able to hold HIV infection rates among adults under 1 percent, many developing-country governments have failed to do so and are now struggling with much higher infection rates. This is most evident in some southern African countries, where up to 20 percent or more of adults are infected.

A similar situation exists with population growth. While populations in nearly all industrial countries except the United States have stopped growing, rapid growth continues in nearly all the countries of Africa, the Middle East, and the Indian subcontinent. Nearly all of the 70 million people being added to world population each year are born in countries where natural support systems are already deteriorating in the face of excessive population pressure, in the countries least able to support them. In these countries, the risk of state failure is growing.

Some issues seem to exceed even the management skills of the more advanced countries, however. When countries first detected falling underground water tables, it was logical to expect that governments in affected countries would quickly raise water use efficiency and stabilize population in order to stabilize aquifers. Unfortunately, not one country—industrial or developing—has done so. Two failing states where overpumping and security-threatening water shortages loom large are Pakistan and Yemen.

Although the need to cut carbon emissions has been evident for some time, not one country—industrial or developing—has succeeded in becoming carbon-neutral. Thus far this has proved too difficult politically for even the most technologically advanced societies. Could rising carbon dioxide levels in the atmosphere prove to be as unmanageable for our early twenty-first century civilization as rising salt levels in the soil were for the Sumerians in 4000 BC?

Another potentially severe stress on governments is the coming decline in oil production. Although world oil production has exceeded new oil discoveries by a wide margin for more than 20 years, only Sweden and Iceland actually have anything that remotely resembles a plan to effectively cope with a shrinking supply of oil.

This is not an exhaustive inventory of unresolved problems, but it does give a sense of how their number is growing as we fail to solve existing problems even as new ones are being added to the list. The risk is that these accumulating problems and their consequences will overwhelm more and more governments, leading to widespread state failure and eventually the failure of civilization.

Analytically, the challenge is to assess the effects of mounting stresses on the global system. These stresses are perhaps most evident in their effect on food security, which was the weak point of many earlier civilizations that collapsed. Several converging trends are making it difficult for the world's farmers to keep up with the growth in food demand. Prominent among these are falling water tables, the growing conversion of cropland to nonfarm uses, and more extreme climate events, including crop-withering heat waves, droughts, and floods. As a result, world grain production has fallen short of consumption in seven of the last eight years, dropping world grain stocks to their lowest level in 34 years. Corn prices nearly doubled and wheat prices nearly tripled between late 2005 and late 2007.

Just when it seemed that things could not get much worse, the United States, the world's breadbasket, is planning to double the share of its grain harvest going to fuel ethanol—from 16 percent of the 2006 crop to 30 percent or so of the 2008 crop. With this enormous growth in the U.S. capacity to convert grain into fuel, the world price of grain is moving up toward its oil-equivalent value. This ill-conceived U.S. effort to reduce its oil insecurity has helped drive world grain prices to all-time highs, creating unprecedented world food insecurity. Under this stress, still more states may fail.

State failure can come quickly—and often unexpectedly. In looking back at earlier civilizations, it was often a single environmental trend that led to their demise. But countries today are facing several simultaneously, some of which reinforce each other. The earlier civilizations such as the Sumerians and Mayans were often local, rising and falling in isolation from the rest of the world. In contrast, we will either mobilize together to save our global civilization, or we will all be potential victims of its disintegration.

Plan B—A Plan of Hope

Plan B is shaped by what is needed to save civilization, not by what may currently be considered politically feasible. Plan B does not fit within a particular discipline, sector, or set of assumptions.

Implementing Plan B means undertaking several actions simultaneously, including eradicating poverty, stabilizing population, and restoring the earth's natural systems. It also involves cutting carbon dioxide emissions 80 percent by 2020, largely through a mobilization to raise energy efficiency and harness renewable sources of energy.

Not only is the scale of this save-our-civilization plan ambitious, so is the speed with which it must be implemented. We must move at wartime speed, restructuring the world energy economy at a pace reminiscent of the restructuring of the U.S. industrial economy in 1942 following the Japanese attack on Pearl Harbor. The shift from producing cars to planes, tanks, and guns was accomplished within a matter of months. One of the keys to this extraordinarily rapid restructuring was a ban on the sale of cars, a ban that lasted nearly three years.

We face an extraordinary challenge, but there is much to be upbeat about. All the problems we face can be dealt with using existing technologies. And almost everything we need to do to move the world economy back onto an environmentally sustainable path has already been done in one or more countries.

We see the components of Plan B—the alternative to business as usual—in new technologies already on the market. On the energy front, for example, an advanced-design wind turbine can produce as much energy as an oil well. Japanese engineers have designed a vacuum-sealed refrigerator that uses only one eighth as much electricity as those marketed a decade ago. Gas-electric hybrid automobiles, getting nearly 50 miles per gallon, are twice as efficient as the average car on the road.

Numerous countries are providing models of the various components of Plan B. Denmark, for example, today gets 20 percent of its electricity from wind and has plans to push this to 50 percent. Some 60 million Europeans now get their residential electricity from wind farms. By the end of 2007, some 40 million Chinese homes will be getting their hot water from rooftop solar water heaters. Iceland now heats close to 90 percent of its homes with geothermal energy. In so doing, it has virtually eliminated the use of coal for home heating.

With food, India—using a small-scale dairy production model that relies almost entirely on crop residues as a feed source—has more than quadrupled its milk production since 1970, overtaking the United States as the world's leading milk producer. The value of India's dairy production now exceeds that of its rice harvest.

Fish farming advances in China, centered on the use of an ecologically sophisticated carp polyculture, have made this the first country where fish farm output exceeds the oceanic catch. Indeed, the 32 million tons of farmed fish produced in China in 2005 was equal to roughly a third of the world's oceanic fish catch.

We see what a Plan B world could look like in the reforested mountains of South Korea. Once a barren, almost treeless country, the 65 percent of South Korea now covered by forests has checked flooding and soil erosion, returning environmental health and stability to the Korean countryside.

The United States—which over the last two decades retired one tenth of its cropland, most of it highly erodible, and shifted to conservation tillage practices—has reduced soil erosion by 40 percent. At the same time, the nation's farmers expanded the grain harvest by more than one fifth.

Some of the most innovative leadership has come from cities. Curitiba, Brazil, a city of 1 million people, began restructuring its transport system in 1974. Since then its population has tripled, but its car traffic has declined by 30 percent. Amsterdam has developed a diverse urban transport system, where nearly 40 percent of all trips within the city are taken by bicycle. Paris has a transport diversification plan that also includes a prominent role for the bicycle and is intended to reduce car traffic by 40 percent. London is relying on a tax on cars entering the city center to attain a similar goal.

Not only are new technologies becoming available, but some of these technologies can be combined to create entirely new outcomes. Gas-electric hybrid cars with an enhanced battery and a plug-in capacity, combined with investment in wind farms feeding cheap electricity into the grid, permit most daily driving to be done with electricity, and at a cost equivalent of less than $1-a-gallon gasoline. In much of the world, domestic wind energy can be substituted for imported oil.

The challenge is to build a new economy and to do it at wartime speed before we miss so many of nature's deadlines that the economic system begins to unravel. This introductory chapter is followed by five chapters outlining the principal environmental, demographic, and economic challenges facing civilization. Then there are seven chapters that outline Plan B, the roadmap of where the world needs to go and how to get there.

Our civilization is in trouble because of trends we ourselves have set in motion. The good news is that momentum is building in efforts to reverse damaging environmental trends. Just to cite one example, in early 2007 Australia announced that it would ban incandescent light bulbs by 2010, replacing them with highly efficient compact fluorescents that use only one fourth as much electricity. Canada quickly followed with a similar initiative. Europe, the United States, and China are expected to do the same soon. The world may be approaching a tipping point on a political initiative that can drop world electricity use by nearly 12 percent, enabling us to close 705 coal-fired power plants. This "ban the bulb" movement could become the first major win in the battle to stabilize climate.

Participating in the construction of this enduring new economy is exhilarating. So is the quality of life it will bring. We will be able to breathe clean air. Our cities will be less congested, less noisy, less polluted, and more civilized. A world where population has stabilized, forests are expanding, and carbon emissions are falling is within our grasp.

Top Twenty Failing States, 2006

1	Sudan	113.7
2	Iraq	111.4
3	Somalia	111.1
4	Zimbabwe	110.1
5	Chad	108.8
6	Ivory Coast	107.3
7	Democratic Republic of the Congo	105.5
8	Afghanistan	102.3
9	Guinea	101.3
10	Central African Republic	101.0
11	Haiti	100.9
12	Pakistan	100.1
13	North Korea	97.7
14	Burma	97.0
15	Uganda	96.4
16	Bangladesh	95.9
17	Nigeria	95.6
18	Ethiopia	95.3
19	Burundi	95.2
20	Timor-Leste	94.9

Source: Fund for Peace and Carnegie Endowment for International Peace

Note

* Chapter from Lester R. Brown's publication Plan B 3.0 Mobilizing to Save Civilization, W.W. Norton, 2008.

Global Footprint Network: Our Role in Ending Overshoot

Mathis Wackernagel

From Al Gore to Leonardo DiCaprio, people everywhere are talking about global warming. Mainstream newspapers and broadcasts are leading with the headlines. Businesses, governments and individuals all over the world are measuring their carbon Footprints. The climate crisis has captured the public's attention and as a global community we are finally starting to seriously examine our impact on the planet.

Many people don't realize that climate change is just one part, or a symptom, of a bigger issue: humanity's metabolism is becoming too big for planet Earth to support it. But hardly anybody is talking about it—until now.

This is why we are advancing the Ecological Footprint, a resource accounting tool that can help us measure and manage this crisis. It tells us the whole story about human demand on the biosphere. It tells us what we need to know in practical, actionable terms. It tells us in accessible ways that humans are consuming resources at a faster rate than the Earth can replenish. This ecological overshoot is leading to problems such as disappearing forests, declining fisheries and global warming.

The Footprint calculates our impact in terms of planets. It tells us that if everyone in the world lived as Europeans do, it would require three planets to support their lifestyle. Canadians would need 3.5 planets, and Americans? Five. The underlying message is—we only have one planet, so we must find ways to live within Earth's limits.

Global Footprint Network is a non-profit organization dedicated to making the Ecological Footprint as prominent a metric as the GDP and making one-planet living a feasible way of life.

Launched in Oakland, California in 2003, Global Footprint Network began out of the spare bedroom of my house and within four years it has bloomed into a $2 million organization with more than 85 global partners, 18 staff, and offices in Europe and the U.S.

Our mission is to help countries, businesses, and institutions operate within the Earth's limits, and build worldwide commitment to battle this problem.

Our vision for getting it done is to institutionalize the Footprint in key, influential national organizations and governments so that they can effectively manage their ecological assets the same way they manage their finances. We seek to work so strategically and aggressively that we create a critical mass of powerful institutions using the Ecological Footprint to make decisions, redirecting billions of dollars of investment flows and public monies to promote sustainability.

In 1990, I co-invented the Ecological Footprint tool with my colleague William Rees. Since then the Footprint has emerged as the world's premier measure of humanity's demand for resources and their availability on Earth. We launched Global Footprint Network in response to a growing demand for an organization dedicated to stewarding and advancing the Footprint tool, taking it into board rooms and meetings with heads of state, and providing support for the network of users—Footprint consultants and practitioners, business executives, government leaders, individuals, and organizations employing the Footprint as a decision-making tool.

The Footprint tells us that currently humanity's demand on the planet is exceeding the planet's ability to meet this demand by 25%. And while over 6 million people worldwide have measured their Footprints online, using the Footprint quiz at www.ecofoot.org, the reality is that individual actions are only one part of the solution. What about influential nations? What about multinational corporations? What about international agencies?

At Global Footprint Network we believe that to effectively create large-scale shifts within the human economy, we must engage with top-level decision-makers in all these arenas. We believe that in the same way we have built marvelous institutions to stabilize financial capital, with central banks and their prominent leaders like Greenspan, Bernanke and Trichet protecting the Dollar and the Euro, we can and must support our existing institutions in finding ways to stabilize, strengthen, and protect our planet's natural capital.

If you think of the Ecological Footprint like a financial statement—comparing our demand on, and nature's supply of, ecological resources—it is as if today we are living off the planet's credit card, essentially liquidating the Earth's ecological assets. This phenomenon is called "Ecological Overshoot" and while this can be managed for a short while, it ultimately depletes and degrades our most essential resources, such as our atmosphere, forests, fisheries, and agricultural land.

Using the Ecological Footprint, large institutions can specifically measure their demand on the planet. They can also use the Footprint to assess their sustainability performance, set realistic targets, monitor projects and programs, communicate successes, and identify the impacts of their choices.

Our theory of change is designed to make the most of the Footprints' appeal and impact by focusing Global Footprint Network's activities in the following three ways:

- Supporting the Footprint movement through developing methodological standards; growing and servicing our partner network; creating online communication tools; and developing new, groundbreaking Footprint applications.
- Igniting a global conversation about the Earths' limits by disseminating outreach tools and conducting media campaigns, such as the Living Planet Reports that we co-produce with the WWF (World Wide Fund for Nature) and that resulted in their most popular media event in history in 2006.
- Addressing opportunities for lasting, systemic change through our Ten-In-Ten Campaign—to institutionalize the Footprint in 10 key nations by 2015—and by annually calculating and publishing the Ecological Footprints of 152 nations.

Our approach is working. We are engaging with major corporations that not only want to change their own companies, but want to be leaders in transforming their industries. These are companies like Kaiser Healthcare that understands the link between human health and environmental health, or SITA, France's largest waste management company. Our work results in huge reductions in Ecological Footprint. The GPT Group, a large commercial real estate firm in Australia, has set a goal of reducing the Footprint of its portfolio of real estate holdings—worth US $15 billion—by 20 percent. We also built an online calculator that helped GPT's shopping mall retail tenants reduce their construction and operational Footprints by up to 40 percent. Aurora, a US $1 billion dollar housing development in Australia, is projected to achieve a 40 percent reduction in its housing and transportation Footprint. BC Hydro, a large utility company in British Columbia, has committed to "no net increase" in its Footprint for the next 20 years, even as it expands its electricity production.

In addition to our own work in this arena, we more than 85 partner organizations around the world that are also dealing directly with huge institutions and this is creating a large ripple effect. The Ecological Footprint inspired our partners WWF and Bioregional to develop the concept of One Planet Living, which has swept the UK and is spreading around the world. One Planet Living inspired Tony Blair to commit to a One Planet Economy and to spearhead the UK government's new mandate to building only 'zero carbon homes' within 10 years. David Miliband, former minister of environment and now UK's Foreign Secretary has been one of the Ecological Footprint's supporters. And finally, the City of London won its bid for the 2012 Olympics based on the concept of a One Planet Olympics. Imagine the transformational impact that the concept of One Planet Living could have on the one billion people around the world who will be watching the Olympics.

There is no doubt we are at the center of a large and growing global movement.

Our progress working with national governments and international agencies is widespread, and in my mind, very hopeful. When we launched the Ten-In-Ten Campaign, in 2005, it seemed ambitious to have 10 countries to adopt the Footprint as a decision-making tool by 2015. But in just two years we have 23 national prospects. Two of which—Wales and Ireland—have already adopted the Footprint as an indicator of sustainability. Five of which—Switzerland, Japan, the United Arab Emirates, Mozambique, and Belgium—we are actively working with on research collaborations. And others like Australia are incorporating the Footprint into their government agencies like EPA Victoria.

Getting buy-in for using the Footprint at the international level requires acceptance by statistical offices, policy advisors, academia and business, which is not an easy task. Add on the additional challenge that the Footprint is operating from the meta-view and working from the inside out against the largest system in the world—the human economy and our collective relationship with the Earth.

Yet, we are committed to this work because we believe that securing our ecological assets is critical for human well being, and for the viability of a future where we can breathe clean air and drink clean water. Every time a company or a nation begins making a shift, Global Footprint Network comes one step closer to creating a world in which we can all live well, within the means of one planet.

WHY DO WE NEED THE ECOLOGICAL FOOTPRINT?

One fundamental requirement for sustainability is to use renewable resources slower than nature can replenish them. Societies who do not meet this minimum condition run ecological deficits.

To know whether we meet this requirement and to properly manage our ecological assets, we need to measure our use of nature. We need resource accounts that keep track of how much nature we have versus how much we use. Such accounting operates just like financial accounting: it keeps tally of the available capital, revenues and expenditures. As with financial assets, it is possible to spend more of our ecological assets than is being regenerated – for some time. But such overspending depletes the capital and cannot be sustained in the long term. Continued ecological deficit spending leads to environmental bankruptcy, eroding economies, quality of life and societal stability.

In short, like any successful business that keeps track of revenues and expenditures, society needs robust accounts of its demand on, and supply of, ecological assets. This is what Ecological Footprint accounts offer.

WHAT EXACTLY DOES THE FOOTPRINT MEASURE?

The Ecological Footprint is an indicator that measures people's demand on nature. This demand includes both the resources we consume as well as the waste we produce. We obtain these resources from forests, cropland, fisheries, and grazing land, among other ecosystems. The built environment compromises the land's ability to provide biological resources. Additionally, ecosystems absorb and assimilate the waste we produce as a result of resource consumption. The Ecological Footprint adds up these ecosystem areas to measure total human demand on nature. In other words, Ecological Footprint analysis builds on "mass flow balance," and each flow is translated into the ecologically productive areas necessary to support these flows.

Ecosystems have a limited ability to supply us with natural resources (this is based on factors such as available water, climate, solar energy, technology and management practices etc). This is called biocapacity. When a population's Ecological Footprint exceeds the biocapacity, biological resource 'overshoot' occurs.

Global Footprint Network calculates the Ecological Footprint of nations on an annual basis. From this data we undertake global analysis. Overshoot measured on a global scale is an indicator of unsustainability. Data shows that humanity's resource demands and waste production began to exceed planet Earth's ability to meet this demand around 1986. Today humanity exceeds the planet's ability to provide biological resources by 30 percent – thereby dipping into the natural capital stock. While the world average capacity was 1.8 hectares per person, the world average Footprint was 2.2 hectares per capita.

The sustainability challenge is no longer about future generations; that was 10–20 years ago. Now it is about present generations. It is about giving everyone the tools to do what they can to be part of the solution.

It is no secret that we are standing in the face of unprecedented challenges, and they are incredibly time sensitive. If we do not make large-scale changes now, we will bankrupt the biosphere. Banking on the possibility that we can just continue as usual and use the resources of two planets by 2050 is utterly unrealistic. We know that we must address our collective Footprint or much of what we cherish and depend on today may vanish within this century. But in my opinion, a game that cannot be won is not worth playing and I believe we have developed a way to keep score that is inspiring people to play, people all over the world, and to give their very most creative energy so that the whole of humanity can win.

Eco-Social Markets, a Global Marshall Plan and Social Entrepreneurs

Franz J. Radermacher

Introduction: The Challenges Ahead

The world faces great difficulties concerning the environment, the climate issue, the opening gap between rich and poor, imbalances between cultures, the world financial system und questions of war and peace. And obviously, free markets are not the answer to the world's problems. Consequently, new worldwide initiatives, such as the Eco-social Forum of Europe, the Global Economic Network, the Coalition for the Global Commons and Mohammad Yunus' initiative for social enterprises are urgently needed to tackle the un-desirable global developments, which also become apparent in the insufficient implementation of the UN Millennium Development Goals. It is also very helpful that The Goi Peace Foundation operates in this respect in its many networked activities.

I. The Eco-social Market Economy

I. 1. The Eco-social Market Paradigm

The Eco-social Forum of Europe, the Club of Rome, the Global Marshall Plan Initiative and others since long argue that a reasonable future for humankind needs a revolution-evolution in Global Governance. Elements are climate justice, incorporation of external effects via prices into the world economy system, so that "prices tell the truth" etc. Only then can enterprises and entrepreneurs really fulfil their potential for a better world. Protection of the environment and blocking of slave-type child labour must become a part of WTO and the world financial system.

At the very least, we need governmentally controlled labelling systems that tell consumers what they want to know about the rules and conditions under which products were produced. It is often not adequate to compare goods and services (only) at the level of function—as is the WTO's credo. Often, the processes, under which goods and services have been created, are of similar importance as the function.

Overall, the task is to provide the globalized economy with an adequate global regime for the markets, promoting world peace, justice and sustainability and the realization of an open society. Such a regime does not exist today, on the contrary. Needed, in a long-term perspective, is a worldwide Eco-Social Market Economy, linking markets and competition with high social, cultural and ecological standards for the welfare of all humans. Key to a consensus on such standards, and to overcome global poverty at the same time, are co-financing measures supplied by the rich countries in favour of the developing countries, supported by an adequate regulatory framework. In return, as part of a contract, established by all partners voluntarily, developing countries would adopt these standards, despite the concomitant loss of competitive advantages. Better standards imply in particular better governance structures in all countries, and improve local government. This approach reflects the reasoning behind the EU enlargement processes, the successful Montreal Protocol for the protection of the world's ozone layer, but also that behind the US Marshall Plan for Europe after World War II.

I. 2. A Major Challenge—The Ethical Question

The Eco-Social Market Economy model and the Global Marshall Plan/Planetary Contract approach are both based on a clear ethical foundation. This is the world ethos position, common to all great religions, to humanism and also present in the UN Earth Charter. Two principles are basic, which can both be deduced from the Golden Rule, namely the principle (1) to care for the environment and the world's resource base and keep it intact and (2) to take care for the dignity of all humans. These principles immediately translate into corresponding requirements concerning the governance of companies, which are today reflected in concepts such as ethics for business or corporate social responsibility (CSR). However, voluntary business codes, as important as they are, are usually not sufficient to address global needs. Internationally agreed upon rules, transparency and compliance mechanisms are key. This is where an eco-social market approach and business ethics meet. Because under suitable frameworks, markets will reward, what is ethically desirable. We have to work harder to achieve this situation.

II. The Global Marshall Plan Initiative

II. 1. The Conceptional Approach

A Global Marshall Plan/Planetary Contract represents an intermediate step towards a worldwide Eco-social Market Economy. According to authoritative sources, 980 Billion US-Dollars will be needed on top of the current international development aid until 2015 to reach the UN Millennium Development Goals. Moreover, the usage of these funds must follow different mechanisms than currently applied, and in close interaction with the world's civil society. Some countries have already made pledges, which reduce the amount of money needed additionally to about 860 Billion US-Dollars from 2006. Under an adequate regime, and focusing on developing countries that are willing to meet the requirements mentioned, this sum could be raised from 2008 through instruments such as Special Drawing Rights of the International Monetary Fund, a worldwide levy on financial transactions (Tobin tax), a worldwide levy on trade (Terra tax), a worldwide levy on kerosene, a reasonable trade system for CO_2 emission rights, adequate debt relief measures for the poorest countries, insolvency laws for states and, finally, the establishment of an International Financial Facility as proposed by the former British Chancellor of the Exchequer Gordon Brown.

II. 2. New Forms of Implementation

As important as raising the funds are new forms of implementing the goals, in particular: financing the implementation of the UN Millennium Development Goals on a project basis. The effective allocation of funds for self-directed ways of development is maybe the most difficult aspect of a Global Marshall Plan. The responsible bodies for the implementation could be the World Bank and the United Nations Development Program (UNDP) as well as other UN organizations, such as the UNEP environmental programmes, UNESCO or the United Nations Population Fund (UNFPA). On their part, these organizations should rely more on local initiatives and NGOs than they do today, and support adapted technologies, measures to increase local welfare and private initiatives for development. The latter should compete for co-financing funds, allocated in selection procedures controlled by an independent jury. Besides satisfying basic needs, financial aid should be aimed at empowerment, capacity building and ownership.

Practical experience shows that self-directed, self-assured and responsible development is best achieved when participation, education and enforcing the role of women are promoted. Guiding principles for the allocation of funds are subsidiary (bottom-up), transparency and control of financial fluxes to reduce corruption. Concrete examples for accordant fund allocation are micro financing and microcredit or the partnership-helper model (help for self-help). In this respect, there is a close cooperation between the Global Marshall Plan Initiative and the Global Economic Network with economist and Nobel laureate Muhammad Yunus, creator of the Grameen Bank. Muhammad Yunus is a member of the presidency of the Global Economic Network. Muhammad Yunus' new initiative for social entrepreneurs is also in the focus of the Global Economic Network.

Also, there is then pressure towards good governance within countries, making sure all people will have a decent education and sufficient health care service. All this will significantly increase the power of people to help themselves. This will also be supported with the significantly increased level of co-financing of about $100 billion a year. In the concept of the Global Marshall Plan this money not just goes to governments, but to a great extend goes into small and medium-sized enterprises, into microcredits, into regional projects and it goes into improving the ownership situation of poor people. And all use of such funds will fall under strict compliance rules. So, all in all, the Global Marshall Plan will significantly and permanently improve the situation of the poorest.

II. 3. What Do We Hope For?—The Double Factor 10 Perspective

Similar to Europe's economic miracle after World War II, the eco-social reasoning behind a Global Marshall Plan/Planetary Contract will create a gigantic global departure in the right direction, analogous to the EU enlargement processes: economic development, environmental protection, social balance and cultural balance are all promoted simultaneously.

The developing part of the globe closes the gap, and positive growth effects show everywhere. The future formula 10~>4:34 indicates that within the next 50 to 100 years, a ten-fold increase of the global gross national product is achievable, at the same time taking care for an efficient environmental protection and the realization of a sustainable development. The effect of a worldwide investment program in the scope required would, in a relative perspective, be comparable to the effect of constructing the transcontinental railway system in the US at its time, and release unimagined powers for a development in the right direction. While growth rates in the rich world may average between 1 and 2% per annum for about 50-70 years, they will reach 5 to 7% in the poorer parts of the world. The rich North and the poor South will profit equally from the resulting boom. At the same time, the imposed social and ecological standards will contain the current polarization within both the rich and the poorer countries. Thus, more global balance is compatible with significantly increased global wealth and environmental protection and does not entail less social balance within states.

III. Social Enterprises and Social Entrepreneurs—Some Considerations

III. 1. Social Enterprises—A New Initiative by Muhammad Yunus

On the way to a double factor 10, a wealthier and more balanced, more peaceful globe in peace with nature and cultures, entrepreneurs and enterprises will have a central role to play. Muhammad Yunus is now promoting this issue and offering new perspectives. Social enterprises should address social requirements, while entrepreneurs today generally follow other intentions. Certainly, it is encouraging that The Goi Peace Foundation also networks into this direction. And the Eco-social Forum Europe, Global Economic Network, Global Marshall Plan Initiative have these approaches within their spectrum and think that proper frameworks will promote this. However, it is an intellectual challenge to precisely specify and argue for the specific characteristics of social enterprises. There has to be a very precise clarification of the differences to well-established forms of organizations such as co-operatives, foundations and non-profit organizations.

In particular, it is important, but might be difficult to block attempts to camouflage the concept.

The new initiative by Muhammad Yunus is particularly important. It comes at a crucial moment in time. Presently, market fundamentalists are trying to consolidate their ideas on the nature, aims and shareholder-value oriented goals of enterprises and therefore the market via regulative respectively deregulative interventions. Of central importance is the guarantee (better to say "systemic pressure" conditions) of a high return on equity in the sense of a "law of nature," enforced by politics and frameworks. With this in mind, some market fundamentalists presently argue even against co-operatives as valid structures of economic activities. Eventually, they might even go against foundations.

For this and other reasons, it is important to put something against their line of argumentation, which could be abbreviated as TINA (There Is No Alternative). Social enterprises/social entrepreneurs can be an important factor in this "game" of arguments.

III. 2. Relations of Muhammad Yunus' New Initiative to other Initiatives and Concepts

There already exists a global Initiative for socially oriented enterprises, which is a positive force. This initiative follows a more relaxed definition of socially oriented enterprises than Muhammad Yunus is arguing for. So social enterprises/social entrepreneurs in Yunus' sense form—in his own words—a subset of what the initiative for socially oriented enterprises is arguing for.

There is also a relation between co-operatives, in particular those co-operatives which pay no or nearly no return on equity, and social enterprises in the sense of Muhammad Yunus. A difference may be that the social purpose, which co-operatives are following, often has to do with the interests of the members of the co-operative. Often, but not always, those members are also the beneficiaries (however, most often not the only ones) of what the co-operative is doing. An interesting case would be a co-operative (of "richer" entrepreneurs) organized to build a bridge over a river that serves for "poor" people (but for their own companies' activities as well) and later would finance itself from tolls for using that bridge. Ownership here is with the co-operative. Should this be regarded as a social enterprise, particularly in the case that the income from tolls is just sufficient to maintain the bridge? In this case, there is no return on equity and there is no paying back of private equity that forms the basis for this co-operative.

In countries such as Germany, the public side often organizes certain socially important activities, such as local transportation or water and energy supply, via state or town-owned enterprises.

III. 3. Return on Equity—A Critical Issue

Observers have some questions seeing that Muhammad Yunus does not allow any return on equity for social enterprises. No return on equity means that, first, there is no compensation for inflation and, second, there is no compensation with regard to possible returns on alternative investments like supplying money on assets free of risks in a bank. Third, there is no compensation for risk taking, keeping in mind that starting a social enterprise involves risk. Not considering these three types of payments on equity of social enterprises means that social enterprises are, in a sense, heavily subsidiary businesses (by its shareholders). If everything works fine, a payback of private equity put into the business after some years is offered, if profits of the social enterprise allow to do this. These limitations of payback of equity make the argumentation for his concept somewhat difficult.

Muhammad Yunus asks for tax advantages for social enterprises, because they serve a public cause. There are good arguments in this direction, but public debate will be difficult. This idea will find heavy opposition, as we saw it for instance within the European Union concerning the Sparkassen sector, particularly in Germany. The arguments, which are all biased, always go into the direction of economic inefficiency and unfair competition, due to a special treatment of a restricted segment of the market.

There also is a risk that social enterprises could be placed as a kind of second-class enterprise category to serve second-class people in a world of "brazilianisation." Currently, a major challenge is a fair and balanced participation of all people in success to goods and services that can be produced "sustainably" from limited resources. Today most people do only have a very limited access to needed resources and wealth produced. A concept of social enterprises could, in the worst case, institutionalize a class society via companies dedicated to serve the needs of the poor part of the world, while "the other companies" provide goods and services for the wealthy people.

III. 4. How to Deal with Sophisticated Financial Constructs

Muhammad Yunus' idea of social entrepreneurs would be strongest if social enterprises could be constructed in a stronger way. They should be to the highest degree as possible, like other enterprises or other entrepreneurs. Besides the strict application of social and ecological standards widely agreed, there should only be one difference: Money that today is taken out of companies as a surplus beyond compensation of equity for inflation, interest on risk-free assets, and compensation for risk taking of private equity, should remain in the company to be used for dedicated social purposes. Whether one wants additional help by the government concerning taxes and subsidies would then need special consideration and argumentation.

This fair return-oriented approach to social enterprises can be argued for under any circumstances. But what is more important, the possibility to hide additional payments of returns on equity by using tricky forms of financing has to be impossible. One should take care that "normal" enterprises cannot camouflage themselves as social enterprises.

Clever actors may finance social enterprises mainly on debt instead on equity (e.g., by emitting debt obligations that are traded anonymously via the capital market) as is known from strategies today to avoid paying taxes in countries such as Germany. The same structure could be used here to have a social enterprise in the sense of Yunus and still to get returns on equity through the right kind of financial constructions. This could also be done e.g. by buying expensive services or goods from other companies of the shareholders (this has been a usual strategy of hedge funds).

Either one finds a way to make such constructions impossible (a hard job, because tax authorities have the same problem and did not yet solve it) or one has to live with the situation that clever actors can force conditions into a social enterprise, which, on a material level, one does not want to accept in his definition. This is a problem from a logical point of view. Therefore, it should be carefully analyzed as to avoid misuse of the important concept of social enterprises.

Conclusion

A world in trouble needs bold new initiatives. The economy has a major role to play in this. The eco-social market philosophy gives new perspectives in comparison with market fundamentalism and Manchester Capitalism. It is the better system. The Global Marshall Plan is a step in this direction. Social enterprises and social entrepreneurs fit well into this world of thinking, and the activities of The Goi Peace Foundation as well.

Featuring a New Culture of Agriculture

Franz-Theo Gottwald

It appears that the world is heading for a new food crisis—triggered by several interrelated factors:

- Changes in lifestyle of several hundred million people toward diets that contain higher amounts of animal proteins,
- crop failures due to climate change,
- speculation in the raw material market,
- increased use of agro fuels.

Viewed from the climate change aspect, the International Commission on the Future of Food and Agriculture (www.future-food.org) has analyzed the situation in the following way:

Current global trade and economic policies are enforcing a centralized, fossil fuel-driven food and agriculture system that is directly at odds not only with the ecological imperative but also with the time table and reduced emission targets that most governments are committing to in international fora. This huge contradiction must be addressed if we are to meet the challenges of climate change and global warming.

At the same time, the present food system is also extremely vulnerable to climate change, which this report also demonstrates. Almost every corner of the globe has already been touched by dramatic weather shifts that have affected crop production and food distribution.

Additionally the commission outlines some of the false agricultural solutions that are being promoted in the name of "clean" or "green" energy—namely, genetically modified organisms (GMOs) and large-scale production of agro fuels. Most importantly, it demonstrates that ecological organic food systems are a real solution to current climate concerns in terms of mitigation and adaptation and an energy transition to a post-fossil fuel era (Manifesto, 2008, p. 10).

Ecological, Organic Food Systems

Ever since its inception in 1985, the Schweisfurth Foundation has worked toward a new culture of agriculture that contributes to sustainable food security. A number of practical projects in the fields of soil fertility, plant health and animal well-being as well as a holistic regard for food quality, have shown that a shift from chemical, energy-intensive agricultural practices to ecological, organic food production is globally feasible and makes economic, social and ecological long-term sense.

The overall concept for this new approach to agriculture is the ecology of integrated cycles and close sourcing.

The Schweisfurth Foundation compiled a *Vision for the Future Viability of Food Production, Processing, and Marketing* (2002). It enlists seven benchmarks formulated to restore quality through an ecology of integrated cycles and close sourcing.

- Future viability is the idea underlying the production, processing, and marketing of food. Agriculture and food production that remain viable in the future realize:

  – sustainability
  – the principle of responsibility
  – efficient economic practices
  – health and well-being
  – marketability
  – multifunctionality

They intelligently link regionalization and globalization and use modern technology.

- Food must be produced as organically as possible. The organic quality of food comes from sustainable production, which protects the natural basis of existence and preserves plant and animal diversity. Ecological agriculture guarantees the living conditions and habitats that are appropriate for each species of plant and animal involved. With ecological agriculture and food production, people can take responsibility for nature—for human beings, flora and fauna, water, air, and soil.

An ecology of integrated cycles and close sourcing makes these goals achievable. According to this ecological principle, most of the food raised, processed, and sold in a given area comes from that region. Its freshness and taste are guaranteed. An ecology of integrated cycles and close sourcing encompasses thinking and behavior consistent with natural cycles, from the cultivation of fodder crops to the use of organic waste.

- Consumers desire high-quality food. It must be natural and good tasting. Because organically produced foods are rich in nutrients, they help lower health costs naturally.
- Restoring quality through an ecology of integrated cycles and close sourcing is economical. Short distances are not cost intensive. They incur no costs that society at large must bear for practices harmful to plants, animals, or the environment.
- The ecological efficiency achieved by sustainable culture and food production mainly strengthens small business and the crafts by easing pressure on municipal budgets and sharpening competitiveness within and between regions. A regional network economy stimulates employment and fosters innovation.
- The organic production, processing, and marketing of organic foods are competitive: It satisfies consumer desire for security, transparency, and trust. Food produced and processed through an ecology of integrated cycles and close sourcing has many merits. Abundant regional food production leads to strong customer relations and informed consumption.
- Organic food production, processing, and marketing are multifunctional. They benefit several other areas important to societies. For example, this system saves energy, reduces transport costs, creates jobs, preserves fields of occupation, protects apprenticeships, and promotes regional development (cf. Vision, 2002. pp. 11–13).

This vision hand-in-hand with the preservation and expansion of small and medium size rural farms as well as small and medium size enterprises in processing and regional marketing, is the basis for a new concept of agriculture.

Food Is a Moral Commodity

This new culture of agriculture integrates discussions on fairness, sustainability, generational justice, climate protection, health and regional food security. This has turned food into downright moral commodities. Its message is explicit: plant, animal and human health must be protected. Morally questionable actions such as use of potentially dangerous chemicals, feed enhancers, genetically modified or nanoscale enhancers or additives cannot be tolerated. It is an organically oriented culture.

Organic agriculture's influence upon conventional food production practices has become palpable as of late. Big processing companies such as Dr. Oetker have been developing organic products to secure a share of the booming organic market. Major marketing chains like Carrefour or Wal-Mart have been building organic product lines. The pendulum between global and local has been going in the direction of the local aspect. Markets are changing. Conventional producers take on ethical topics. Practically all discounters have been increasing their organic product selections. Nowadays they have even begun to advertise with their fair-trade products.

The food sector is exponentially moving toward becoming an ethical market: "in the old days, there was a small number of customers buying organic millet in small natural food stores, while nowadays it can practically be found in every supermarket" according to the social economist Nico Stehr and the communications scientist Marian Adolf of Zeppelin University in Friedrichshafen. While a few years past organic millet and raw yoghurts waited for customers in hidden Third-World-Stores, small sales booths, or tiny organic stores, a dramatic change has taken place. Today organic and fair-trade products serve millions of customers and enjoy triple growth rates. This development is not only limited to food items, but extends to many other products whose mix of raw materials as well as production processes are scrutinized from an ethical point-of-view. Market volume of these products and services has been growing exponentially and rapidly.

Lately, the ethical aspect has become one way of judging goods and services. New about this ethical dictum is its scope, its vehemence, and its direct applicability via sales figures as well as growing globalization of these values, standards and regulations. Today it is no longer sufficient to complement company marketing strategies with altruistic events or sponsorships, nowadays total quality management requires a sustainability department, while corporate social responsibility—particularly within the higher echelons—is a definite must. Company efforts to do justice to ethical dicta with regard to price and quality are not solely due to intrinsic motives. They are due to changing consumer demands and also due to markets in general that force companies into action. The following argument in favor of a morality of markets goes far beyond a short-term reaction to a media fad. It points toward a new step in the development of the capitalist economic system, particularly with regard to relative market power.

What Does "Good Economy" Mean?

Nico Stehr und Marian Adolf explained the term as the kind of holistic corporate responsibility that customers expect from their food producers and food marketing agents. Corporate Social Responsibility (CSR),

Corporate Citizenship (CC), and Corporate Governance (CG)—these unwieldy terms define leadership and management duties dealing with integral corporate responsibility.

The multiplicity of concepts applied by corporations trying to live up to standards of responsibility is very confusing. This confusion stems from the vast differences in company cultures that have developed in market economies. They share the concrete preservation of responsibility, technically labeled Corporate Responsibility (CR). This responsibility may be more aligned with environmental topics (Corporate Environmental Responsibility, CER), or Corporate Culture may be directed toward being good in their dealings with communities, town councils and counties where the company is situated (Corporate Citizenship) and thus wishes to be seen as a "good citizen" of the local society.

In its *Green Book* the EU commission describes Corporate Social Responsibility as a "concept allowing corporations to voluntarily integrate social concerns into their activities and into mutual dealings with stakeholders." In this context, the term stakeholders refers to all societal groups and institutions coming in various types of contact with the corporation: Communities, educational facilities, clubs, environmental groups, and action groups.

The term "Corporate Citizenship" is used in a similar vein. It denotes demands pertaining to "good citizenship" made upon entrepreneurs with regard to their joint responsibility for a healthy development in the company's social environment. This inclusion of social responsibility may lead to a new form of social administration.

With regard to Environmental Responsibility it is paramount to reduce levels of pollutant emissions as well as exploitation of natural resources in such a way that neither endangers economic capabilities, nor produces social hardships like increased job loss. Moreover, the central question of eco-social development is a way of incorporating calls for equality in order to reduce ecological pressures and respect the stability of national economies, despite increasing world populations and urbanization.

Increasingly management of large food producing companies have been establishing "Rules for Good Governance" (Corporate Governance). These are predominantly companies in the food sector that are especially vulnerable to public scrutiny and criticism due to their ecologically and ethically problematic manufacturing processes, that might entail health problems (e.g. candy); or because they themselves or a company within the same line of business have come to the media's attention in the past due to ethically questionable or even criminal business practices (e.g.

spoiled meat); also possibly due to their special excessive marketing powers, since power should always be tempered with moral responsibility. One only has to think of food producing giants like Nestlé or the economic power of Rewe, Edeka, and the Metro Group.

There are a number of criteria for "good business practices" or "living responsibility." Working with production companies from various sectors, André Habisch, Professor for Christian Social Ethics and Social Policy at Eichstaett-Ingolstadt Catholic University identified seven criteria:

1. **Family-friendly Policies.** A company creates a framework to help workers who want to start or take care of an existing family.
2. **Local Regulatory Functions**: A corporation may be active in local environmental protection activities or engage with community education policies. Companies in Bavaria have set outstanding examples in the "Umweltpakt Bayern" (Bavarian Environmental Compact) and the Stiftung Bildungspakt Bayern (Bavarian Educational Compact Foundation), to name just two examples.
3. **Cultural Activities and Sponsorship**: This type of work transcends regional activities and sponsorship. Cultural activities also include in-house cultural efforts as shown in the architecture and decoration of company offices and factory buildings.
4. **Research and Development**: A responsibly acting corporate citizen in this sector would come to a consensus via dialogue with stakeholders, i.e. inclusion in research and development of the ultimate users through consumer discussion panels. In view of biotechnology or nanotechnology research and development, this is becoming an ever more significant distinguishing mark of ethical vs. bad corporate management.
5. **Human Resources Activities**: Decisions in this sector deal with the number or type of apprenticeship training openings as well as continuing and adult education programs available to employees. Additionally, policies for employees over 50 years of age are set.
6. **Corporate Volunteering**: This criterion expands company horizons beyond the confines of corporate premises. This concept is called corporate volunteering. A number of larger corporations have begun to encourage their employees to take on volunteer jobs, e.g. in civic foundations or clubs. This kind of activity goes beyond merely enriching community life by assuring essential life-sustaining functions like the work of the volunteer fire department.
7. **Donations, Support or Sponsorship**: A good corporate citizen has a systematic program in place, for instance tailored to local or regional needs via round table-discussions.

Most of these criteria hold true for a number of food sector companies whose representatives gave lectures on agricultural and food ethics at the Schweisfurth Foundation between 2004 and 2007. Companies like Frosta AG; Hipp-Werk Georg Hipp GmbH & Co.KG; Private Weissbierbrauerei G. Schneider & Sohn GmbH; Rapunzel Naturkost AG; Deutsche See; Thoenes Naturverbund; Life Food GmbH, Taifun; Regal Springs, Switzerland, have developed modes of operation to express their "culture of care."

Ethical World Trade

Since many food and beverage products are imported from developing countries, ethically responsible trade is part of practiced responsibility. The importer of coffee, tea, mangoes or bananas faces four challenges:

1. **Fair Prices**: Prices for raw materials often are extremely low and prone to strong fluctuations. This has a direct impact upon further development in producer countries and often entails heavy monetary indebtedness of developing countries, especially in the Sahel region of Africa. This leads to an ethical challenge: How can trade in raw goods contribute to the stabilization of prices and equitable raw material trade agreements? This ethical challenge can be extensively substantiated through application of the moral fairness guideline.
2. **Environmental Damages and Resource Depletion**: Cultivation, harvest and transport have to be organized in an ecologically sustainable way.
3. **Dignity and Human Rights**: Practicing corporate ethics means the existence of codices of conduct, social stipulations, agreements, campaigns, and if necessary, trade sanctions in case of infringements upon human dignity or human rights of small farmers and field laborers, especially if producers from indigenous populations are involved.
4. **Peace Activism**: The fourth benchmark for traders in raw materials is carefully avoiding anything that might trigger bloodshed, or more positively stated, that they, acting as "good corporate citizens" will act as peace keepers in those regions where the agricultural goods are produced. Especially as it is certain that under changing climatic conditions, increasing water shortages, for instance, may lead to warlike disputes in agricultural areas. Therefore, future corporations in their role as corporate citizens will have to actively work towards pacifying these regions, and will be judged by their contribution to peaceful developments.

Internationally, the Schweisfurth Foundation is engaged in assisting companies, labor organizations, political administrations and other NGOs in creating and integrating instruments designed to meet these four challenges. One instance would be collaborations with various stakeholders in China's meat industries, where the Foundation endeavors to foster organic meat production and the implementation of strict animal protection standards. This is just one example of the Foundation's philosophy of "peace and dignity for all living beings."

Ethical Management

Value-conscious management is at the core of "good economic activities." Studies conducted by the Schweisfurth Foundation have proven that corporations like Kraft Foods or Danone and other large food producing companies can be role models: What counts are their ethical management practices.

Setting an Example: Corporate leaders should set positive examples in their daily work, guided by demonstrations of respect, appreciation, transparency and open and fair discussions.

Actions Speak Louder than Rhetoric: It is not the leadership's speech bubbles, but rather the actions that count. Statements on values made today are forgotten tomorrow. What matters is how values are dealt with, if they are respected or trampled underfoot—this is what employees remember for years to come.

Job Profile: Executive positions should be filled with an eye to solid individual value systems, not just a professional, success-studded resumé.

Merits: A value-oriented leadership is part of a system of merits. Being conscious of value is rewarded, while any infringement will entail demerits and will endanger any further advancement on the job ladder.

Setting Limits: Possible risks to advancement opportunities, reputation and business interests due to infringements should be discussed openly.

Sanctions: Misconduct will lead to disciplinary action. Violations will be dealt with even if they do not infringe upon written laws.

In order to set clear and binding standards for corporate leadership, practical corporate experience has shown that a value-management system should be in place.

Successful business marketing involves as many employees as possible in order to determine how they would perceive a pleasant corporate atmosphere, especially as this will act as a further bonding agent between company and workers. These outcomes are set down and published in an Ethics Charter that is available and binding for all. This presumptive charter would set down the following points:

Marketing Conduct: Geared for long-term success, quality management, conduct in dealing with customers, suppliers, competitors; orientation toward innovation and growth; involvement in other corporations.

Conduct toward Employees: Sets standards for internal communications, target agreements with managers and department heads, schooling and continuing education, manager selection and training, employee and manager assessment, wages and salaries, dismissal and dismissal procedures, working hours and family concerns, company suggestion plan, work safety, employee representation, employee conduct, culture of discussion, ambition and consideration, company loyalty, corruptibility, hierarchy, know-how communication, social conduct of employees.

Conduct toward Country and Society: Compliance with public regulations, conduct toward public administrations, social commitments.

It can be stated that even if corporate ethics have begun to shift toward the ecology and even if agriculture and food industry have started to accept responsibility for their own future, nonetheless, small and medium sized processors and regional distributors conduct sustainable development in a more ethical and definitely more sustainable fashion than large size companies (cp. Gottwald/Boergen, ISOFAR, 2008).

This is the reason behind the Schweisfurth Foundation's increasing emphasis on rural and artisanal food production as part of a sustainable global future.

Political Leadership for Food Security and Food Democracy

As early as 1995 Marc Rosegrant et al. of the International Food Policy Research Institute presented **Vision 2020** that requires conscious implementation in six sectors:

First: Vision 2020 can only be implemented if by that time, national and local governments function more effectively. Without good governmental and administrative actions with regard to food security, posting and enforcement of property rights, agrarian reforms, funding options and access to markets will not improve or become easier. However, consumer advocates, NGOs and environmental protection agencies have to be fully engaged in assisting governments in developing countries in the fulfillment of their duties and responsibilities.

Second: Vision 2020 can only be implemented once enormous strides have been made in basic education, preventative health care and fair income distribution. One essential requirement is a new distribution scheme giving the poor access to productive resources like soil or rich fishing grounds. One example might be Brazil, where soil distribution laws grant squatters' rights to small farmers, thus allowing them to cultivate unused tracts owned by large landed property owners as an aid to survival. However, this requires proper policy regulations concerning information and education. The most interesting aspect in this connection is the empowerment of women. It is imperative that men support and further female power and influence wherever possible. In view of the eminently important slow-down of population growth, this kind of social revolution would be inherent with progress and simultaneously would assure food security for the 21st century.

Third: Vision 2020 can only be implemented if agrarian research and ecological counseling programs have been expanded significantly in developing countries. Agrarian research has to come up with answers to problems of food insecurity, poverty and depletion of natural resources and damage to the environment. The developing countries have to increase their national spending for agrarian research to one percent of agrarian production now, and to two percent in the future. Clearly defined policies, which take into account risks as well as opportunities with regard to the future of biotechnology research, are still awaiting definition and implementation.

Fourth: Vision 2020 can only be implemented if natural resources are managed in a sustainable way. This requires increased local control and improved local manpower in organization and management. Farmers and communities have to be encouraged to implement integrated soil-fertility-programs, thus ensuring them of legal soil rights and improved access to loans, strong markets for fruits and vegetables, investments in infrastructure and fertilizer subsidies in case of high prices due to inadequate or poorly functioning markets. The international community has to push through a global program of coordination and checks in order to prevent ocean overfishing beyond sustainable limits. Water policy reforms are required for the improvement of available sources of water, provision of attractive incentives for improving allocation procedures to water users, development of more efficient technologies for water supplies, granting of secure rights to water and tempering price gouging.

Fifth: Vision 2020 can only be implemented once small loan and savings institutions like the Grameen Bank have been allowed to develop quickly and in many different locations. This development requires legally enforced modifications to all those frameworks that favor large and capital-intensive applications rather than small and labor-intensive ones. As models in Bangladesh and India have shown, a relatively insignificant amount of easing in the area of private investments through new micro-credits will give rise to a number of small, labor-intensive, competitive rural organizations especially in food trade, processing and marketing.

The sixth and final point states that Vision 2020 can only be implemented if international cooperation and assistance are improved. Above all, international development organizations and bilateral donors will have to agree to concentrate their development work on countries willing to fall in line with the other five target areas of Vision 2020. Rich countries—and this means the G8 countries above all others—have to increase their development aid from 0.3 to 0.7 percent of GDP and will have to store a minimum amount of excess food for emergency situations (Lutzenberger/Gottwald, pp. 129–131).

Everybody Counts

But in a culture of agriculture not only governments are enjoined to work toward global food security, each and every consumer has to take on an active role.

The International Commission on the Future of Food and Agriculture made a list of six People's Actions required for ensuring food security in times of changing conditions. Since 1990, the Schweisfurth Foundation has been incorporating these tenets into its planning on publications, exhibitions, awards, and education campaigns for young adults:

1. Maintain and nurture biodiversity—this begins with promoting biodiversity of seeds and breeds in farming and your own back yard.
2. Shift from chemical, energy intensive agriculture practices to ecological, organic food production.
3. Choose water prudent agriculture—conservation and water harvesting should be the primary aims instead of intensive irrigation and groundwater mining.
4. Choose and favor farmers' markets and local, organic, fresh seasonal products and short chains. In this way, the energy backpack is lightened.
5. Initiate and support incentives that make the shifts to rebuild local food economies. Farmers must be allowed to be the guarantors of the quality of the seed and food they produce without being squeezed out by the bureaucratic industrial standards of seed registration and food safety.

6. Create democratic spaces for farmers, local communities and consumers to decide how to make the transition to a post fossil fuel food system based on localization and sustainability (Manifesto, 2008, p. 45).

It is especially the last point, which emphasizes the importance of regions and communities. Only spatial closeness will allow areas to develop that are suitable for a democratic, sovereign and equitable way of supplying good food for all. Responsibility rests with all consumers who, together with food producers and distributors, have been invested with the task of assuring that basic needs will be met to guarantee a future safe from hunger and worry. The Schweisfurth Foundation, in recognition of these new values of regionalization, uses educational means, policy counselling and pilot projects to empower new movements like the Bundesverband der Regional-bewegung, which are designed with regionalization in mind.

A new civilization of ecological and social economies in and with rural areas, and a new culture of agriculture are the cornerstones for a sustainable civilization in the 21st century.

References

Fischler, F., Gottwald, F.Th., Ernaehrung sichern—weltweit. Oekosoziale Gestaltungsperspektiven. Bericht an die Global Marshall Plan Initiative. Hamburg: Murmann 2007.

Gottwald, F.-Th., Boergen, I., "Innovations within the Organic Food Sector—Basis for Novel Business Relations between Agricultural and Processing Enterprises." In: Cultivating the Future Based on Science. Vol. 2: Livestock, Socio-Economy and Cross Disciplinary Research in Organic Agriculture. Proceedings of the Second Scientific Conference of the International Society of Organic Agriculture Research, Modena. 2008. S. 536-539.

The International Commission on the Future of Food and Agriculture, Manifesto on Climate Change and the Future of Food Security. Florence: Arsia 2008.

Rosegrant, M. et. al., Global Food Projections to 2020. Implications for Investment, Washington, D.C. 1995. In: Lutzenberger, J., Gottwald, F-Th., Ernaehrung in der Wissensgesellschaft. Frankfurt: Campus 1999.

Schweisfurth, K.L. et al, Toward Sustainable Agriculture and Food Production. A Vision for the Future Viability of Food Production, Processing, and Marketing. Schweisfurth Foundation, IFOAM 2002.

Complementary Currency Systems

Jacqui Dunne

> *"--There is a loftier ambition than merely to stand high in the world.*
> *It is to stoop down and lift mankind a little higher."*
>
> —Henry Van Dyke

2014—A Probable Future

Embu, a 23-year-old Kenyan Bantu-speaking woman and mother of one takes the microphone and beams a broad, proud smile at the assembled group of representatives. They've traveled from far and wide across the expansive Nyanza Province, which borders on Lake Victoria, for this important quarterly meeting. Delegates from across the culturally diverse region, with a mixture of Luo, Gusii, and Kuria tribes, sit in excited anticipation to hear the financial reports and updates on their area's comprehensive network of co-operatives and trade associations. Preliminary accounts and animated gossip, along with obvious evidence from the vibrant commerce that is transacted daily, bodes well for good news and a well-deserved celebration later that evening.

While waiting for the eager chatter to die down some attendees quickly check their account balances on their mobile phones. Sammy sees that the consignment of goatskins and meat from his co-op to their neighbors across the border in Tanzania has been paid in full in the local currency, the Zutu, which circulates in the eco-region around Lake Victoria. This trading currency was designed to facilitate local commerce by keeping the Zutu circulating within their larger community. This has brought tangible wealth to the region in the past couple of years.

Their local currencies are backed by time—one hour of work equals one unit—or by a commodity, such as timber. A special savings currency called the Muti, named after the Zulu word for tree, is backed by shares in re-forestation plantations. Sammy works there part-time. The future earnings from the felled trees in twenty years time will be helpful in looking after his parents' retirement and, additionally, the new woodlands are reversing decades of soil erosion, enticing indigenousness species back into the region.

His mobile e-purse carries several currencies—three national, euros, Kenyan and Tanzanian shillings, as well as several local, including the Zuta and the Muti. There is an education currency called the Saber, which has leveraged the ten million euros that was granted five years earlier, twelve times over, each and every year. Based on his hours of mentoring younger students, helping them with their English and math homework, Sammy earned Saber credits, which have enabled him to pay the tuition for his long-distance learning degree in book-keeping and business law.

Food, which was a major problem for decades, is now grown locally, either within the local forest or on organic farms, rather than imported. The vibrant forest supports a constructed ecosystem to provide bananas, coconuts, and other tropical fruits and nuts. Little labor is required since it is self-sustaining. The organic farms provide yields as high as conventional 'green revolution' intensive farming methods while helping to build soil. The overall economics of the system, that includes grains, vegetables and also livestock, far exceeds that of the massive farm just outside the village that previously occupied and was destroying the local farmland. Labor is paid for using a time-backed local currency, where one hour of service equals one unit of the local currency. This money can be used to purchase a wide array of products and services in the local community and by its design tends to remain there.

Bëbëlë, another meeting attendee, takes a moment and looks around the assembly hall with a certain satisfaction. The old building, which was constructed by the British in the early 1960s, has been totally retro-fitted with passive energy features by Bëbëlë and his team. Energy use in the community has been drastically slashed while the residents still live and work in comfort. The new adjacent structure where tonight's banquet will be held actually generates energy to feed into the local utility grid. Even though the temperature today is going to be hot with a large assembled group inside these design modifications allow them to remain cool without the need for air conditioners. All appliances, when required, are highly efficient, often using as little as a tenth of the energy of comparable products built in 2000.

Embu clears her throat and raises her arm to call the house to order. While waiting for silence she reflects on the terrible period of racial tensions and political strife following the 2008 general elections. She smiles with contentment as she surveys the gathering, which only a few years earlier was torn asunder by distrust and suspicion, as she gets ready to start the meeting. The entrepreneurship and innovation that is clearly evident within the hall was ignited through an integrated series of trainings and programs. These encouraged each individual to have the self-assurance to trust their own observations of what was appropriate action, given their unique real-world awareness, experience and knowledge. This new found confidence—to be able to address issues on a grassroots level, along with an integrated plan of training, education, access to information and the introduction of appropriate low-tech technologies and new monetary innovations—was the lever on which their universe has shifted forever.

The air is electric with anticipation as the applause for Embu dies down.

"My dear colleagues and friends, I know you are all excited to get the financial reports and stories from our various co-op and team leaders on their collective breakthroughs and success for the past few months. I know you've been talking among yourselves and have a sense of the good news we have to share together," she begins.

"But there is something far more important I want to tell you. We have been contacted by some wai-Kukuyu in Nairobi. They live in terrible misery with little food and no real opportunity, in the center of the capital in a heap of rubbish and filth."

"We have been asked to come and share our knowledge and capabilities with them. As we are country folk and not knowing the ways of the big towns, I was able to contact the people in a far away place called Curitiba, Brazil—on the other side of the world—who were able to restore their own big town with its terrible poverty, disease, and no hope twenty years ago, by using local currencies and local people's ideas ...just like us."

"The news is I have asked and they have agreed to come to Kenya to help the Kukuyu," her voice breaks with emotion.

There is a gasp of surprise and awe from the assembled group.

"So, my question to you, delegates and friends, can we, will we, use our time and abilities to help our brothers and sisters in Nairobi. Are we willing as Kenyans, no better still, as follow human beings, to make a difference and share the knowledge and resources that was so generously given to us? Are you with me?"

With that, all 300 attendees leap to their feet and roar a resounding "yes!!"

While the scenario above explores a possible future, legend has it that the ancient Greek mathematician, Archimedes, by realizing and making use of the multiplying power of a lever, was able to move an entire sailing ship filled with men with but a single rope. He did so by identifying a well-placed position from which to intervene—a "leverage point"—a place within a system (whether a living body, corporation, city, economy, or ecosystem) where a small shift in one thing can produce major changes throughout. His discoveries led to his bold proclamation: "Give me a place to stand and I can move the world."

One of the greatest leverage points for substantive and enduring transformation in our world today resides in our monetary system. Money is an essential aspect of modern life; a key consideration and determinant in the affairs of state and in the state of human and global affairs. Yet, despite its preeminent role in our lives, the inherent potential of money has only just recently begun to be appreciated and utilized. Making use of new understandings with regard to money provides options and means by which to intercede in and effectively address a broad range of vital concerns and to vastly improve human and global conditions.

Money, like "tools," is a generic concept. Just as we have hammers, drills or paint brushes for particular applications, many types of money are both possible and required to address different needs. The predominant form of money in use in our world today—national currencies—notwithstanding their various names, nations of origin and motifs, are all of one type of monetary design, put in place centuries ago at the beginning of the Industrial Revolution. This industrial age money was designed to address a limited set of specific objectives of that bygone period: competition, industrialization and nationalism. We now know that money can be intentionally designed and tailored to promote many kinds of objectives and behaviors, including cooperation as well as competition, community-building as well as business, long-term as well as short-term investment patterns, etc. But not one type of money, just as no single tool, can do it all.

At the core of this shift in awareness is the discernment that money is a human construct. It lies in the domain of agreement, like political parties and marriage. Money is an agreement within a community—be it geographical, social, or internet-based—to use something as a medium of exchange. During World War II, for instance, commodities such as cigarettes and women's stockings were used as a medium of exchange in lieu of national currency when it was scarce. Historically, everything from shells to stones has been used as money.

A modern and popular example of such a commercial application of a new complementary currency is frequent flyer miles, which the airlines started as a marketing/ loyalty scheme. Now, participants can use frequent flyer miles to purchase everything from rental cars to hotel rooms to groceries. Today, neighborhoods, villages, and even bio-regions are currently creating new currencies to deal with their particular issues by designing their own local monetary systems. They use these to link their unused resources with their unmet needs. These innovations generate greater abundance and more options.

These new currencies do not replace national money, such as the yen, dollar or euro; they work in tandem with them. There are now some 3,000 complementary currencies around the world. These are providing economic solutions for the global crisis in education, health-care, joblessness, care of the old and infirm, and environmental degradation without having to create bond measures, raise taxes, redistribute wealth, or rely on federal assistance.

To illustrate the power and diversity of such complementary currencies, we take a look at Curitiba, Brazil, which faced massive problems resulting from crushing poverty; Time Dollars, a currency based on an hour of time; and the Swiss WIR, a business-to-business currency. In conclusion a proposal for an educational currency is explored.

Curitiba, Brazil

Garbage was a major problem in Curitiba, the capital of the southeastern state of Paraná, Brazil. Its urban population had mushroomed from 120,000 in 1942 to a staggering 2.3 million in 1997. Many of the inhabitants lived in favelas, shantytowns made out of cardboard and corrugated metal. Garbage collection trucks could not get into these favelas, as the streets were not wide enough to travel through. As a consequence, the garbage piled up and disease broke out.

Jaime Lerner, who became mayor of Curitiba in 1971, did not have access to funds to apply customary solutions, such as bulldozing the area or building new streets. Bond measures, further taxation, or federal assistance were simply not options. Another way had to be found to deal with the garbage problem.

It was decided to place large metallic bins on the streets at the edge of the favelas. Anyone who brought in a bag full of pre-selected garbage received a bus token. Those who collected paper and cartons were given plastic chits, exchangeable for food parcels of seasonal fresh fruits and vegetables. In addition, a school-based garbage collection program supplied poorer students with notebooks.

Tens of thousands of children soon picked the neighborhoods clean. Parents made use of the tokens to take the bus downtown, oftentimes to find work. The bus tokens were soon accepted at local markets and exchanged for food. In one three-year period, more than 100 schools traded 200 tons of garbage for 1.9 million notebooks. The paper-recycling component alone saved the equivalent of 1,200 trees—each day.

These improvements were accomplished without having to redistribute wealth, raise taxes, issue bonds, rely on charity or loans, or depend on the federal government, or international organizations, such as the World Bank, or the International Monetary Fund (IMF). The improvements burdened no one. Everyone benefited.

Eventually, more than 70% of Curitiban households became involved. The 62 poorer neighborhoods alone exchanged 11,000 tons of garbage for nearly a million bus tokens and 1,200 tons of food. The results in purely economic terms are worth noting: from 1975-95, the Domestic Product of the city of Curitiba increased by some 75% more than that of the entire state of Paraná, and 48% greater than that of Brazil as a whole. The average Curitibano made more than three times the country's minimum wage, but his or her real total income was at least 30% higher still. This 30% difference was income directly derived from nontraditional monetary forms, such as the exchange of garbage for food. The outbreak of diseases diminished. Other results in human terms for these Curitibanos—in the renewal of dignity, and faith in the future—can only be imagined.

Other programs were created as well, designed specifically to finance the restoration of historical buildings, create green areas, and provide social housing—all by means that did not financially burden the municipality. In 1990, Curitiba was given the highest environmental award by the United Nations Environmental Program (UNEP).

This city discovered a means by which to match unmet needs with unused resources. Challenges, such as garbage collection, environmental pollution, city restoration, job creation, education, disease intervention, and hunger, were tackled by making use of a complementary currency—a monetary initiative that did not replace but rather complemented the national currency system. This innovative approach enabled one developing, formerly impoverished city to vastly improve conditions in the remarkable span of a single generation.

Curitiba represents an important, 25-year practical case study. It offers testimony that a "dual-currency" approach—one that uses both the traditional national currency and a well-designed complementary currency—can address a broad range of issues to the benefit of all.

Time Dollars

Time Dollars was created by attorney, Dr. Edgar Cahn. As a Fulbright scholar, co-founder of the National Legal Services, a speechwriter and counsel to former Attorney General Robert F. Kennedy, and a close associate of Sargent Shriver on the War on Poverty and the Peace Corps, Cahn has dedicated much of his life to those less fortunate than himself.

One of Cahn's important observations is that formally paying people by whatever means also empowers them. He asserts that "counting what people do is a way of valuing what they do." Given the scarcity of national currency, Cahn came up with a complementary medium of exchange—time. The basic unit of account is a Time Dollar, equivalent to one hour of service, which can be spent for goods and services that are available within a given community. This complementary currency system allows transactions to occur that would likely not otherwise take place and provides a means by which to acknowledge and honor the contributions and skills of people, matching their offerings with the needs of their community.

Cahn cites a ten-year study conducted by researchers from Harvard, Columbia, and the University of Michigan, which endeavored to identify what helps make neighborhoods safe. The answer to this $51 million study was not more police or government programs; rather it was "collective efficacy," a fancy term for neighbors looking out for each other's kids and stopping their misbehaviors. Time Dollars are a proven way to boost such relationships.

The cost of starting such a program is minimal. Small communities can use a blackboard or a piece of paper to keep a tally; for larger-scale projects, a timekeeper computer program can be downloaded for free from the Internet. It is scalable to accommodate any level of participation and any number of person-hours that may be needed.

As with other complementary currencies, the effects of Time Dollar systems go far beyond a simple exchange of goods and services. A survey was conducted to compare U.S. retirement homes using Time Dollars with those that did not. It was found that Time Dollars bring members of a retirement home closer together. When there is a birthday, it becomes a party that includes the entire home. A potluck dinner now takes place each week. A communal garden has begun. People now say hello, interact and watch out for one another. In short, community is created.

Time Dollars also reinforces volunteerism. One could argue that the services provided by volunteers are done altruistically, without the need for any compensation or complementary currency system. Evidence demonstrates, however, that the acknowledgment of the services rendered via a complementary currency makes a big difference in terms of the willingness to volunteer. Indeed, research by the University of Maryland Center on Aging has shown that about a third of the people taking part in the Time Dollar system had never volunteered for anything before. It also shows that the volunteer dropout rate—which in most programs typically reaches 40% per year—is only 3% in these programs.

Time Dollar systems are becoming more popular worldwide and now operate in over 17 countries. There are an estimated 79 systems in operation in the United Kingdom, where they are referred to as "Fair Shares" or "Time Banking" with another 80 in development. In Japan, there are 70 Time Dollar systems. There are an estimated 65 established programs in the United States, with another 70 in formation. Other countries that have recently adopted the system include Senegal, Ghana, and New Zealand. In total there are approximately 350 mature systems worldwide.

Time Dollar or Time Banking systems are being used in an ever-growing number of different applications. For example:

Elderplan. This is a health insurance company in Brooklyn, N.Y. that now accepts 25% of the premiums for its senior health programs in Time Dollars. Preventive measures, such as fixing a broken bathtub rail, are provided through Elderplan's Care Bank, a Time Dollar exchange. The Elderplan model is now expanding through all five boroughs of New York City.

Time Dollars Youth Court. Founded in 1996, Youth Court is now one of the cornerstones of the juvenile justice system in Washington, D.C. Juveniles accused of nonviolent offenses are tried before a jury of their peers—other juveniles who have been convicted of similar offenses. Those found guilty are sentenced to a mixture of community service, life skills counseling, tutoring younger students, a requisite apology, and service on a Youth Court jury themselves. Volunteer and respondent jurors earn Time Dollars, which they can redeem for recycled computers, savings bonds for college, educational trips, and events.

The effectiveness of this program is attracting a good deal of attention. Participation in the Youth Court reduces first-year recidivism by half. The Youth Court now processes approximately 60% of nonviolent, juvenile offenders' first cases. The program has been officially sanctioned by the D.C. Superior Court to work with the criminal justice system in a "partnership for the purpose of jointly developing a diversion program which provides a meaningful alternative to the traditional adjudicatory format in juvenile cases." Similar programs are now being implemented in South Africa and Jamaica.

Other Time Dollar applications. In exchange for refurbishing bicycles that are then sent to Africa, some prisoners in the United Kingdom and the United States can now earn Time Dollars, which are transferred to their own families. A tutoring program in some Chicago public schools pays older students Time Dollars to tutor younger students. The older students can then use their Time Dollars to obtain refurbished computers, thus compensating them for their knowledge and service. A credo of Time Dollars states, "You have something your community needs, you should be rewarded for offering it."

A new proposal called Carebanking. This is a quasi-franchise social venture enterprise to address the problems associated with aging. Edgar Cahn remarks, "CareBanks builds on the proven efficacy of Time Banking. This social venture element supplies sustainability, reliability and civic engagement to cope with the Age Wave tsunami."

In recognition of the social contributions offered by Time Dollars, three separate Internal Revenue Service (IRS) rulings make this complementary currency officially tax-exempt in the United States.

The WIR

Switzerland enjoys one of the most stable economies and highest standards of living in the world. Tourism, Swiss chocolates, precision watches, a trusted banking system, and political neutrality during and following World War II are often cited as principal reasons for this nation's economic well-being. While each of the above have no doubt played their role, it may come as a surprise to learn that a unique, little-known, but very robust commercial complementary currency has been significantly contributing to the country's economic stability.

Switzerland is home to the oldest functioning complementary currency system in the Western world. Called the "WIR" (an abbreviation for Wirtschaftsring-Genossenschaft), it roughly translates as "Economic Mutual Support Circle." Wir is also the pronoun "we" in German. The WIR was founded in Zurich in 1934 by 16 members to procure and develop employment possibilities, promote local industries and trades, and support business ventures.

This business-to-business complementary currency is run by and for a community of businesses as a mutual-credit system. WIR can be obtained by selling goods or services to fellow members: the seller obtains a WIR credit, the buyer receives a corresponding WIR debit. Additionally, a client can obtain credit from the WIR Bank at a very low interest rate (1% per annum). Such loans are usually guaranteed by real estate or other assets. The value of the WIR is pegged to the Swiss franc—that is, one WIR = one Swiss franc—but all debits in WIR are settled in WIR.

Members tend to participate in WIR exchanges for the following reasons:

- It is very cost effective: commission on sales and payment expenses are limited to 0.6% on deals completed in WIR
- It gives access to a large, varied, and prescreened—and, therefore, dependable and credit-worthy—client base; this helps to engender trust, a key ingredient with all currencies
- Credit in the WIR system is cheaper and more readily available than in national currency
- WIR provides small businesses additional means by which to get established, even during economic depressions or high-interest-rate periods, when national currencies are typically less available or more costly to obtain
- Many auxiliary services are provided—for example, direct mail, publicity among members, publications—all of which encourage and support small- to medium-sized businesses

The WIR also provides a macroeconomic advantage to both WIR members and the Swiss economy in general. A key feature of the WIR is that currency issuance automatically tends to be countercyclical to the typical business cycle. During a recession for example, when regular banks are not lending, businesses can instead borrow WIR to meet their needs. When the economy improves again, the WIR volume spontaneously reduces, so it actually expands and shrinks counter-cyclically with the official Swiss Franc economy, as needed. This feature is a powerful stabilizing mechanism in tempering the inevitable boom-and-bust peaks in the Swiss business cycle.

A quantitative study on the WIR's macroeconomic impact was conducted by Dr. James P. Stodder, a professor at the well-respected Lally School of Management and Technology at Rensselaer University. Stodder's study concluded that the WIR system is indeed countercyclical, contributing measurably to the stability of the Swiss economy and employment rates: "Growth in the number of WIR participants has tracked Swiss unemployment very closely, consistently maintaining a rate of about one-tenth the increase in the number of unemployed." This means that when the conventional Swiss franc economy slows, job losses are partially avoided by involving more people in the WIR economy.

Professor Tobias Studer, from the Center of Economic Studies at Basel University, Switzerland, considers the Stodder study a breakthrough: "For the first time, an independent American researcher has arrived at a surprising conclusion: far from representing a factor of disturbance for the national monetary policy, the credits created by WIR constitute a support of the National Bank (the Swiss central bank) in pursuit of its monetary policy objectives."

Within its first year of operation in 1934, the WIR listed more than 1,000 account holders who actively exchanged goods and services, and who celebrated its formation at the first "WIR Industrial Fair" in the city of Basel. There are now over 60,000 members actively participating in WIR nationally, including approximately 25% of all small and medium-sized Swiss businesses. For the year 2006, its trading volume reached 1.67 billion Swiss Francs ($1.4 billion). WIR now owns its own bank building as well as six regional offices and operates in four languages.

Even in one of the most conservative, hard-nosed capitalist countries in the world, complementary currencies have taken hold and make both business and macroeconomic sense.

Switzerland is not the only capitalist nation to realize the benefits of complementary currencies. Japan, one of the top three largest economies in the world, is now using these on a nationwide basis to address a wide variety of needs.

The Saber

The Saber (pronounced saa-bear, meaning "knowledge" in Portuguese), is a specialized education paper currency allocated to primary schools, particularly in economically depressed areas where funding is typically not available in sufficiency. This currency is first given to the youngest students (seven-year-olds) who transfer it to older students (for instance, ten-year-olds) in return for tutoring help with their schoolwork. The ten-year-olds can then do the same thing with 12-year-olds in compensation for the hours spent mentoring, and the latter with 15-year-olds, and so on. At the end of this "learning chain," the Sabers would go to 17-year-olds who could use them to pay for part or all of their university tuition.

In the above example, the Saber offers a number of advantages. It circulates among five students, the last of whom enters university; it allows for better education through learning by teaching; it offers a greater chance for students to go to university; and it allows educational funds to be used for many more students than if they were used for just one, thereby creating a "learning multiplier."

The university would be able to exchange the Sabers for conventional money through the Education Fund but at a discount of, say, 50%. This process is possible because most of the costs at a university are fixed, and, similar to empty seats on an airplane, the marginal expense of an additional student has little impact on those costs.

A Learning Multiplier

Several decades of research has shown that learning retention depends less on the person or the topics involved than on the delivery system. What is striking is that our traditional education system commonly uses the two least effective methods available: lecturing and reading, through which respectively only 5% and 10% of what is being taught will be remembered. At the other end of the spectrum an impressive 90% retention rate applies to whatever one teaches others.

The total learning multiplier per dollar for the education budget allocated to this project would, therefore, be a factor of ten (five times for the exchanges among students of different ages, multiplied by two for the arrangement between the Education Fund and the university, since they discount the Saber by 50%). This ten-fold learning multiplier was calculated in terms of the financial effect of $1 billion spent through the Saber system, delivering a total of $10 billion worth of education. Factoring in however, the increase in learning retention rates from 5-10% (normal education procedure) to 90% (teaching others), another ten-fold multiplier effect develops. In other words, spending $1 billion through the Saber system could be roughly estimated to generate as much as $100 billion worth of retained-learning, in comparison to that obtained through conventional means.

The Saber program could also be expanded beyond the conventional classroom: eight-year-olds could teach their newly learned reading and writing skills to parents or illiterate grandparents; students could help the elderly or handicapped, by reading to the blind or recording oral histories of a neighborhood. These programs would encourage inter-generational relationships and further learning, not to mention creating extra assistance for the elderly without burdening governmental budgets.

Saber and Demurrage

Demurrage—a time related penalty for not using the currency—can be used to control the balance between the number of students each year wanting university seats and their availability. A demurrage fee would be applied to encourage students to use Sabers for the year that is printed on the Saber itself, for example, year 2010. If they were not used to pay for tuition before or during that year, they could be exchanged for Sabers of the following year—the year 2011—but with a penalty of 20%, when a new expiration date is stamped on the paper currency. This gives a strong incentive to use them on or before the 2010 deadline.

Saber and Inflation

Three factors make the non-inflationary dynamics of the Saber fundamentally different from those of regular money. They are:

1. Sabers are ultimately redeemable into money only by universities, and only for educational purposes
2. The quantity of Sabers issued would be equal to the universities' capacities to increase their number of students, thereby avoiding the inflation problem generated by a currency that is created in excess of the goods or services available. Extra students would be using seats that would otherwise be empty
3. The demurrage fee of 20% ensures that the Sabers circulate only for a limited and controlled time period, further reducing the possibility of excess currency

At the time of writing, the Saber proposal is being championed in Brazil by Professor Gilson Schwartz from the University of São Paulo. There is also interest in this concept in several other countries.

Creating a world in which we can all meet our basic needs, to live with dignity and in balance with the world requires honoring a more integrative perspective of money systems and economics. This can be provided, in large part, by complementary currencies, along with other monetary innovations. If Curitiba, Brazil, a city overwhelmed by poverty and garbage in a nation with few resources to assist it, was able to transform its difficult and challenging conditions in less than one generation with simple monetary mechanisms, imagine what is possible for communities, such as Embu's, our cities, our nations, and our world.

References

No More Throw-Away People: The Co-Production Imperative by Edgar Cahn.
Money: Understanding and Creating Alternatives to Legal Tender by Thomas Greco.
Origin of Wealth: Evolution, Complexity, and the Radical Remaking of Economics by Eric D. Beinhocker.
Of Human Wealth: New Money for a New World by Bernard Lietaer and Stephen Belgin.
Money and Sustainability—The Missing Link. A Report to the Club of Rome by Bernard Lietaer and Stefan Brunnhuber with Robert Ulanowicz and Sally Goerner.

PART II

INNOVATING NEW ECONOMIC PRACTICES FOR SUSTAINABILITY

A. THE ROLE OF BUSINESS IN SUSTAINABLE DEVELOPMENT AND PEACE-BUILDING

Twenty Ideas that Changed the Way the World Does Business

Mal Warwick and Deborah Nelson et al.

In 1987, when a small group of visionary business leaders and investors came together in the mountains of Colorado to form what became Social Venture Network, the phrases "corporate social responsibility" and "socially responsible business" were terms of ridicule in the mainstream U.S. business press. The icons of values-driven business, such as Ben Cohen of Ben & Jerry's and Anita Roddick of The Body Shop, were routinely mocked on the business pages and the evening news and at corporate gatherings. Today, just two decades later, four of every five companies on the Fortune Global 500 now issue annual reports on their non-financial performance, consumers in Europe and North America are favoring demonstrably responsible companies, and business schools the world over are scrambling to offer courses on sustainability and Corporate Social Responsibility.

We know that Social Venture Network (SVN) had a lot to do with that change, because we were there. In this chapter, we'll spell out twenty of the Big Ideas championed by our members, encouraged and often incubated within SVN—ideas that helped foster that world-altering trend.

Pioneering a New Path

Co-founded by Wayne Silby and Joshua Mailman in 1987, Social Venture Network (SVN) connects, leverages, and promotes a global community of leaders working to create a more just and sustainable economy through business. Today, SVN is a support system for a diverse community of more than 400 members, including company founders, social entrepreneurs, investors, and key influencers.

Today, the concept behind SVN might seem commonplace, but its genesis two decades ago was the result of a revelation. Mailman explains: “We decided that it was imperative for us to use our resources to create a new paradigm: one in which business operates to add value to society—without compromising the well-being of future generations.”

Since SVN began, the attitudes of its founding members have been increasingly embraced not only by businesses and nonprofits, but also by the public at large. “The way that people think about business and social change is merging,” Mailman explains. “SVN helped innovate that shift through its focus on values.”

Indeed, thanks to the visions and actions of Silby, Mailman, and thousands of other pioneers and innovators who have participated in the network, SVN has catalyzed fundamental social change during its 20-year history. Because of connections forged among like-minded members, SVN has helped launch such organizations as Investors' Circle, Business for Social Responsibility (BSR), Net Impact, Business Alliance for Local Living Economies (BALLE), SVN Europe, and Social Impact Leadership Coalition (SILC).

Socially Responsible Investing

The financial industry isn't known for being especially caring, but after years of working with investors, Amy Domini and Joan Bavaria found that they cared about a lot more than just money. Socially responsible investing (SRI) is based on the idea that the way you invest your money matters, and that investments should be in line with the values of the individual or corporation that makes them.

Domini, who founded Domini Social Investments in 1991, began questioning investment practices while as a stockbroker in the 1970s. “When I was asked to recommend a company that was on the verge of getting a big military contract, I realized I didn't want to ask the caring people who were my clients to invest in killing machines,” she says.

Joan Bavaria had a similar experience, leading her to create Trillium Asset Management Corporation, the first socially conscious management firm solely dedicated to socially responsible investing. Since founding the firm in 1982, she's seen SRI change not only the way people invest, but also the way companies run their businesses.

Business as Change Agent

Ben & Jerry's Homemade is a quintessential example of a company that paved the way in using business to effect positive social change—a point the company makes on every pint of their now 40-plus flavors of ice cream.

Co-founder Ben Cohen is nationally known as a leader and pioneer in socially responsible business, both from his work with Ben & Jerry's and with Business Leaders for Sensible Priorities. From the beginning, he understood the potential of using business as a medium for social change. "We realized one of our major assets was packaging," Cohen says. "It could be used as a form of alternative media."

By the 1990s, Ben & Jerry's had become one of the most popular ice cream brands in the United States. With their success, Ben and Jerry had proven that consumers are eager to purchase products that are aligned with their values. From strict recycling rules to the employee-driven Green Team, Ben and Jerry's earned the respect of consumers by walking their talk.

"Business is the most powerful force in society," Cohen says. "It has the highest potential for solving social problems. Once consumers saw examples of prosperous companies integrating social concerns into their business practices, they were emboldened to demand the same of other businesses. Businesses could no longer say it was impossible."

Seeding the Organic Revolution

As Gary Hirshberg, President and CEO of Stonyfield Farm, saw the demand for organic products grow steadily over the past 20 years, it was clear that the "organic revolution" was well under way. But as more and more consumers began to see organic foods as the natural choice, Hirshberg knew the revolution needed to grow to scale.

Beginning in 1983, when Stonyfield was a seven-cow farming school, Hirshberg and his partner Samuel Kaymen operated the yogurt company using core values of environmental sustainability. "We were children of the 60s and had no choice but to question the conventional models and try to integrate these values," Hirshberg says.

By putting values first and marketing second, consumers became passionately loyal to the brand, driving the company's growth into the largest organic yogurt company in the world. And there was another side effect: "Our net profits were actually better than our competitors'," Hirshberg says. "What began as a set of practical steps to change the way we did business resulted in a better business and a model for other companies to follow." Stonyfield continues to set an example through socially responsible practices such as donating 10% of profits each year to efforts that help protect or restore the Earth and using yogurt lids to educate consumers about environmental issues and motivate them to take action.

M.B.A. in Sustainability

In the 20 years that Gifford and Elizabeth (Libba) Pinchot spent as consultants for Fortune 100 businesses, they found that many executives trained in business schools held beliefs counterproductive to a healthy environment and a just society. They realized that if business leaders were ignoring their broader responsibility to society and the environment, something about the business school system had to change.

"The only solution was to reinvent the MBA," Libba says. "First by doing it and then by helping other schools."

On 9/11/2001, Libba was in Ecuador when she heard the devastating reports of the terrorist attacks back home. Overcome by the news, she decided she should pursue her dream of a business school focused on sustainability. On that same day, Gifford was in Connecticut facilitating an investment discussion, along with many SVN members. After hearing news of the traumatic attacks, the group took the next four days to flesh out Gifford and Libba's idea for a sustainable business school.

In 2002, Bainbridge Graduate Institute (BGI) opened, offering the first MBA program in the U.S. that focuses on leading socially and environmentally responsible businesses. Unlike other schools that offer concentrations in sustainability, BGI incorporates social and environmental responsibility into every class, including finance, marketing and organizational systems.

As Libba explains, "BGI is an incubator for business education so other schools can teach these principles. Many faculty from other institutions immerse themselves in our monthly residential program and many schools are asking BGI for help in designing sustainable MBA programs."

Tread Lightly

Jeffrey Hollender witnessed the effects of an unhealthy environment when his son was hospitalized after suffering an asthma attack in their home. An asthma specialist confirmed the cause was 100% environmental and part of the cure included using non-toxic cleaners.

Hollender knew something needed to be done. He took action by beginning a mail order catalog business selling environmental solutions. "As we grew and explored issues," he says, "we saw that toxic chemicals and the products that use them were hugely important yet were things that few people knew about."

Now the nation's leading brand of non-toxic and environmentally safe household products, Seventh Generation is making a difference by saving natural resources, reducing pollution and keeping toxic chemicals out of the environment. "Every consumer who buys a Seventh Generation product is making sure that the world their children are growing up in will be that much less contaminated," Hollender says.

"SVN has connected us to a big storehouse of wisdom as we explore a brave new business territory that's largely uncharted," Hollender says. "The vision behind our idea is a world where people don't carry hazardous chemicals in their bodies, the environment is free of toxic pollutants, and the economy diligently conserves its natural resources for consumers and future generations. We want to make it easier for consumers to create this world through their purchasing decisions and everyday activities."

Spirit in Business

A student of Zen Buddhism, Bernie Glassman felt he needed to bring the essence of Zen, which is the realization of the interdependence of life, to everyone from the poor and homeless to business people and political leaders. He realized his vision by creating the Greyston Mandala, a network of businesses and nonprofits engaged in community development in Yonkers, New York.

Greyston brings together for-profits, non-profits and spiritual centers to help low-income communities transform themselves. "I honor businesses for what they do, I honor nonprofits for what they do, I honor government for what it does, and then I invite everyone to the table so that together we can come up with innovative and broad-based solutions that can serve as many people as possible," Glassman says. "The fewer or less diverse voices you invite to the table, the smaller and narrower your solution will be and the fewer people it will serve."

The Greyston Foundation has become a national model for inclusive community development. An important element of the foundation's model is the Greyston Bakery, a company that lives its values by prioritizing both profits and social contributions. Their tagline, "Great desserts by great people doing great things," reflects the essence of the company. Led by CEO Julius Walls, Jr., Greyston Bakery uses profits to fund the community development programs of the Greyston Foundation, such as job training for adults, after-school programs for children, and building affordable housing for low-income families. They also have an open hiring policy that provides jobs and training for individuals who have struggled to find employment.

Employee Ownership

Employee ownership is a powerful way for business leaders to create a more just economy. From employee stock ownership at Eileen Fisher to 100% employee ownership at King Arthur Flour, smart companies are embracing this practice for the values it represents and the added benefit of increased productivity.

The National Center for Employee Ownership, founded by Corey Rosen in 1980, helps encourage more companies to explore employee ownership by providing accurate, unbiased information and research on ESOPs, equity compensation plans such as stock options, and ownership culture. As a U.S. Senate staffer in the 1970's, Rosen helped draft legislation on ESOP's at a time when very few companies even knew what an ESOP was.

Successful clothing designer and entrepreneur Eileen Fisher developed a successful ESOP that put nearly a third of the company in the hands of her 624 employees. King Arthur Flour—America's oldest flour company—has benefited enormously from employee ownership.

In 1996, owners Frank and Brinna Sands were looking at how best to ensure the company would thrive for the next 200 years. Seeing their employees as family and wanting to give something back to them, the Sands began to transition to an ESOP structure under the leadership of CEO Steve Voigt. In the ten years since, King Arthur Flour—now 100% employee-owned—has grown from 60 to nearly 200 employees and generates $55 million in annual sales. Voigt attributes much of this growth to the entrepreneurial employee-ownership culture.

Rosen believes employee ownership has the capacity to create drastic change in the way wealth is distributed. "Around the world, the gap between rich and poor has become increasingly wide," he says. "Employee ownership is a means to harness the market to provide for greater equity, in the literal and fairness sense, for everyday employees." Today, 25 million employees are owners in the companies they work for.

Family-Friendly Workplace

While working for Save the Children in the Sudan in the mid-1980s, Linda Mason raised $15 million and served over 400,000 famine and war victims. Upon returning to the U.S., Mason saw that the United States had its own crisis—poor-quality childcare. The number of mothers in the workforce was rapidly increasing, and the supply and quality of existing child-care was inadequate.

In 1986 Mason and her husband Roger Brown formed Bright Horizons Family Solutions, which is now the world's leading provider of employer-sponsored child-care, early education and work/life solutions. "Our goals were to create an organization that would simultaneously honor and respect early childhood educators, be a great place to work, and be an environment that would allow employees to flourish," Mason says.

Bright Horizons now manages more than 600 child-care centers for many of the world's leading corporations, hospitals, universities, and government agencies. "When Bright Horizons started, it was difficult to get major corporations involved," says Mason. "But now most corporations realize their bottom line is tied to being family-friendly and respectful of families."

Mason and Brown's innovative business followed the path set by Arnold Hiatt at Stride Rite, who pioneered child-care at the workplace. In response to families encountering problems finding both child and elder care, Hiatt opened Stride Rite's first company-run day care center in the U.S. in 1971 and then opened its Intergenerational Day-Care Center in 1990.

Local Living Economies

As a pioneer of the local living economy movement, Judy Wicks believes community self-reliance isn't just a utopian vision, but the key to our very survival. "The corporate-controlled global economic system, based on the continual growth of large corporations and long distance shipping, is using up more natural resources than the earth can restore and contributing to global warming," Wicks says. "The solution is clear—we must decentralize business ownership, food production, and energy production into self-reliant local economies."

For Wicks, this vision grew from the business she founded in Philadelphia in 1983, White Dog Café, and its mission to serve customers, community, employees, and nature. Food is purchased from local farms where animals are raised on sustainably grown pasture and produce. Long distance purchasing is limited to what is not available locally. Operations are powered by electricity from wind power generated in Pennsylvania.

After achieving success with the café, Wicks had an epiphany. "It wasn't enough to have good business practices within one's own company," Wicks says. "We had to work cooperatively with other businesses to build a whole local economy based on these values." Taking what she learned to a higher level, Wicks started the White Dog Foundation, which uses 20% of the Café's profits to build a local living economy, including connecting local farmers with other restaurants.

At SVN, Wicks teamed up with David Korten, author of *When Corporations Rule the World;* Michael Shuman, author of *Going Local;* and Laury Hammel, owner of the Longfellow Clubs and a longtime activist in founding business organizations, such as BSR and its New England predecessor.

Wicks and Hammel co-founded the Business Alliance for Local Living Economies (BALLE) at the 2001 SVN Fall Conference and currently serve as its co-chairs. "With over 50 local networks and more than 15,000 members across North America, BALLE is starting to change the economic story that shapes business and consumer behavior, as well as government policy, by building awareness of the implications of each choice we make between a global corporation and a local business.

Clean Technology

In 1976, physicist Amory Lovins wrote a famously controversial paper suggesting that more power plants were unnecessary and unaffordable. A "soft energy path" that emphasized efficient use, less-centralized supplies, and renewable sources would, he argued, work better and cost less.

Investors are now agreeing. Green energy got $71 billion of global investment in 2006, while central power plants won less than half the world market—beaten by cheaper, faster micropower and "negawatts" (saved electricity). Rocky Mountain Institute (RMI), which Lovins co-founded in 1982, continues to lead this and other business transformations that create abundance by design.

An independent, entrepreneurial, nonprofit think-and-do tank, RMI fosters the efficient and restorative use of resources to make the world secure, just, prosperous, and life-sustaining. RMI's 60 staff members have helped corporations design $30 billion worth of super-efficient facilities in 29 sectors.

One of RMI's four for-profit spin-offs is E SOURCE, an electric-efficiency information service that laid the foundation for the multi-billion-dollar negawatt industry. Another, spun off in 1999 to promote the tripled-to quintupled-efficiency Hypercar® vehicles that Lovins invented in 1991, now does business as Fiberforge. It's commercializing a manufacturing process for near-aerospace-grade advanced-composite structures at automotive cost and speed. Such ultralight cars will halve their weight and fuel use, be safer, yet cost the same to make—and save U.S. oil equivalent to finding a Saudi Arabia under Detroit. Such innovations underlie RMI's Pentagon-cosponsored Winning the Oil Endgame—a roadmap for an oil-free America by the 2040s, led by business for profit.

Green Building

Green building practices have come a long way since the advent of solar panels. Now entire buildings—and the architecture firms that build them—are operating with a focus on sustainability.

William McDonough has been a leader in the sustainable development movement since its inception, designing and building the first solar-heated house in Ireland in 1977 and the first "green office" for the U.S. Environmental Defense Fund in 1985. Time magazine recognized him as a "Hero for the Planet," stating that "his utopianism is grounded in a unified philosophy that—in demonstrable and practical ways—is changing the design of the world."

McDonough's product and process design firm, McDonough Braungart Design Chemistry (MBDC), offers a unique Cradle to Cradle Certification. This stamp of approval provides companies with a means to tangibly and credibly measure achievement in environmentally intelligent design and helps customers identify products that are sustainable.

The phrase "cradle to cradle," a play on the phrase "cradle to grave," refers to the new industrial revolution that McDonough is championing. In his book *Cradle to Cradle: Remaking the Way We Make Things,* he and co-author Michael Braungart argue that we should eliminate the concept of waste altogether, while preserving commerce and allowing for human nature. In the book, they promote upcycling, a method of recycling in which the products of recycling are as good or better quality than the original product. Downcycling, in contrast, refers to recycling in which the recycled product loses some of its original quality.

Social Entrepreneurship

As many of SVN's members were growing their companies, Bill Drayton was formulating work around a different kind of entrepreneurial activity—what is now called social entrepreneurship. "By 1980, there was a new generation coming up that was tired of the inefficiencies of the older order," Drayton says. "We could see that the historical moment had come for transformation."

With that, Drayton launched Ashoka: Innovators for the Public.

Drayton focused on one idea: provide social entrepreneurs with an entire web of resources to help them develop their visions into enterprises that fuel long-term social change. Today, Ashoka provides financial support to more than 2000 leading social entrepreneurs in over 60 countries (known as Ashoka Fellows) elected to join its network. With that, it provides a strong and lifelong community of peers that offers support and advice. Fueled by this powerful mix, Ashoka Fellows bring their enterprises to scale, and in the process, catalyze structural changes in the communities in which they operate and around the world.

"The very small investment needed to launch a powerful new idea and entrepreneur sets in motion a long-term change," Drayton says. "Each social entrepreneur is a role model," Drayton says. "His or her success will encourage many, many others to stand up, care and organize."

Now in operation for more than 25 years, Ashoka's impact is far-reaching. Upon surveying Fellows five years after joining the organization, Ashoka found that 97 percent continue to pursue their vision full-time. 90 percent have seen independent institutions copy their innovation, and over half have changed national policy.

Natural Capitalism

It's no secret that human economic activity is exceeding the planet's limits. As "natural capital" is degraded by the wasteful use of energy, water, fiber, and soil, the value of these assets is rising. That's why a growing number of "natural capitalists" are seeking a change nothing short of a successor to the industrial revolution, toward a world in which business and environmental interests overlap.

The book *Natural Capitalism: Creating the Next Industrial Revolution,* written by Paul Hawken, Amory Lovins, and L. Hunter Lovins in 1999, was praised by President Bill Clinton as one of the five most important books in the world today. While the philosophy behind natural capitalism is firmly based in science and logic, its insights are visionary.

"Somewhere along the way to free-market capitalism, the United States became the most wasteful society on the planet," Hawken said in an article he wrote for *Mother Jones* magazine. "Until the 1970s, the concept of natural capital was largely irrelevant to business planning, and it still is in most companies. Decades from now, we may look back at the end of the 20th century and ponder why business and society ignored these trends for so long."

Through his Natural Capital Institute, Hawken works with institutions and individuals to help them better understand the principles and practices leading to social justice and environmental restoration. "Natural capitalism is not about making sudden changes, uprooting institutions, or fomenting upheaval for a new social order," Hawken says. "Natural capitalism is about making small, critical choices that can tip economic and social factors in positive ways."

Fair Trade

After spending 11 years helping develop cooperatives in Nicaragua, Paul Rice believed that something better was possible for farmers worldwide. In 1998, Rice launched TransFair USA from a converted warehouse in downtown Oakland. Today, TransFair is the only U.S. certifier of Fair Trade products, harnessing the power of business to avoid exploitation in the global supply chain. By auditing transactions between licensed companies and Fair Trade producers, TransFair ensures that each product bearing the Fair Trade Certified label has been produced according to international standards.

"The impact of Fair Trade goes far beyond money," Rice says. "It is dignity, power, and hope. U.S. consumers have become unwilling accomplices because we enjoy the cheap products brought to us by global manufacturing chains. We must give companies incentives and tools to take care of workers and the environment without sacrificing profitability."

By building social responsibility, environmental sustainability, supply chain transparency, and corporate accountability into the new global business model, TransFair has successfully channeled nearly $85 million in above-market pricing to farm workers in some of the poorest countries in Latin America, Asia, and Africa. Every dollar invested in TransFair over the past six years has resulted in $7 of additional income for Fair Trade farmers.

Natural Beauty Care

Founded by Horst Rechelbacher in 1978, Aveda has been at the forefront of natural beauty care. As the son of an herbalist and a naturalist, Rechelbacher was born with a respect for nature and the amazing, healthful properties of natural plant ingredients. As a result, Aveda is one of the world's largest purchasers of organic ingredients, all of which are traceable from soil to bottle.

But the natural beauty philosophy behind Aveda goes beyond what's in the bottle. Rechelbacher believes responsible packaging, manufacturing and corporate practices are equally important. He was the first to incorporate recycled content in beauty packaging.

"We support values that cultivate a sustainable economy and culture," Rechelbacher says. "We find inspiration for doing so in nature and believe that nature is not merely something to be cherished and protected, but emulated as a model of sustainability."

Social Finance

What if a bank cared as much about improving the community as maintaining profitability? That's the thinking behind social finance. Today, such companies as ShoreBank serve as examples of financial institutions that have been able to build individual, family, business, and community strength and sustainability through loans and education.

ShoreBank was founded in 1973 by four small-business loan experts, who dreamed of reversing the decline of Chicago's inner city neighborhoods. They knew fixing the entrenched problems of urban decay would require a different approach and a new kind of institution. In ShoreBank, they created a "community development" bank—one that could make a profit while transforming neighborhoods through enterprise.

At first they focused on retaining and rebuilding the physical environment by providing loans to residents who wanted to renovate the neighborhood's deteriorating buildings. Later, they went on to solicit "Development Deposits" from across the U.S., drawing on socially-minded investors who wanted to support community development and still earn a competitive return.

Today, the ShoreBank family consists of two commercial banks, based in Chicago and the Pacific Northwest, and ShoreBank International, a consulting company that helps financial institutions and their funders, governments and communities around the world provide credit for micro enterprise, small and medium businesses and housing. Starting with its partnership with Nobel Prize winner Muhammad Yunus of Grameen Bank in the 1970s, ShoreBank International has worked with more than 65 banks and development finance organizations in more than 40 countries, advancing more than $300 million in small business loans to date.

In recent years, SVN has influenced ShoreBank to focus on environmental as well as economic sustainability. ShoreBank is living up to its bold tagline, "Let's change the world," by proving that the triple-bottom-line goals of profitability, community development, and conservation are both compatible and mutually reinforcing.

Functional Fashion

When Margot Fraser traveled to Germany in 1966, she never expected to return home with an answer to the world's foot miseries. During a visit to Bavaria, a yoga instructor showed her a pair of sandals, suggesting they might alleviate some of her foot pain. "The design made sense to me, the outline asymmetrical, like a foot, the contoured footbed... it looked like something my feet might enjoy," Fraser says. This was Fraser's introduction to Birkenstock sandals.

After two months of wearing the sandals, Fraser's feet felt alive in a new way. Sensing she was on to something big, Fraser wanted to spread the word to women back home. Unfortunately, the Birkenstock design was everything that fashion wasn't in the 1960s.

"Tiny and dainty were the desired attributes of feet," she says, "Birkenstock certainly didn't fit into that picture."

Convinced of the merits of Birkenstock sandals, Fraser began importing and selling them from home. At first, retailers told her women would never wear these shoes, but by the early seventies, a cultural shift brought along a change in fashion sense. The Birkenstock sandals fit right into the health-conscious style of the new generation. "I knew that this was not a fad, it was part of something bigger, a mind shift that encompassed more than just dress codes; a new, different way to look at life, to seek a connection with nature," Fraser says. "Birkenstock was part of this movement; it opened people's eyes to the mind-body connection."

Fraser's value-based approach to business has brought Birkenstock Footprint Sandals, Inc. from a small home business to the multi-million dollar company it is today. Her company honors its belief in the power of community by sponsoring initiatives such as grants, product donations, and an employee volunteer program that contribute to the well-being of the recipient communities. "We were the pioneers and made it easier for other companies with similar products and ideas to enter the field; the whole comfort footwear market exploded, helping everybody to prosper."

Consumer Power

In 1982, a visionary group of people joined together with one common belief: that an economy that works for the people and the planet was possible. And so Co-op America was born, dedicated to creating a just and sustainable society by harnessing economic power for positive change.

"Our publications show people ways to live with social and environmental concerns in mind. Our Green Festival events work to support green businesses and increase the ever-growing population of green consumers," says Denise Hamler, Director of Green Business Programs for Co-op America and Green Festival.

Co-op America uses a unique approach that involves both consumers and businesses. They educate people about how to use their spending power to promote social and environmental sustainability, help socially and environmentally responsible businesses emerge and thrive, and pressure irresponsible companies to adopt responsible practices. Hamler says, "We need to create and educate a critical mass of educated and environmental consumers. SVN brings together the true social change makers and leaders. These are the people and organizations we want to play with."

Co-op America's programs have had a significant impact on the world in recent years. Their Community Investing program moved more than $1.5 billion into disadvantaged communities in the U.S. and abroad over the past four years; their Fair Trade Alliance mobilized over 250,000 people to advance Fair Trade; and their Climate Action program has rallied businesses, consumers, and investors to address the issue with the speed and power it requires and helped launch a solar company to make it affordable.

Social Change Media

Smart, thorough, probing media arc an essential ingredient to a successful democracy, but in recent years steady consolidation of the mainstream media, together with the recent trend of slashing newsroom staffing and budgets, have put corporate agendas far ahead of the public's interest. To fight this, independent media organizations such as *Utne, Mother Jones,* and *The Nation* are inspiring and informing progressive change by staying devoted to journalistic ideals, often covering stories that traditional media won't touch.

When *Mother Jones* magazine was launched in 1976, the country was ready for a publication that featured investigative reporting on the great unelected power wielders of our time—multinational corporations. *Mother Jones* reporters have consistently broken stories well ahead of the media pack, earning a substantial readership and the respect of both independents and the mainstream.

Viewed individually, each of these 20 ideas has had a significant impact on the conduct of business in the United States—and often around the world as well. Taken together, they have helped change the way the world does business, setting the human race on a path toward sustainability.

Inclusive Business—Profitable Business for Successful Development

Ricarda McFalls

The private sector is a key provider of economic opportunities, training and education, and it can offer many a route out of poverty. Business investments and operations in developing countries generate both economic growth and social development. Deregulation and privatization have led to companies assuming roles that were once the exclusive domain of governments: Worldwide, more than 100,000 state-owned enterprises have been privatized in the last two decades.

There is also increasing recognition by governments, development actors and non-governmental organizations that broad-based private sector development is critical to economic advancement and sustainable poverty alleviation. The private sector already dominates global financial flows to developing countries—net inflows of private capital reached a record level of USD 1.03 trillion in 2007, a 40% increase from 2006. In May 2007, *The Economist* reported that developing countries repaid loans totaling some US$ 185 billion to official lenders, including governments and the International Monetary Fund, from 2003 to 2006. Money is flowing and on balance, country risks are falling.

But what can business tangibly contribute to development? Companies can take the lead in developing Inclusive business opportunities, that is, initiatives that seek to integrate low-income populations into the value chain of companies. They can achieve this by integrating low-income communities into their value chain as consumers, distributors and/or suppliers. For example, developing and sourcing from low-income suppliers can build capacity, generate employment and bring small businesses into the formal economy. Also, companies can develop innovative and affordable products and services that improve the overall quality of life.

They can take a leading operational role in the provision of basic needs such as water, sanitation, energy, housing, health care and communication services. Finally, in order to spread economic opportunity and facilitate future inclusive business initiatives, they can work with others to improve the investment climate, root out corruption and improve overall health and education levels in the developing world.

In essence, inclusive business models try to find synergies between development goals and the company's core business operations. Sound inclusive models can therefore deliver higher socio-economic value for communities while opening new avenues of growth for the company. The notion of inclusive business calls for additional focus and significant innovation in the way companies do business. It is about creating new forms of employment, new markets, and affordable products and services aimed at making business benefit many more people in a way that spurs economic growth and encourages entrepreneurship.

A particular area in which inclusive business can have a significant impact is in the development of small and medium enterprises (SMEs). Local entrepreneurs and SMEs form the backbone of global economic activity. In developing countries, more than 90% of firms outside the agricultural sector are SME and micro-enterprises. These SMEs are the driving force behind innovation, production and employment. As local entities, they draw upon the community for their work force and rely on it to do business. They understand the communities within which they operate and are able to provide goods and services tailored to local needs

Figure 1
Inclusive business maximizes social and economic value

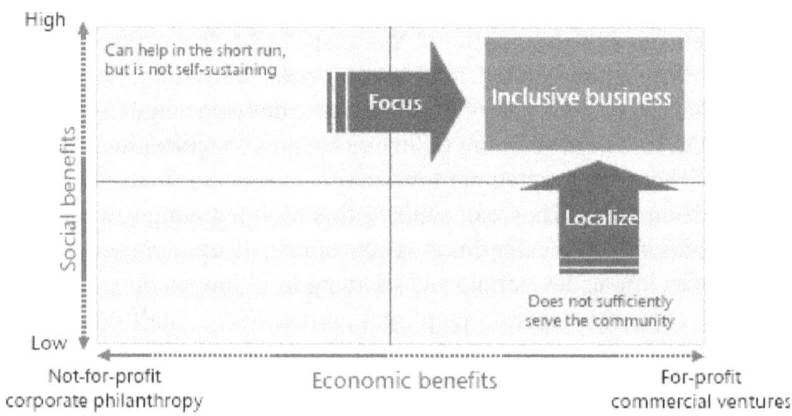

and at costs affordable to local people. However, SMEs in developing countries are often unable to fulfill their potential because of unfavorable regulatory frameworks; inadequate skills and capabilities; poor or obsolete infrastructure and technology; and difficult access to finance.

In this context, it is possible for large corporations to use inclusive business approaches to significantly improve the situation of SMEs. Building relationships with SMEs to source local supplies, or contracting local SMEs to sell and distribute company products strengthens the capacity of the SMEs and creates local livelihoods. Companies can also help build capacity, thereby providing training in basic skills, technology transfers, direct investment in infrastructure, and the sharing and imparting of knowledge.

Keys to Successful Inclusive Business

While the world's low-income segment represents the market for the future, it is vital to ensure that the products offered and the partnerships built meet their needs. True, inclusive business models aim to use commercial means to better people's lives. Developing appropriate products that meet people's needs and integrating low-income suppliers sustainably into a value chain are delicate balancing acts, with the risk that companies market products that are inappropriate for low-income communities or that the local suppliers supply products and services that are inadequate for the operation of the company.

The WBCSD identified a combination of three factors that help build successful inclusive business models: focus, partner, and localize. In essence, companies will need to:

- Focus on core competencies—Companies that concentrate on their key strengths are better able to innovate around those strengths. This helps guarantee consistency between the company's portfolio of activities and the inclusive business model, and will make it easier to take successful pro-poor business mainstream in the future.
- Partner across sectors—Governments and NGOs are increasingly interested in working with business. By involving development organizations that share complementary goals, companies can benefit from on-the-ground expertise and additional resources. Ensuring that they have the trust of the communities they work with is also essential. Likewise, thinking across sectors might lead to innovative partnerships involving companies from different industries, addressing a bundle of needs holistically.
- Localize the value creation—Companies operating in developing countries often lack the usual infrastructure and support systems: market

Figure 2
The 3 building blocks of successful inclusive business ventures

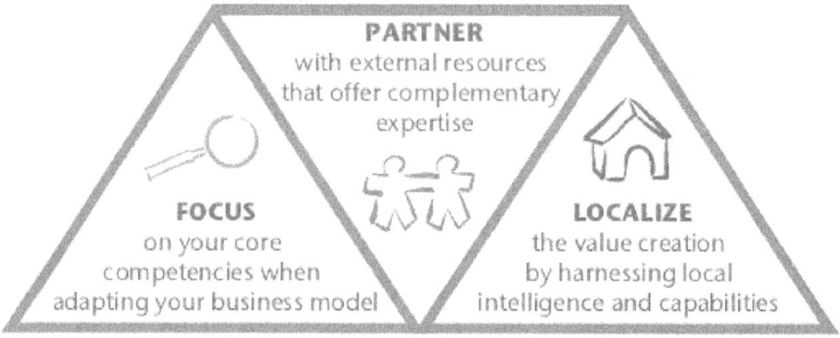

intelligence, manufacturing capabilities or distribution channels. So, they have much to gain from tapping into local networks and local knowledge.

Financing Inclusive Business Opportunities

One of the greatest challenges that surrounds inclusive business is attracting sufficient and appropriate capital to finance such activities, especially in countries with considerable business risk. To overcome this barrier, a mindset shift is required whereby companies embrace new ways of thinking about how business could be done. To make the most of available resources, companies need to redefine how, from whom and for whom they raise capital.

Financing inclusive business does not involve abandoning the traditional modeling process of gauging risk after estimating the capital needs and expected future cash flows. However, it does entail adjustments to factor in indirect and less tangible benefits for the company. The considerable social benefits these projects bring mean that many non-traditional sources of capital may be interested in helping such a business succeed. These sources of capital can help remove obstacles to profitability and bridge the lead-time until a business is fully commercially viable. Both direct funding (project capital), and funding that improves the business environment and supports partner organizations (partner capital) can help to achieve this.

Some companies have begun to shift their thinking from a centralized capital strategy, whereby companies raise their own funds for their business to a distributed capital strategy, in which they also become capital conduits to existing local expertise and capacities. Development agencies are increasingly interested in working with business, and some private foundations are beginning to support for-profit ventures whose goals mesh with their own program objectives.

In order to benefit from this public money, inclusive businesses need to demonstrate tangible social benefits. And for partnerships to work well, managers may need to learn the language and goals of non-business organizations.

The WBCSD's Work in the Domain of Inclusive Business

The WBCSD brings together some 200 international companies in a shared commitment to sustainable development through economic growth, ecological balance and social progress. Members are drawn from more than 30 countries and 20 major industrial sectors and greatly benefit from a Regional Network of some 55 national and regional business councils and partner organizations. Via its Development Focus Area, the WBCSD is seeking to raise awareness of the business contribution to development, helping business and non-business stakeholders understand what is possible by providing case studies, guides and tools that advance our understanding of development challenges and opportunities.

Some 60 WBCSD member companies and Regional Network partner organizations are committed to playing their part in building capacity and empowering people so that they have the opportunity to move out of poverty and into the formal economy. They intend to help create new businesses, markets, employees and customers among low-income communities. They recognize that their efforts must extend beyond corporate philanthropy if they want to build responsible, viable and inclusive business models.

Inclusive Business Opportunities in Practice

The WBCSD's online case study library contains detailed information on what companies are doing to implement the inclusive business concept. Some examples from this collection include:

- BP currently leads several consortia of petroleum companies developing oil and gas fields in Azerbaijan, Georgia and Turkey. Developing an effective local supplier base is core to the success of BP's business and to strengthening the Azerbaijani economy. BP opened an Enterprise Center in Baku in 2002, run on behalf of its international oil and gas partners in the Caspian region. The facility helps local companies develop their business in support of oil and gas projects, particularly those involving international companies. The Center offers training in management, finance, IT, quality control and marketing. Experts also provide technological assistance to improve engineering and manufacturing know-how. Azerbaijani SMEs receive free training in health, safety and environmental policies; are helped to participate in tender processes, access technical requirements of oil and gas operators and identify foreign partners for local projects. The Enterprise Center also supports firms by identifying sources of credit, training and certification. In addition, it maintains a supplier database tracking more than 150 local SMEs.

- Unilever is a world leader in hygiene, personal care, food and cleaning products. Its Indian subsidiary, Hindustan Lever, already enjoys a sophisticated and extensive distribution network encompassing both urban and agricultural areas, yet a core challenge is to develop locally appropriate distribution channels for customers in undeveloped, and often very remote, regions. The goal is to work from within these communities, promoting health while generating sustainable income for the poor. Through its Project Shakti ('strength'), Hindustan Lever now works with 46,000 entrepreneurs, covering 100,000 villages in 15 states and reaching over 3 million households in India. This innovative business model provides significant opportunities for local women to participate in the economy; it empowers local communities and promotes health and hygiene. Hindustan Lever estimates that by 2010 the program will generate an annual combined income for Shakti entrepreneurs of over US$ 25 million a year.
- Following a successful pilot program in Kenya, Vodafone is rolling out a service that allows customers to access cash via their mobile phones. Called M-PESA, the service allows customers to borrow, transfer and make payments using a mobile phone, transforming financial services by making transactions cheaper, faster and more secure. Since its launch in April 2007, M-PESA has attracted over 2 million Kenyan customers, with 200,000 more signing up every month on average. In 2008, M-PESA was also launched in Afghanistan and in Tanzania.

As the examples above suggest, experience by member companies over the past few years has demonstrated that inclusive business has the potential to generate financial and social benefits. For this reason, the WBCSD recently adopted a more proactive strategy to promote inclusive business in the developing world.

In 2006, the WBCSD joined forces with the SNV Netherlands Development Organization, to form the Alliance for Inclusive Business. This Alliance seeks to overcome old paradigms and prejudices that are still today an obstacle to inclusive business. SNV and the WBCSD consider that the best way to overcome these barriers is to present tangible results from the field of successful initiatives. The WBCSD-SNV Alliance therefore brokers and designs specific opportunities that are not only attractive investment options, but also benefit low-income communities.

The Alliance has an initial focus on Latin America and is active in eight countries where the WBCSD has national business partner organizations: Bolivia, Colombia, Ecuador, El Salvador, Guatemala, Honduras, Nicaragua and Peru. To date, the Alliance has contacted more than 300 companies in these countries, generating some 80 inclusive business ideas, of which some 40 are being implemented. The innovative process has attracted the attention of a number of other organizations, including the Inter-American Development Bank (IDB), keen to promote and fund these initiatives. In addition, the Alliance has helped the Ecuadorian government to design and implement a policy of social and economic inclusion. The government has started to promote and support inclusive business, and has signed agreements with several large national companies.

Examples of inclusive business opportunities currently being implemented include:

- Despite the success of microcredit in Bolivia, over 3 million people in Bolivia (roughly 65% of the economically active population) are excluded from microfinancial services because of high transaction costs. This is due to the absence of non-credit financial microservices, and other socio-cultural barriers. And unlike traditional banking, microfinance entities are not connected through information technology (IT) networks which would allow small transactions to be made using a bank card. In March 2007, the Alliance began to collaborate with Bolivian company Síntesis SA, an IT company specializing in online transactions, to fill this void. The Alliance and Síntesis SA are currently involved in designing a pilot project with the participation of microfinance institutions FIE (Private Financial Fund for the Promotion of Economic Initiatives), FADES (Foundation for Development Alternatives) and EcoFuturo. As a starting point, the partners will assess the banking habits of some 100 users of an innovative bank card over a three-month period. The project will monitor some 10,000 transactions made through portable point-of-sale devices, in four towns across Boliva as well as a remote rural area. The devices accepting the cards will be installed in petrol stations, mini-markets, hardware stores, and retail shops.
- The global coffee market is coming under increasing pressure to make improvements in quality and traceability. This is encouraging large export companies to engage directly with small producers. This in turn allows the small producers to benefit from cooperation with large companies that have access to secure sustainable markets, technical assistance and credit. In Peru, the Alliance identified Perales Huancaruna SA (PERHUSA), the country's largest coffee exporter, as a good candidate

for an inclusive business venture with local coffee producers. Following initial discussions, PERHUSA and the Alliance signed an agreement aimed at strengthening the ties between the company and small producers. Having started in mid-2006, this cooperation is expected to increase income—driven by a higher price and quality of the produce and greater technical assistance—for over 3,000 coffee-producing families in the Amazon, Cajamarca and San Martín regions.

- Corporación Dinant is a leading agribusiness company in Central America. Its activities include the production, industrialization and export of fruit and vegetables, oils and other foodstuffs. Looking to the future, Dinant has started to produce biodiesel from African palm and is gearing up to produce it from jatropha curcas. This energy crop has low water requirements and grows in low-fertility soils. However, it requires intensive manpower, providing excellent opportunities for job creation in rural areas. The WBCSD-SNV Alliance, in collaboration with the Honduran Business Council for Sustainable Development (CEHDES), is working with Dinant to set up an inclusive business which will involve 2,000 small producers from the Comayagua region in the production and commercialization of the jatropha seed.

A Favorable Environment for Inclusive Business

The contribution of the private sector to development can be accelerated, but only if there is a sound enabling environment in place. This is as true for SMEs as it is for large multinational corporations. Through endeavors such as those outlined above, companies are discovering that there is no "one-size-fits-all" approach. To be successful in these markets, companies must focus on meeting real needs, using approaches adapted to the markets they target and that integrate well with their core business competences. This is not always easy and can carry with it considerable business risk.

A key prerequisite for the success of the business model is a favorable investment climate that is both stable and predictable. Also here, there is no "one-size-fits-all" approach. Each country faces a different set of priorities; every development strategy must be orchestrated in tune with the local context. Therefore, rather than pressing simply for better governance or better framework conditions, the WBCSD encourages governments to consider key priority areas which, if addressed, could maximize the impact of development efforts and the benefits of increased investment inflows.

In this context, the WBCSD has called upon political leaders to focus their attention on the following priorities:

1) A fair and competitive global market that is non-discriminatory

2) Regulatory frameworks that uphold property rights, promote greater movement of entrepreneurs to the formal economy, and root out corruption
3) Capacity building and access to finance for local enterprises and entrepreneurs
4) Investment in the necessary infrastructure such as roads, energy, telecommunications, and ports

These key areas embrace companies' most pressing concerns. Improving governance not only improves the business environment but strengthens human rights. Building up infrastructure and promoting education are investments that benefit people and thereby also development goals.

While governments create the frameworks that encourage—or hinder—development, the private sector generates entrepreneurship, creates employment, and builds wealth. The WBCSD seeks to advocate for change by working collaboratively with multiple stakeholders to create a more enabling business environment and to identify synergies between official development assistance and foreign direct investment.

Ultimately, companies that move beyond conventional wisdom and work with new partners have an unprecedented opportunity to help people lift themselves out of poverty and into market economies. At the same time they will be developing new markets for their products and services. Unfortunately, it is precisely low-income communities, the ones we have focused on here, which are far too often excluded from functioning markets and are untouched by the benefits these markets can bring. Business, governments and civil society have a collective responsibility to ensure that markets really work for all, thereby making globalization truly inclusive.

Teekampagne—"Citizen Entrepreneurship" for a Meaningful Life

Guenter Faltin

Teekampagne: A Quick Overview

Teekampagne ("Tea Campaign"), founded in 1985, is not a well-known company because it spends so little on advertising. Nevertheless, it has become the largest mail order tea business in Germany. According to the Tea Board of India, it has been the world's largest single importer of Darjeeling leaf tea since 1998.

The idea for the company goes back to the "social entrepreneur" Gottlieb Duttweiler, founder of the "Migros" stores in Switzerland at the beginning of the 20th century. Duttweiler's goal was to provide pure, unadulterated products at an attractive price, through a business model that cut out layers of middlemen between producer and consumer. For this blending of social vision and market economics, he was fiercely attacked by both socialists and capitalists. One camp was defending its doctrine, the other its profits.

The name "Teekampagne" derives from the fact that originally, back in 1985, we sold our tea in "campaigns"—i.e. only at certain times of the year and only in certain places. Since tea keeps well for long periods, we encouraged our customers to buy their year's supply at one of these "campaign" events. Today, our Darjeeling tea is available year-round, or as long as supplies last. But then as now the term "campaign" speaks to our economic vision: to enable our customers to buy pure Darjeeling tea at an extravagantly small price. This vision requires that we "campaign" to educate consumers about our concept: we limit ourselves to one kind of tea, so that we can buy in large quantities and import directly from India, and we sell in large packages; specializing in Darjeeling tea allows us to carry out the strictest inspections and select the very best quality. Informed consumers are our most loyal partners. In fact, they "campaign" for us by word of mouth, saving us from using traditional marketing methods, thus lowering our expenses and the price of the product for themselves. Our customers are our collaborators; their understanding of the economic process has been a necessary condition for our success.

At the cost of small inconveniences (limited choices, planning ahead, putting in a year's supply), customers get an exquisite product at a low price. What, then, is the product?

It is named after the mountainous district of Darjeeling, on the slopes of the Himalayas in northern India. Darjeeling tea is considered the best tea in the world. It is cultivated at extreme altitudes, on steep slopes, under intensive sunshine in a generally cool climate. This gives it a distinct and unique flavor. The natural harvest quantities are limited.

Quality is paramount. Before we buy, we conduct many inspections to insure the best quality—a quality which requires the use of much and highly qualified labor to create and maintain. In addition, we look into our growers' use of agricultural chemicals, even in the case of organically grown leaves, to deter fraud. Each batch of tea is checked several times for hundreds of chemical residues (herbicides and pesticides), and we only buy the very cleanest teas. The results of our chemical tests are published on each package—we were the first tea company in the world to do this (even though many told us this would only frighten customers). The customer can also trace where the tea in each package comes from and when it was plucked. In addition, we have long campaigned for producers to do without chemical pesticides and fertilizers altogether; by the year 2010, all of our teas will be organically produced.

The practice of "sustainable development," of course, has many dimensions and cannot be limited to reducing the use of chemicals, reducing packaging, and reducing transportation. Importantly, in Darjeeling, a sufficient tree population is essential to halt soil erosion on its steep slopes. With this in mind, Teekampagne initiated and still finances a reforestation project entitled "Save the Environment & Regenerate Vital Employment" (Project SERVE). In 1996, the World Wide Fund for Nature, India, agreed to manage our project locally, affirming our efforts with its international prestige.

Unfortunately, what is marketed as "Darjeeling" is not always Darjeeling. The Tea Board of India, the official Indian tea authority, has estimated that up to 40,000 tons of tea are sold world-wide under the name of

"Darjeeling," although the district itself only exports 10,000 tons a year. To protect itself against this blending of Darjeeling with cheaper tea from other areas, the Tea Board introduced a special trademark, certifying that the tea sold with this trademark is 100% pure Darjeeling.

We were the first tea company in Germany to be awarded this seal of purity. We decided to use it as our company logo, instead of creating one of our own, to help with the planters' efforts to prevent adulteration of their Darjeeling with teas from low-lying areas. (All marketing experts considered this a foolish decision).

With this, we practice fair trade in a different and more comprehensive way than is usually conceived. In addition to using the trademark and protecting the purity of "Darjeeling," we finance a reforestation project, and we also pay higher prices than other traders would if they purchased 400 tons a year. And there is an additional, important aspect: we don't charge our customers higher prices for fair trade. Instead, our business model allows us to charge lower prices by breaking with expensive conventions (advertising, expensive packaging, etc.).

The education reformer Ivan Illich who I got to know in the early 1980s, used to argue vehemently against charging extra for fair trade. In this practice, he argued, the customer pays not only for the product but also contributes to an invisible "charity box," a modern version of buying "indulgences" (paying money to save your soul)—a trade that Martin Luther was already inveighing against. Although charity has some positive effects, it does NOT challenge the business models that put pressure on commodity prices in exporting countries and inflate prices for consumers at the other end. Since it does not represent a systemic change of business practices, it is also not sustainable: it may stop when the charitable giver's attention is drawn to another urgent need. We practice fair trade with a different method: we do not charge the consumer so that we can feel good about ourselves; instead, we challenge costly conventions, and the savings benefit everyone.

"Trade, Not Aid" is an effective and sustainable way of benefitting the region of Darjeeling as well as our customers and partners. We wanted to help create a trading situation, using market principles, that benefits both the producer and the consumer. There is much research to demonstrate that in developing a regional economy which has the potential to survive, charitable donations and political subsidies often do more harm than good. Our aim is to raise consciousness about, and increase the demand for, genuine high-quality tea; embracing the Indian trademark as the sole guarantor of genuine Darjeeling quality is an effective strategy in support of Indian tea producers. A better quality will be achieved through hiring more labor, which increases some production costs, but will result in disproportionately higher sales revenues for the producer. Higher prices for better-grade tea, on the one hand, and greater demand for labor, on the other, allow the influential trade unions in Darjeeling to negotiate better wages and working conditions.

One tangible result we observe is that the employees on the Darjeeling plantations already enjoy better working conditions relative to other parts of India. High-quality production is also important for another reason: cheap mass production puts a downward pressure on prices worldwide, creating a glut in which supply exceeds demand. Neither the consumer nor the producer benefits from the creation of an inferior, adulterated product.

Such a product also tends to suffer from the "terms of trade" problem: as long as a finished product is created in the buyer country, exporters of raw materials will find it difficult to get a decent price. In the case of tea, merchants in the buying countries do this by blending teas of different qualities and places of origin, as well as by creating a variety of flavors through aromatic additives. By contrast, Teekampagne buys and markets Darjeeling as an end product. There is a much smaller span between the price paid to the producer and the price charged to the customer, while the overall cost to the consumer remains low. This is a "win-win" concept that benefits all sides. Our customers, too, can feel good about their cup of tea, knowing that their purchase sustains the people of Darjeeling.

Anyone Can: How I Got There

Although I was attracted to the field of economics quite early, starting at age 14 to invest my pocket money in the stock market, this was regarded as an inappropriate, even evil, activity in small-town Bavaria of the 1950s, and my family and teachers were emphatic in their disapproval. Naturally, I went on to study economics—only to find that the university curriculum had managed to turn an exciting subject into a boring and meaningless chore. I finished my coursework quickly, completed a doctoral dissertation in order to savor university life a little longer and, at age 31, as a sharp critic of how economics was taught, found myself being offered a tenured professorship, with a lifetime job guarantee from the government. When I accepted this position, I promised myself that I would study and teach the subject in a way that would keep my students awake and engaged. I already considered entrepreneurship, in its combination of theory and practice, the most vibrant field in which to bring economics to life, and I thought long and hard about starting a company. But how? I pored over the question which kind of business might offer good prospects. During visits to Tanzania and India, I was stunned to see how much more people have to pay for products like coffee, sugar, and tea in Germany, compared to the prices paid for them in the producing countries. In the case of tea, especially, the difference was huge. With only rudimentary knowledge about the tea business, I began to crunch numbers for tea and compare them with those for products in other fields. It turned out that the tea trade had very little price competition and relied on very traditional methods. After I analyzed the costs of trading tea, I realized that by challenging a number of conventions in the tea business, I could create a business idea that might (and did) look crazy to everybody else, but made superb economic sense: one variety of tea; only big packets: "buy your supply for a year." What looked like a joke at the beginning became a big success story. I learned that you can conquer a well-established market with a good idea; that the quality of an idea is more important than the availability of resources; that you do not need to know everything about business administration to succeed as an entrepreneur; that imagination and disciplined persistence trump everything else. I learned that (almost) anyone can be an entrepreneur. And I learned that you can not only keep your students awake, but that you can also have fun and do a lot of good at the same time.

Puzzling Out Simplicity

Neil Churchill, an entrepreneurship expert, once said that for a good idea to turn into a reality, up to 50,000 pieces of information need to be processed. It may take up to 10 years before an idea turns into a successful startup.

The history of ideas, experiences and insights that created Teekampagne resembles a puzzle, put together both playfully and persistently, and it certainly took years before the pieces came together in the simple, yet elegant picture we can see today. Some of the first pieces came about when I was a student at St. Gallen business school in Switzerland: I shopped at a Migros store, where one Swiss Franc bought you two and half chocolate bars. How come? In his early years, Duttweiler, selling from trucks, had rounded off prices to whole numbers (to save time on giving customers change), which resulted in charmingly odd product weights and measures. And why was Duttweiler so fanatical about purity of products and value for money? Why did he succeed, contrary to all conventions and expectations? My travels abroad added more pieces, leading to my discovery that the high price of tea in Germany was a function of expensive packaging and complex distribution systems. But how could one convince customers to choose only one kind of tea and buy enough for an entire year? Could one succeed in the marketplace by appealing to customers' reason, rather than distracting them with promises? Was it possible to educate, rather than seduce, the customer? To create (and rely on) economic literacy, rather than count on customers' ignorance? Treat the customer as a true business partner, rather than a prey?

Our initial gamble was that customers would reward an effort to enlighten them about their own best interests; that they would embrace a new concept which would offer them significant advantages. At its very core, this was an attempt to create the economic framework for a new, rational simplicity. Today, Teekampagne has over 180,000 customers, 93% of them by word of mouth.

One kind of tea; large packages; direct import and direct sale; purity; ecology; transparency. Seems simple. Why was this a radical idea? How can simplicity become a business concept?

Reasoned simplicity is indeed central to our business venture and to our philosophy of entrepreneurship. Think creatively, choose consciously, live wisely: these ideas can be found in Eastern philosophy, as well as among the ancient Greeks, in the tradition of the Enlightenment, but also among the 19th century Romantics. One of the thinkers we have found inspirational is Henry David Thoreau (1817-1862) of Concord, Massachusetts, best known for his book *Walden*; or, *Life in the Woods* (1854). Thoreau tells us that the richness of life consists of rich ideas and insights, not of an accumulation of material things. We should possess and consume few but excellent things. Teekampagne has embraced this idea. We offer "luxury through simplicity." In doing so, we not only make excellent tea available at a reasonable price. We also propose a new, and yet old, philosophy of life, which includes intelligent economics and consumption.

Rational simplicity is crucial to a person's well-being, as well as to our planet's survival. Declining resources, along with overpopulation and pollution, make a return to simpler approaches to life an absolute necessity. Proponents of simplicity enrich their lives by unburdening them. They try to calm "this chopping sea of civilized life" by choosing wisely among the thousand-and-one items offered daily. "'Simplicity, simplicity, simplicity!' I say, let your affairs be as two or three, and not a hundred or a thousand; instead of a million count half a dozen, and keep your accounts on your thumb nail," Thoreau advises. The message sounds astonishingly modern: live with a few excellent things, and live more deliberately.

Breaking with Convention: Simply Better Economics

"Simplicity" brings up some images that raise skeptical eyebrows: the well-situated professor advocating asceticism, or the holy man in his hair shirt; even the admirable Gandhi at his hand loom is not everyone's idea of the good life. To keep your eyebrows at rest, let me spell out how the principle of rational simplicity actually makes for better economics and for a superior enterprise. Here are some key features of our business model:

(1) Simplicity means saving on unnecessary costs (e.g., packaging), while focusing on the most important functions (e.g., purity, transparency). Avoid waste! In our current project, the CO_2 Campaign (importation of high-efficiency, energy-saving light bulbs), the Chinese factory that makes the bulbs also packages them in the exact same cartons in which they arrive on the German customer's doorsteps. No additional repackaging (common in conventional distribution systems) occurs along the way.

(2) Simplicity means efficiency: polishing away at the business model, until everything irrelevant (merely conventional) has been removed. The key aspects are in plain view.

(3) Simplicity means plain speech, factual information, rather than advertising lingo. Customers are treated as rational beings; they are informed, not manipulated.

(4) Simplicity means responsibility: satisfying a customer need with a good product, rather than creating a need that may be frivolous, wasteful, or even hurtful.

(5) Simplicity means being clear about one's cause. If it is a social cause (e.g., environmental responsibility, fair prices, etc.), its cost should be borne not by the customer but through a rational business model that produces savings. These savings then support the cause.

(6) Simplicity means helping the customer understand how things work: economic mechanisms as well as processes of production and distribution. An enlightened customer who can explain to others why Teekampagne can deliver great tea at low prices becomes an ally and ambassador for the company.
(7) Simplicity means respecting the intelligence of others.
(8) Simplicity means avoiding unnecessary complexity. Many founders fail because they are overwhelmed by the challenge of complexity that comes with growth along conventional business models.
(9) Simplicity means taking the long view. This sounds like a paradox: of course we could increase our profits quickly by selling inferior teas, adding inexpensive flavoring (which German law would even allow us to call "naturally identical aromas"), and giving them fantasy names ("Tropical Dreams"). But in the end, we would become like all the others and lose our competitive advantage. We would also lose our identity and our integrity. Taking the long view requires the discipline to resist temptation.

Finally, rational simplicity acknowledges the fact that we live in a global economy that is characterized by fierce competition, by a never-ending battle for customer attention. You can seek that attention with gigantic marketing budgets—or you can gain it by being different, by being unconventional, by being clearly and unequivocally on the customer's side. Customers respond with respectful affection and become durably attached to your company; they become a community. This is the way of the future.

In the end, rational simplicity means better economics.

I am an economist. Some have called me an idealist—not intending to pay me a compliment. If what I have described is indeed "idealism," it is simply the belief that reason will have the upper hand. Our company's continuing success proves that this is not an unreasonable assumption.

Teekampagne and the Notion of "Social Entrepreneurship"

"Social Entrepreneurship" is a concept that seeks to describe how social problems and social needs can be addressed with the tools and methods of business entrepreneurship, such as creativity; opportunity recognition; unbureaucratic procedures; looking beyond resource constraints; focus on the customer or client; 'can-do' ambition and resolute optimism. Although the concept arose out of an academic discourse about philanthropic and not-for-profit enterprises, it has now expanded to include a discourse about the non-individualistic ends served by for-profit enterprises and about the social responsibilities and/or obligations of business in general. I would even go so far as to speak of a "convergence theory:" every enterprise should be conceived as a "social enterprise" in some sense; for-profit and not-for-profit enterprises should have more in common than is suggested by the fact that the one seeks to maximize profits (and distributes them to owners or shareholders), and the other seeks to optimize service to its cause.

I am troubled by the word "should," however. It smacks of the kind of moral admonition that spoils so much of the discourse about business ethics. People (and businesses) quickly tire of being told what they "should" do; it is much more effective and sustainable in the long run to acknowledge and appeal to their self-interest: to show them what they can do that benefits both themselves and others. In the case of "social entrepreneurship," therefore, it is more instructive to look at businesses that already function well as social enterprises, and to figure out what they do.

Universities could be one example. In the United States, private universities are technically not-for-profits, but many have for-profit subsidiaries whose revenue stream helps to lower the cost of tuition and fees. Is Harvard University a business or a charity? It is both. With its need-blind admission practices, it will educate anyone with sufficient talent, regardless of that person's economic resources. Is it run like a business? Absolutely. Does this business serve a greater good? Indeed it does.

The search for conceptual commonalities between for-profit and not-for-profit enterprises recognizes that all good enterprises go for a cause, that they make meaning. The focus on commonalities may also help us around the intellectual trap of claiming altruism as the sole spring of not-for-profit economic activity; we can acknowledge the legitimacy of self-interest as a motivation for economic engagement, while pointing out that there is such a thing as enlightened self-interest that includes but transcends economic individualism; that seeks to serve the interests of multiple constituencies. "Cui bono? Who benefits?" may be a more pertinent question to ask about an enterprise than whether it distributes dividends or pays taxes.

In the for-profit business world, too, it is worth looking at businesses that function as "social enterprises." But what does that mean? Does it mean "giving back" some profit to a local community? Does it mean supporting a social cause, either from the company's profit, or by a surcharge on its product, or both? Or does it mean working with a different business model altogether?

My colleague Mohammad Yunus, for one, has been insistent about calling Teekampagne an example of "social entrepreneurship." We are a for-profit business and pay taxes, but if I ask the "cui bono?" question, I do see that our economic activity has quite a few beneficiaries. The list could include (but not necessarily be limited to) the following:

(1) Our customers get an exquisite product (of unparalleled purity) at a low price.
(2) The producers of our tea (owners as well as workers) get a decent price for their efforts.
(3) We run a profitable company that employs people and gives work to other businesses.
(4) Our Project SERVE has benefits for Darjeeling: we have planted 2 million seedlings so far, 70,000 last year alone, and such related projects as our model village Tinchulay or the Batasia Eco Garden produce long-term economic and educational results.
(5) Our business model benefits the environment: using large packages reduces trash and cuts back on shopping trips; shortening the path from the producer to the consumer saves energy as well as money.
(6) Resources have been made available to endow the "Stiftung Entrepreneurship" ("Faltin Foundation for Entrepreneurship") in Berlin. Its purpose is to show that important causes, addressed with creative ideas and artistic imagination, are at the root of entrepreneurial success, and to build bridges between business and social entrepreneurship.
(7) Students and collaborators of mine have started successful companies of their own that apply the "campaign" principle of rational simplicity:
   a. Artefakt is a company that markets high-quality olive oil through the campaign method;
   b. Zait directs high-quality olive oil, wine, and other gourmet products directly from the producer to the consumer;
   c. Ratio Drink AG sells organic apple juice concentrate (add tap water and drink!);
   d. Rapskernoel.Info offers cold-pressed organic canola oil;
   e. EBuero, which has 250 employees in Berlin alone, as well as branches in -several European countries, offers low-cost virtual office support to anyone who needs a secretary.
   f. Teekampagne's latest venture is the already-mentioned CO_2 Campaign, the distribution (in large packets) of high-quality energy-saving light bulbs. (When our bulbs were featured—not advertised!—on prime-time German TV on July 16, 2008, our internet server collapsed under the inquiries that night.)

The most lasting benefit is still evolving: my long-standing university workshop on generating and refining entrepreneurial ideas, in which I apply everything I have learned from my Teekampagne work, has encouraged a growing number of persons (not just students, but people of any age) to develop business ideas of their own. More importantly yet, it has sharpened my own concept of what I call "citizen entrepreneurship" or "entrepreneurship for all."

"Citizen Entrepreneurship:" Self-Determination as a Philosophy of Life

"Everyone can be an entrepreneur," says Yunus. He has demonstrated in Bangladesh how even the poorest of the poor can take charge of their own life with micro-loans and a support system that helps them succeed. But is that experience universally applicable? In most countries, but certainly in the industrialized world, doesn't it require a lot of resources and expertise in business management to start a company?

Not necessarily.

First, let me point out that the customer can already be a co-entrepreneur. For instance, the Teekampagne customer orders a year's supply and provides storage (thus relieving us of this task). The Ratio Drink customer buys organic apple juice concentrate and adds water. In both cases, the customer understands the specific business concept and has a general understanding of how markets work. In both cases, the customer may become an ambassador for the company and the product. In both cases, the customer adds value and gets value in return. The customer thinks and works alongside the entrepreneur.

Secondly, what I teach in my workshops and what Teekampagne (along with its offspring) demonstrates is that an intelligent, sufficiently refined and developed idea is more important than the availability of resources or a complete understanding of business management. As to resources, experience shows that really good ideas do not necessarily require a huge amount of startup funding or, if they do, funding will follow and find them. With regard to business management, acquiring what some consider the "necessary" expertise can actually stand in the way of refining and implementing the business idea. Management expertise can be delegated and bought with relative ease; working through and refining concepts is something we need to do ourselves.

Thirdly and finally: Does it require genius to come up with a great business idea? Of course not. Idea generation and refinement can be learned and taught; in many instances, a successful business idea is the application of existing knowledge to a new field, the combination of existing ideas, or an improvement of something that already exists. What is required, however, is a focus on function and a willingness to break with convention. If Darjeeling is sold in 2 oz. packages, in stores, and in pretty wrapping, is that a convention or a necessity? Once I understand that such convention is not necessary for getting the tea to the consumer, I can begin to develop a different business model.

If entrepreneurs do not require huge capital or expertise or genius ideas to get going, what do they need? They need three things: appropriate methods and techniques to enhance initial ideas; perseverance; and faith in their ability to determine the course of their own lives.

The moral philosopher Adam Smith, known mostly for his book *The Wealth of Nations* (1776), already envisioned a form of "citizen entrepreneurship:" the ability of individuals to participate in the marketplace as agents of their own fate. "Every man ... lives by exchanging, or becomes in some measure a merchant," says Smith, developing what his biographer Jerry Muller has termed "a vision of 'commercial humanism'" that is morally uplifting as well as practically empowering. To practice economic self-determination has long been recognized as a necessary (though not sufficient) condition for personal and political self-determination ("an empty sack cannot stand upright," we are told by Smith's contemporary and acquaintance, Benjamin Franklin). So considered, economic self-determination can become the basis of a life plan that conceives of a well-lived life as a multi-dimensional work of art. In our own day, the futurist Max Horx describes the ideal type that embodies this idea: "Our culture of individualism will produce a type of entrepreneur who will work for more than money, who wants to be good because he is ambitious—ambitious in a new, qualitative sense: he wants to create an individual life that is a work of art, as harmonious and exciting as possible." The citizen entrepreneur is that type: free to create, free to gain, and free to share.

Finally: have fun, in the sense of excitement, fulfillment, pride of accomplishment. Nothing is more exciting than to send a brainchild into the world and see it prosper. My students who started working on entrepreneurial projects did not just start new companies; they also re-fashioned themselves as human beings. They became more focused, more curious, and more communicative; their optimism and 'joie de vivre' was infectious; they even looked better. Were these changes the natural result of success? No—all of this happened before it was even clear whether their business idea would ever survive in the market. Was it because they were having fun? Yes, that too—but what really happened was that their life achieved a new direction and purpose; it gained meaning and perspective. Some are getting rich now; but that is not what makes their faces shine. They have become the entrepreneurs of their own lives.

References

Faltin, Guenter 2008. Kopf schlaegt Kapital, Hanser, Muenchen.
Fleischmann, Fritz 2006. Entrepreneurship as Emancipation: The History of an Idea (lecture held on 12th of July 2006).
http://labor.entrepreneurship.de/tiki-index.php?page=Ressourcen.
Horx, Matthias 2005. Wie wir leben werden. Unsere Zukunft beginnt jetzt. Campus Verlag, Frankfurt am Main.
Kawasaki, Guy 2004. The Art of The Start. Penguin, New York.
Yunus, Muhammad 2008. Die Armut besiegen. Hanser, Muenchen.

Peak Oil and Resource Wars: How Can the Business Sector Contribute to Sustainable Peace?

Daniele Ganser

In this chapter I want to look at the question how the private sector can contribute to the promotion of sustainable peace. I will approach the issue in three steps. In a first step I will ask whether we have specific examples from recent history which suggest that the promotion of peace and social norms should at all be a task for the private sector. I will conclude that it is indeed in the best interest of the private sector to promote peace indirectly through Corporate Social Responsibility (CSR). In a second step I will focus on the problem of resource wars and the challenge of peak oil. I will conclude that the far reaching dimensions of peak oil have so far not yet been fully integrated into the CSR discourse, and that resource wars must be expected to intensify in the first half of the 21st century. In a third and final step I will look at specific companies, most of which from my native Switzerland, and ask what procedures they have developed to promote peace.

The Role of the Private Sector in Questions of War and Peace

During much of the 20th century the private sector was expected to do, above all, three things: create a profit for the shareholders, provide jobs for the workforce, and pay taxes to the host country. Still today these tasks rank among the core responsibilities of every company. If a company therefore fails in any or several of these tasks and for consecutive years is unable to make a profit, is forced to lay of workers, or worse, goes bankrupt, the company and its management are being perceived as a failure. Questions of war and peace, on the other hand, have throughout the 20th century been in the classical domain of the state which controlled the army, the police and the right to declare war or make peace within the framework of international law. The business sector did not have then, and it does not have today, a primary responsibility for questions of war and peace. These remain with the state.

Within a changing global business environment, increased pressure from ethical investors, the media, Non-Governmental Organisations (NGOs) as well as academics, the private sector today is still expected to fulfil its three core tasks, hence make a profit, create jobs and pay taxes. But in addition to these three "classical economic tasks," three additional "modern economic tasks" have been added to the "to do list" of companies during the last two decades. The first is environmental responsibility. Companies are today expected not to harm nature in any way, and companies that engage in illegal logging of the rainforest for instance face sharp criticism and sometimes even lawsuits. The second is social responsibility. Companies are today expected to live up to high social standards, and companies that are seen to disrespect women's rights or promote child labour can come under severe public pressure and suffer from consumer boycotts. Last but not least on the extended "to do list" is the promotion of peace. Companies that are perceived to be war profiteers and who can only create jobs, profits and taxes if at the same time both death and destruction increase in other countries, can come under sharp criticism or even parliamentary investigations.

This increase of expectations towards the behaviour of companies has risen the challenges for modern management. Companies are being perceived as unethical players if they get caught violating ecological or social standards, or worse still, profiting from war. If such bad news about a well known brand name reach a larger audience and spread across the globe, significant blowbacks can result.

One of the best known examples is the recent history of the American shoe manufacturer Nike. The company was in the 1990s faced with the criticism that in several shoe manufacturing plants in Asia social standards were violated. In the beginning Nike was not fully aware of the potential blowbacks of such operations and unwisely declared, that although Nike products were indeed being manufactured in these plants in Asia, the US company was not responsible for the social standards within these plants, as they were not owned by Nike but were only subcontractors. The public in the US and Europe was not convinced by this argument. Nike's market share started to fall as Nike was perceived as unethical, while competing companies including Adidas and Puma presented themselves as socially responsible producers. In order to regain its market share Nike was forced to style itself as a social business operator, introduced social labour standards in all its production plants, including those of the subcontractors, and in 2001 published its first "Social Report."

A similar experience was made by the Swiss underwear producer Triumph. Specializing in the production of expensive underwear for the high end sector Triumph had some of its products manufactured in Burma, profiting from the low labor costs in that military dictatorship. Thereafter a group of NGOs, united in the so called "Clean Clothes Campaign" (CCC), attacked Triumph in January 2001 publicly with the slogan "Support Breasts, not Dictators." Triumph got under very heavy pressure as its consumers did not want to see beautiful underwear associated in any way with brutal dictators. Triumph hired the consulting firm Hirzel-Neef-Schmid Konsulenten from Zurich who advised Triumph to immediately retreat from Burma and publicly embrace social and ecological values as part of the company's culture. One year later Triumph closed its last production center in Burma.

The recent historical data on Nike and Triumph illustrates, that the respect for social norms play a significant role when it comes to the reputation of a well known brand name. The same holds true for environmental standards. The Dutch-British oil company Shell faced significant public pressures in 1995, when it wanted to sink its old swimming oil storage facility Brent Spar in the Atlantic ocean off the coast of Scotland. While the British government agreed to the plan the NGO Greenpeace protested and accused Shell of violating environmental standards. Greenpeace activists occupied the Brent Spar for more than three weeks, accompanied by a worldwide, high-profile media campaign. As more and more consumers perceived Shell as unethical and started to boycott Shell service stations and the share price dropped, Shell withdrew their plan to sink the Brent Spar in the Atlantic. Shell insisted in its public communication that ecological values were of great importance to the company culture. Brent Spar was dismantled on the coast of Norway, much of the material was recycled. That Greenpeace had exaggerated the amount of oil left in Brent Spar when it was about to be sunk in the sea played next to no role in the historical development of the event.

Even more delicate than violating social standards or polluting the environment is war profiteering, as the recent historical data suggests. This happened to the Swiss aircraft manufacturer Pilatus. The company specializes in building small but powerful business airplanes and military trainers used also by the Swiss Air Force. Some of its airplanes were exported to Mexico, allegedly only in order to support the Mexican Air Force in its training. Yet when in Mexico in 1994 the Zapatista Army of National Liberation (Ejercito Zapatista de Liberacion Nacional) started its uprising against the government and demanded social reforms, the Mexican government equipped the Pilatus aircrafts with guns and bombs and used them in their fight against the Zapatistas. Ever since the brand name Pilatus is being associated by critics with war profiteering, regardless the current policy of the company which focuses on the civil aircraft market.

Much more attention attracted the case of the US company Kellogg Brown & Root, a subsidiary of Halliburton Energy Services, which was accused of war profiteering in the context of the Iraq war. Following the US invasion of the country in 2003 Kellogg Brown & Root received a multi-billion contract to rebuild the damaged oil infrastructure in Iraq. This lead to sharp criticism and clashes in Washington, as the governmental contract funded by US tax money had been awarded to Kellogg Brown & Root without competitive bidding. Now former US Vice President Dick Cheney, CEO of Halliburton from 1995 to 2000, was accused by US-Senator Patrick Leahy of having covered up the details of the deal which had lead to war profiteering. The Vice President thereafter insulted the Senator during a meeting in the US parliament with the vulgar statement: "*! yourself," whereupon the office of Senator Leahy declared: "The vice president seemed to be taking personally the criticism that Senator Leahy and others have levelled against Halliburton's sole-source contracts in Iraq." Journalist Dan Briody concluded that the case of Halliburton and its subsidiary Kellogg Brown & Root ranges so far among the most critically discussed issues of war profiteering in the USA.

The recent historical data on Nike and Triumph suggests that disrespect for social norms can lead first to sharp public criticism, and then to a loss of market share and profits. The same holds true for disrespect for ecological norms, as the recent historical data on Shell illustrates. The effects of war profiteering finally can result in damage to the brand name or political clashes, as illustrated by the recent historical data on Pilatus, Halliburton and Kellogg Brown & Root. Such and similar cases have lead to an ongoing academic debate on the role and responsibility of the private sector in the modern society.

In order to avoid clashes with their consumers or worse, many companies today stress their commitment to the so called "Corporate Social Responsibility" (CSR), according to which a company promises to its stakeholders not to engage in war profiteering and to always respect social and ecological standards. Swiss businessman Stephan Schmidheiny, himself a pioneer in the global CSR movement, in this context stressed that it is very important for the private sector to analyze the societies in which they operate. "I have always observed and studied social movements, seeking to detect the first signs of change in what seemed to be a static context," declared Schmidheiny in 2003. "This is one of the reasons why I recommend to my fellow business leaders that they become interested in the society around them. It is the best early warning system to detect both risks and opportunities." Schmidheiny had himself gone through a learning process during which he had been attacked for violating ecological standards with his company Eternit Group which manufactured products containing asbestos, later found to have negative effects on human health. Schmidheiny changed his business. "I took the decision to get out of asbestos based on the human and environmental problems associated with the mineral." He participated in the Earth Summit Conference of the United Nations in Rio de Janeiro in 1992, later founded the World Business Council for Sustainable Development (WBCSD) in Geneva, and gave most of his money to the VIVA Trust, which owns some 45 companies that profitably operate in Latin America according to very high CSR standards under the label GrupoNueva. Schmidheiny's conviction has remained that CSR is not first of all an altruistic approach to doing business, but simply the best business strategy available in a fast changing world.

Resource Wars and the Strategic Challenge of Peak Oil

Resource wars, defined as the armed struggle for oil, gas, water, timber and diamonds, range amongst the most complicated phenomenon for contemporary peace research, as business interests and governmental warfare overlap and mutually reinforce each other. A well known example is the recent history of the South African diamond company De Beers, which in the 1990s bought diamonds from Angola while that country was in a civil war. De Beers bought the precious stones from the UNITA rebels under Jonas Savimbi, who in turn used the income from the diamond trade to buy arms and control the diamond territory. From 1992 to 1998 the UNITA is estimated to have earned 3.7 billion dollars from the diamond trade which helped to finance the war. When NGOs including Global Witness criticized De Beers for selling "blood diamonds" to their customers, consumers in Europe and North America reacted with disapproval, as they did not want to have anything to do with the support of the brutal civil war in Angola. When furthermore the UN Security Council in 1998 made the purchase of diamonds from UNITA illegal, De Beers agreed to disengage from the resource war and in the South African city Kimberley started a dialogue with NGOs and governmental representatives in order to find a system to distinguish between normal diamonds and "blood diamonds," with the intention of no longer doing business with the latter.

Even more delicate and complicated than the struggle for diamonds is the global struggle for oil, in the context of which oil companies have already been accused to intensify wars. The Swedish oil company Lundin Petroleum has made such an experience, as Christine Batruch, head of Lundin's Corporate Social Responsibility desk explained in a recent article. In 1997 Lundin bought the right to search and export oil from Sudan. When the Sudanese civil war intensified, NGOs criticized Lundin for supporting the Sudanese government in its brutal war for the control of the country's oil. When the pressure increased Lundin sold its rights and left the Sudan in 2003. Chinese oil companies, including the China National Petroleum Corporation (CNPC), faced no comparable public pressure and continued their support for the Sudanese government in exchange for the right to export oil to energy hungry China.

The British-Dutch oil company Shell was confronted with similar accusations in Nigeria, another oil exporting country suffering from violent internal conflicts. Critics argued that the money which Shell paid to the Nigerian government funded the troops of the regime which in turn cracked down on local dissidents. Shell insisted that corruption in the country was widespread, and that as a foreign business company they had little influence on what the ruling government did with the money earned from the oil export.

Next to Sudan and Nigeria also Indonesia has suffered from resource wars. In the United States in 2001 the International Labour Rights Fund (ILRF) accused the oil company ExxonMobil on behalf of eleven villagers from Indonesia's Aceh province for complicity in murder, torture, kidnapping, and sexual abuse by Indonesian soldiers. ILRF claimed that ExxonMobil had supported the Indonesian military in its civil war in Aceh, during which civilians were raped, tortured and murdered. ExxonMobil during the lawsuit confirmed that it operates the large Arun natural gas deposits and an associated liquefied natural gas (LNG) plant located in Lhokseumawe, Aceh's industrial center on the northeast coast. Arun has been a major source of profit for both the company and the Indonesian government. Yet like Shell in Nigeria

ExxonMobil insists during the ongoing lawsuit in front of U.S. District Judge Louis Oberdorfer that the company had no control over what the Indonesian military did.

While the influence of oil companies on resource wars remains a subject of ongoing controversial debates, it is uncontested that oil is of the greatest importance to the world economy. All industrialized countries, and hence all of Europe, Japan and North America, as well as the upcoming industrial powers China and India, are dependent on a cheap and reliable supply of oil.

Seen from a historical perspective the oil age is but a short period of approximately 150 years in human history, during which a more or less cheap and reliable supply of oil was able to satisfy a constantly growing demand. At the time of the beginning of World War One in 1914 global demand amounted to 1 million barrels per day, with each barrel containing 159 liters of oil. This amount increased to six million barrels per day by the time the Second World War ended in 1945. Yet only very few observers have noticed that during the Cold War global oil consumption has literally exploded, with consumption standing at 22 million barrels per day in 1962, mounting to 61 million barrels per day in 1986, and reaching a staggering 85 million barrels per day in 2006.

This increased dependence on oil has a massive potential to fuel resource wars, as it is a commonly known fact that demand is constantly increasing while oil is only a finite resource. Oil experts and geologists today are focusing less on the question of when global oil supplies will run out, but on when the supply of regular crude will have reached its half-life—i.e., the moment when global oil production will be at its absolute maximum. This historical moment is known as global peak oil. Its precise historical date is contested, but many experts expect it within the next twenty years. "Worry now. The problem is enormous," warned Robert Hirsch, Senior Energy Program Advisor at the consulting firm SAIC, during a Pentagon-sponsored energy conference in April 2006. Addressing the US Congress Hirsch claimed: "The world has never confronted a problem like peak oil."

Colin Campbell, a retired British petroleum geologist had warned of peak oil already in 1997. "The World is not running out of oil. Or rather, not for a long time. What it is running out of is cheap oil, and soon," stressed Campbell. The peak oil phenomenon will make resource wars much more difficult to resolve for peace researchers, as a very strong demand and the danger of falling supply will exercise a dominant role in international politics. "I hope, too, that governments will somehow get the message and not leave everything to the open market that is ill-equipped to deal with the depletion of a finite resource on which we have all come to depend," remarked Campbell who during his career had worked for the oil companies British Petroleum, Texaco and Amaco.

While much of the current analysis of resource wars rightly stresses the importance of Corporate Social Responsibility, it is unlikely that CSR will have a significant effect on global oil production after peak oil. For then, amidst a constantly falling supply and the looming danger or reality of wars and recessions, a considerable amount of oil will be taken by force in total disregard of CSR values. US physicist David Goodstein comes to the conclusion: "We, our children, or our grandchildren face some very difficult times."

The French oil company Total therefore stresses on a special homepage on the topic, that "At the beginning of the 21st century, we are at a turning point." We are not running out of oil, but we will reach peak oil, despite the fact that most people outside the industry have never heard of the word. "Exploration and discovery of new fields is not capable by itself of renewing reserves," warns Total. "Even if we can still count on improvement in recovery rates, oil will be exhausted several decades from now. But before this point of total exhaustion, the threat of shortages in the immediate future hangs over us, that is to say in the next 5 years for the pessimists and the next 25 years for the more optimistic: supply will no longer be capable of responding to an ever-increasing demand: we will have attained the Hubbert Peak for oil. The 'post-oil' era, therefore, should be of concern to us, even today."

The Private Sector and Its Contribution to Peace and Security

The private sector at times is fast to adapt to changing environments and circumstances, and every country features a group of pioneers who manage to be both profitable and to live up to the highest CSR standards. In an attempt to find out how the Swiss private sector views its contribution to world peace, the author contacted a number of companies in the context of the research project "Business of Peace Network: The Private Sector Can Make a Difference." Upon conclusion in 2006 the project lead to a publicly accessible homepage. Some of the results of this research shall be presented hereafter.

Among the companies questioned ranged Jenni Energietechnik which produces solar systems to heat water. The aim of the company is to reduce the dependence on oil by promoting the use of sun power. "It is still not very well known, that the long term supply of oil is not at all as secure as many people think, and that in many countries brutal wars are being fought over the remaining oil resources," Josef Jenni, CEO of Jenni Energietechnik, told the author. "I think that we must first of all make an effort to solve conflicts through dialog and without violence. And that secondly we must promote renewable energies including water-power, wind-power, sun-power, geothermal-power, biomass and biogas ... With my company I help Switzerland to import less oil, which often comes from unstable and conflict ridden regions of the world. In this way I am not only trying to make a profit, but also to contribute indirectly to peace."

German author Franz Alt has elaborated on this thought and in 2002 published the book *War for Oil or Peace through Solar-Power*. While the argument at first sight seems clear cut and convincing, the challenges to replace an oil based energy infrastructure with a sun based energy infrastructure are nonetheless enormous, and can arguably not be implemented before the onset of peak oil. In Switzerland, less than one percent of the energy is produced from renewable solar-power, while oil covers 57 percent of the energy supply. Oil is thus the undisputed leader of the national energy structure, as is the case with most industrialized countries.

Another Swiss company named Precious Woods has also tried to confront the challenge of resource wars, in this case the global fight for timber, and searched for solutions. "The illegal trade with resources has in many cases become the most important source of income for conflicting parties, and in some cases prolonged the war in order to enrich the warlords" explained Andres Gut, CEO of Precious Woods, to the author. "It is well known that president Charles Taylor has engaged in legal and illegal forms of logging in Liberia, then sold the wood to the rich industrialized countries, and thereafter with the money earned supported the Revolutionary United Front (RUF) in its civil war in neighboring Sierra Leone, which became notorious for murder, torture, rape and even amputation of the limbs of its enemies. Through such spirals of violence human lives as well as the ecosystem in which the war takes place are being destroyed. Obviously such developments are absolutely not in the interest of an intelligent and social entrepreneur." In order to find a more productive approach according to CSR principles Precious Woods decided that tropical forests must be protected by using them in a sustainable way. Thus the company bought land in Brazil where it grows and cuts tropical forest according to the guidelines of the Forest Stewardship Council (FSC). This allows the entire ecosystem as well as the employed workers to coexist in a sustainable way. "We want to demonstrate that the sustainable use of timber has not only ecological and social advantages, but also financial rewards, as it is more profitable than the short sighted destruction of old ecosystem," explained CEO Gut.

The Swiss economy is known, above all, for its financial sector, and much less for those companies that deal with wood or solar-power. "I think that also the financial sector can contribute to the promotion of peace" explained Andreas Knoerzer, director sustainable investments at Bank Sarasin in Basel in a conversation with the author. "Many customers are concerned about war and terror and long for security. Security in a very general sense, but including security of their investments." In order to meet this demand for ethical investment Bank Sarasin already in 1994 developed two investment funds called Sarasin OekoSar and ValueSar, which explicitly exclude the arms industry and invest only in shares of companies with an excellent CSR record. "This is but a beginning, but together with many of our customers we believe that this is an important step into the right direction," concluded Knoerzer on behalf of Bank Sarasin.

The data available on the global financial sector confirms that a careful analysis of the flow of money is indeed of the greatest importance for contemporary peace research. Investments in companies with an excellent CSR record can promote social and ecological responsibility and reduce the danger of war-profiteering. At the same time investments, though profitable, into the little transparent arms industry can lead to the exact opposite result. Among those accused of war-profiteering in the financial sector ranges the private-equity investment company Carlyle Group, founded in 1987 in the New York hotel The Carlyle, which engages in lucrative but little transparent investments, as journalist Dan Briody found.

Among the largest investors on the financial markets today range the pension funds, who manage the pensions of many thousands or even millions of employees. In Switzerland the company Ethos specializes in managing the funds of some 80 different Swiss pension funds, investing a total of 900 million Swiss Francs according to CSR principles. "Pension funds, more than anybody else, have to invest with a long term perspective in the interest of its members, thus the Swiss population," explained Dominique Biedermann, CEO of Ethos, to the author. "As an investment foundation we represent the interest of those pension funds who are interested in peaceful coexistence and sustainable development. We and our members are very interested in the state of the World in 2050, and the state of Switzerland in that same year."

Conclusion

Based on the historical data used for this analysis, much of which comes from the field of contemporary history, the following conclusions result. First, that the private sector can contribute to sustainable peace, as the historical data of pioneering companies demonstrates, and that companies with an excellent CSR record will rank as the best performers in this group attracting ethical investments. Peace research must therefore focus much more on the dynamics of the modern global economy. Second, that resource and energy wars must be expected to intensify within the next decades, partly due to the industrialisation of China and India which will significantly increase demand, and the onset of peak oil which will lead to a decline in oil supply with as yet uncalculable consequences. Third, that the reputation of companies associated with resource wars and human rights violations will suffer, while CSR companies will be perceived as ethical players. Swiss businessman Stephan Schmidheiny underlined this line of thinking when he stressed: "Companies are meant to serve society, not the other way around; and companies that do not—and are not seen to—serve society will fail."

The Business Case for Involvement in Conflict Prevention, Peace-Building and Post-Conflict Reconstruction

Steve Metcalfe

Introduction

The International Business Leaders Forum is an international not-for-profit organisation set up in 1990 by The Prince of Wales and a group of chief executives of international companies, in response to the emerging challenges of economic growth and change in the global economy.

IBLF works with companies, governments and NGOs in more than 60 countries around the world, in areas such as health, human rights, enterprise development, governance and corruption, youth employment and partnerships.

Its mission is to promote responsible business leadership and partnerships for sustainable international development, particularly in new and emerging market economies.

Supported by over 100 of the world's most influential international companies and private investors, IBLF has a track record of enabling sustainable solutions to local and global development challenges.

IBLF believes that the support and engagement of the business sector is necessary to achieve the Millennium Development Goals, reduce global poverty and promote economic stability.

The Business Case for Involvement in Conflict Prevention, Peace-Building and Post-Conflict Reconstruction

During the past decade the forces of political transformation and economic globalisation have created a world of new opportunities and hope for some, but increased instability and insecurity for others. Violent conflict continues to affect the lives of millions of people, undermining human progress and economic development.

This has important implications for the private sector, which has become an influential player in many conflict-prone or conflict-ridden countries. From Azerbaijan to Zimbabwe, the potential and reality of violent conflict is becoming an unavoidable business issue.

The long-term effects of conflict on the economic prospects of a country are hard to quantify, but it is clear the private sector is negatively impacted by conflict, which leads to elevated security costs and insurance premiums, as well as affecting productivity as employees and property are targeted by criminals and armed militia. In Colombia, for example, UNDP estimates that between 1.5% and 4.5% of GDP is lost as a result of the conflict.

The private sector—ranging from large multinationals to informal micro-enterprises—has a vital role to play in creating wealth and promoting socio-economic development. It also has a role in contributing—both directly and indirectly—to the prevention and resolution of violent conflict. There is growing evidence that as market economies become more widespread and as business becomes a more central component in societies around the world, the importance of this role is increasing.

Companies also have a moral imperative and leadership responsibility to promote peace, given the increasingly central position of the private sector as decision-makers and influencers at the national and international level.

Certain companies and industry sectors, most notably the defence, natural resource and infrastructure industries, have a particularly important responsibility to understand and address their direct roles as potential causes of conflict. Others, such as banks, travel and tourism companies and companies providing products and services to humanitarian agencies, also have a direct and growing role in conflict prevention and resolution.

Almost all companies, in any industry sector, have an interest in helping to build peaceful and prosperous societies and a role to play by contributing to: equitable econ-omic development; human development, especially education and health; environmental sustainability; good governance; social cohesion and respect for human rights.

IBLF's Work in the Area

IBLF has a track record in countries as diverse as the Balkans, Colombia and Nigeria in developing and promoting the role that businesses can play in conflict prevention, peace building and post-conflict reconstruction.

IBLF believes that there are many strategies that companies can use in order to minimise the negative impacts on society and optimise the positive ones. They are applicable for companies operating in any industry sector, country or community, but have particular relevance in conflict-sensitive or conflict-ridden situations.

The principles can be summarised as:

- Strategic commitment—CEO and board level leadership on corporate responsibility issues, supported by internal management systems, compliance, incentive and training structures to embed policies into the company's daily activities.
- Risk and impact analysis—Assessment of the conflict-related risks and impacts of the company's core business and social investment activities on a systematic and comprehensive basis.
- Dialogue and consultation—identification of and engagement with key stakeholder groups on a regular and consultative basis.
- Partnership and collective action—development of mutually beneficial and transparent partnerships with other companies, civil society organisations and government bodies to address sensitive political and public policy issues and to invest in practical projects.
- Evaluation and accountability—identification of key performance indicators for measuring and monitoring the company's social, economic and environmental impacts and reporting on these to internal and external stakeholders.

Examples of Regional Work

In Colombia, IBLF has helped leaders from businesses, government and civil society improve the role that business can play in helping to mitigate the impact of Colombia's armed conflict on the vulnerable and socially excluded, and as a result encourage conditions for lasting peace and greater prosperity.

In 2006 IBLF, working with Fundación Ideas para La Paz and the UN Global Compact, brought together over 200 leaders in Bogotá, Washington DC and London to discuss the issue and help build trust between the different sectors. The dialogues produced agreement from all sectors that business does have a key role in the peace-building process in Colombia, but also the recognition that historic levels of mistrust at present hinder the contributions that companies operating in Colombia could make.

Companies involved in the Colombian dialogues included The Coca-Cola Company, Anglo American, BP and SAB Miller.

In the *Balkans*, IBLF has helped promote closer links between business and society through a series of workshops and training sessions across the region. Following the war and subsequent peace agreements in the region in the late 1990s, IBLF has encouraged cross-sector dialogue and partnerships to assist long-term development, post-war reconciliation and economic reintegration.

For example: in Croatia and Serbia, IBLF has run partnership-building and capacity-building programmes over the last two years. In Bosnia and Herzegovina and Croatia, IBLF helped launch local chapters of UN Global Compact. And in Serbia, IBLF helps promote business engagement in development through the local Responsible Business Initiative.

In the *Philippines*, IBLF has worked with Philippine Business for Social Progress to co-ordinate a collective business contribution to conflict resolution and development in the war-torn areas of Muslim Mindanao. See separate case study.

In *Nigeria*, IBLF has worked to help businesses engage in more open and systematic dialogue with different stakeholder groups. IBLF worked with extractives companies in the mid-1990s on issues such as human rights, conflict prevention and partnership capacity building with the United Nations.

More recently, IBLF has helped guide extractive and energy companies in their work in the country through the Voluntary Principles on Security and Human Rights. IBLF co-manages the Secretariat for the Voluntary Principles, which aim to maintain the safety and security of extractive operations, whilst ensuring that human rights and fundamental freedoms are respected. As of 2007 there are four governments, 16 companies, seven NGOs and three observers that participate in the Voluntary Principles.

Case Study One—Post-Conflict Reconstruction in the Philippines

The Autonomous Region in Muslim Mindanao (ARMM) represents a number of provinces within Mindanao, in the Philippines that chose to come together under a set of powers delegated to it by the national government.

Since 2000 Philippine Business for Social Progress (PBSP) and the International Business Leaders Forum (IBLF) have been engaged in a Business and Peace Programme, which had at its heart the mobilisation of the business community in the Philippines and beyond to support business leaders in ARMM to develop economic activity and enterprise as a contribution to social stability and as a counter-balance to conflict.

With financial support from the British Embassy in Manila and support from the British Chamber of Commerce range of local capacity building and business network initiatives have been conducted and key ARMM business leaders have been brought together as an advisory and advocacy group. In early 2005 PBSP and IBLF renewed their commitment to the programme and the British Embassy has granted funds to enable a further three-year programme to be fulfilled.

Phase 2 of the Business and Peace Programme was formally launched at a reception in Manila in December 2005, attended by some 120 representatives from business, government and the ARMM authorities.

In October 2004, a group of representatives from PBSP, IBLF and the Tritex Corporation (the owners of the Mindanao Textile Company) visited Mindanao (including ARMM) to assess progress and to understand better the opportunities and challenges in further stimulating ARMM's economic development. During this visit the group also attended the 3rd Annual ARMM Business Congress in Jolo. Since then PBSP has continued its activities under the Business & Peace Programme, IBLF has conducted an intense round of consultations in Manila, New York, Washington DC and Brussels on possible international trade concessions for ARMM and the group has jointly visited ARMM on several more occasions, the last being in early March 2006.

HSBC, Nestle and Unilever have taken part in the Young Muslim Professionals for Business and Peace programme, an internship project that provides an opportunity for young Muslim professionals working in ARMM to experience how international companies operate and bring their experience back to their own companies in Mindanao. Between 2001 and 2006 22 interns were deployed, and about 50 more are planned for the next two years.

In addition, senior executives from Shell and Nestle will in 2007 conduct IBLF Crossing Borders visits to Mindanao, enabling them to see at first hand the relationship between business and development issues.

Business Opportunities in ARMM

The key business opportunities in Mindanao seem to lie in:

- being the source of high quality produce from the land and the sea. Much produce currently grows quite naturally, but there is opportunity to develop commercially viable quantities for local, national and international markets, provided the necessary skills and technology can be transferred there.

- adding value to local produce through local processing, canning and development of additional produce, rather than just shipping out raw materials.
- organic production to take advantage of the growing premium-priced market around the world.
- establishing manufacturing and assembly operations with an enthusiastic workforce, eager to learn.

Underpinning these opportunities is the flexibility of the ARMM Authority, which has already shown a capacity to respond quickly to the needs of business in its regulatory framework.

Barriers to Business in ARMM

The main barriers to economic development continue to be:

- the external perception of instability and unreliability,
- the high cost of transportation around the islands and to the mainland,
- the relatively high mandatory labour costs, as compared to other countries in theregion and elsewhere,
- the loss of quotas under WTO agreements,
- no perceived competitive advantage for national or international companies to source from or invest in ARMM.

The Business Case for Supporting Mindanao

There is a growing understanding that business has both a vested interest in and a responsibility to contribute to sustainable development around the world. In particular:

- business operates best in an environment of social stability;
- instability puts at risk a company's people, property, production, markets, supplies and distribution;
- conflict has no defined borders and impacts locally, nationally, regionally and internationally;
- ARMM provides an excellent opportunity for business to engage with and learn how to do business with a Muslim community to mutual advantage;
- ARMM offers real business opportunities and potential competitive advantages.

Support Action by PBSP and IBLF

In response to the needs, opportunities and challenges in taking ARMM's economic revival to a new level of performance, PBSP and IBLF have been actively co-operating in the following areas:

- continuing the programme of local capacity building;
- assisting ARMM business leaders in responding to expectations of business behaviour and practice;
- raising awareness of the needs and opportunities of doing business in ARMM to a wide audience of businesses, government agencies, development agencies, and multilateral agencies;
- making the business case for national and international companies to engage in ARMM's economic revival;
- exploring the possibility of negotiating special trade concessions for ARMM from the United States and the European Union;
- seeking opportunities for ARMM business leaders to present their case for support and stimulate new business relationships in the Philippines and in the wider international business community.

Local Capacity Building

In early 2005 PBSP and IBLF renewed their joint commitment to their Business and Peace Programme in Mindanao and set out a further three-year schedule of activity. This will continue to cover:

- building local capacity through workshops, training and internships for business leaders and young Muslim professionals;
- encouraging and facilitating networks of contact between business leaders in ARMM and other parts of the Philippines;
- providing platforms on which ARMM business leaders can present themselves nationally and internationally;
- liaising and co-operating with development agencies and others to maximise the impact of projects in ARMM;
- responding to specific needs and opportunities to help ARMM to develop economically.

Conclusions

> *"The Business and Peace Programme has clearly demonstrated how the private sector can be a peace-building agent through the adoption of core business practice and social investment initiatives, as well as active involvement in policy advocacy to help achieve human security goals in conflict areas."*
>
> —PBSP chair Manuel Pangilinan, December 2005.

BLF and PBSP's work in the region has shown that there is a very special, if not unique, opportunity to use ARMM as an example of how a previously excluded community can be brought into the mainstream of economic activity by allowing it to contribute its particular skills and resources as equal partners in business activity.

Case Study Two—Risk and Reputation Management in Vietnam

The Challenge

Vietnam's leather and footwear industry comprises some 400 enterprises employing 430,000 people annually, a high proportion of whom are women aged between 18-25. The working conditions experienced by these women are often characterized by high-levels of heat, noise and pollution. They often lack safety procedures, fire protection and are potentially exposed to high levels of solvents such as toluene, SO_2, NH_3, and other chemicals, in addition to spending long hours at work in non-ergonomic production positions.

As a result of prolonged exposure, workers in the shoe industry are prone to developing oral, optic, ear, nose, throat, or gastric diseases, as well as anemia, endocrine, gynecological, dermal and bone and joint problems. For example in the Yen Vien Footwear Company, where regular health checks are carried out, of 899 health workers, 38% were found to be infected with either ear, nose or throat diseases.

The fact that approximately 80% of Vietnamese producers are subcontracted to foreign firms further complicates the picture. Local producers are often found to be juggling up to four different codes of conduct stipulated by sourcing companies, which themselves are challenged by trying to control issues such as labor force age, compensation and working conditions in companies which they neither control nor own.

Making It Happen

The Vietnam, Business Links Initiative (VBLI) is a collaborative project aimed at improving working conditions in Vietnam's footwear industry, run by a number of multinational companies, Vietnamese government bodies and international organizations.

VBLI works with national firms, many of which are in the supply chains of multinationals and grappling with both the issue of occupational health and safety (OHS), as well as the proliferation of policies to which they must adhere. VBLI argues that addressing such issues can create competitive advantage both for individual companies and for the Vietnamese footwear industry as a whole as the manufacturing sector struggles to compete with China, the giant next door. Increasingly, Vietnamese industry is seeking to gain advantage through quality and assurance to buyers that they will not be plagued by reputational risks if goods are sourced from them.

VBLI has established a number of key objectives to improve the working conditions in the Vietnamese footwear industry:

- Raising awareness of the importance of occupational health and safety issues;
- Effective management of the choice, storage, uses, handling and disposal of the chemicals—and their containers—applied in the manufacturing process;
- Reduction of noise, heat, dust and fumes in the workplace;
- Providing the framework for the transfer of knowledge and skills on occupational health and safety between the participants in the program;
- Strengthening the capacity to monitor, inspect and regulate working conditions, to enhance the implementation of Vietnam's labor laws and to reflect the continuous development in international standards;
- Ensuring the long-term sustainability of the program.

Core facets of the first phase of the VBLI program, which has just been completed, included:

- Drafting a Code of Conduct: a commitment to good practice that factory owners sign;
- Developing a Management Support System (MSS) of basic guidelines on occupational health and safety for factory managers—this has been tested in five pilot factories, has been approved by the Ministry of Industry, and has been disseminated to over 60% of the country's footwear factories;
- Creating and running training courses for factory owners, managers, supervisors, and workers—courses offered include those on OHS management, chemical safety and the safe use and maintenance of equipment.
- Conducting research and delivering reports on needs and challenges of the footwear industry in Vietnam;
- Conducting factory visits;
- Creating the basis upon which a nationwide monitoring and inspection system can be developed. 60% of Vietnam's footwear factories participated in this initial phase and 120 factories received training.

Results

VBLI was evaluated after its third year when it was reported that:

- 64% of managers said increases in productivity over the past three years had occurred as a result of improved working conditions;
- 53% of managers said that orders had increased due to these changes;
- Impact on beneficiaries/companies had been positive: 79% of managers reported that their enterprises had strengthened health and safety

personnel; 90% of leaders and 61% of managers confirmed observance of state regulations on overtime—this reduction in extra-legal overtime was attributed by workers to VBLI's work, their own increasing awareness, and greater legal enforcement;

- 82% of leaders and 81% of managers reported that involvement with VBLI's program had strengthened information dissemination and communication on OHS issues within the enterprise;
- 100% of leaders and 91% of managers reported that investment in OHS was a priority.

The initial 3-year phase of the project was funded by a combination of governments and businesses at a cost of US$100,000 a year. The second phase of the program will be funded along similar lines.

Lessons

- Perceptions in Vietnam—The VBLI experience demonstrates the need to adapt to different cultures and to anticipate geographically specific hurdles. One of the lessons taken from VBLI was the need to make a sound business and governance case to the appropriate parties in a country lacking expertise and appreciation of social or environmental issues.
- Cross-sector collaboration—It is now acknowledged that it was essential to involve all parties, including government, at the outset in order to go to scale. While progress is slow and factories often revert back to convenient methods of production, understanding from the outset that systemic change has to be gradual and built on a firm foundation, which includes government policies and laws, is critical to future outcomes.
- Transfer of skills—The problems faced by the footwear industry are much the same as those being grappled with by the garment industry, which accounts for some 15% of Vietnam's national exports and comprises some 1,200 textile firms, 65% of which are small- and medium-sized enterprises. The extension of the VBLI program to this industry is a major focus going forwards.

PART II

INNOVATING NEW ECONOMIC PRACTICES FOR SUSTAINABILITY

B. CORPORATE RESPONSIBILITY—BUSINESS FOR THE COMMON GOOD

Giving More than Money: The Corporate Social Responsibility Strategy of Deutsche Bank

Hanns Michael Hoelz

In February, 2007, the United Nations climate commission submitted a shocking report: about 500 experts forecast gigantic hurricanes, a significant rise in sea levels, and periods of extreme drought due to global warming. They also underlined, more clearly than ever before, the extent to which man is responsible for these dramatic developments. Since then, the subject of climate change has been a major talking point. Specialists are not the only people who agree that this will be one of the most important subjects over the coming years, along with an ageing population and globalisation.

Global warming, poverty, and social discrimination—the responsibility for finding a solution to these worldwide problems lies not only with politicians, but also within the economic sector. In order to achieve the objectives set by scientists, governments have to pass effective laws and regulations, develop programmes and cooperate more closely than ever before on an international level. Companies in turn must intensify their efforts to act responsibly within society. Few topics are currently occupying managers around the world to the same extent as Corporate Social Responsibility (CSR). Trade fairs and conventions debate the issue, as do lead stories and editorials in the international media. The general tenor of the debate is that a healthy society needs a healthy economy—and vice versa. Corporate Social Responsibility only becomes useful and successful when it benefits both the community and the company. The prerequisite for this is that companies must pursue an active and innovative strategy, and their social commitment must be aligned to company strategy.

Deutsche Bank—A Pioneer of Corporate Social Responsibility

Deutsche Bank has been setting the benchmark in this field since well before the latest UN climate report was issued. Beyond results and shareholder value, we have always been at the forefront of developing groundbreaking social and cultural initiatives. These are not only an integral part of our corporate culture, but also reveal our underlying attitude.

Our numerous Corporate Social Responsibility initiatives offer "inspiration and perspective," and thus support our business. They have added a new meaning to the Bank's claim of "A Passion to Perform." The four pillars of our brand serve as a first point of reference for single initiatives.

- *Pursuing excellence*—attracting top talent, making staff members competent sparring partners for modern, demanding clients, supporting employees in becoming convincing leaders in their communities, and ensuring their loyalty in the long run—these are the prerequisites for our continued business success. The same spirit underlies our Corporate Social Responsibility programmes. Whether our employees volunteer to work as mentors, pass on their professional know-how to teachers in schools, are "hands-on" helpers in community centres, or participate in other volunteering projects, they always aim to contribute more than money.
- *Leveraging unique insights*—As a European player founded to facilitate trade relations with international markets, Deutsche Bank has always believed in valuing differences and in leveraging the insights and expertise a diverse workforce is able to generate. Impressive evidence of our global diversity is our presence in 73 countries, our staff from 130 nations, our multinational top management team, various employee networks and minority initiatives, as well as our social commitments aimed at helping people help themselves and promoting international understanding. Highlights of specific initiatives include the ongoing socio-political discussions initiated by the Alfred Herrhausen Society for International Dialogue or the "I Have a Dream" global internship program targeted at minority students.
- *Delivering innovative solutions*—It is by challenging the status quo and by leveraging the intellectual capital of our global staff members to deliver superior client solutions that we have become the undisputed leader in our home market and an internationally recognised pioneer in the area of product innovation. Numerous awards bear testimony to our success, among them the IFR "Bank of the Year" Award. Examples of our groundbreaking innovations are the financing of renewable energies and the underwriting of the microfinance consortium.

- *Building long-term relationships*—Reliability and eye-level dialogue define the fourth pillar of Deutsche Bank's brand platform. For shareholders, our stock is a valued investment; our employees are justly proud of working for a top global player; and to our clients, Deutsche Bank is a trusted, long-term business partner. With our corporate social responsibility programmes, we go the extra mile to sustainably strengthen the communities in which we operate: regionally, by supporting a number of community development projects, and globally through our commitment to international sustainability guidelines and environmental programmes.

The pillars of our brand build a consistent frame of reference and set out the cornerstones, not only of our business initiatives, but also of our corporate social responsibility programme.

Corporate Social Responsibility—A Corporate Centre Function

Corporate Social Responsibility (CSR) is a corporate centre function, reporting directly to the Management Board/CEO of Deutsche Bank. Its tasks are to champion responsible business practices and to raise awareness of the bank's commitment to society, as well as to define guidelines for the implementation of these goals and to support such activities in the bank's business units and regions. Five foundations represent CSR across the globe to help implement the bank's global strategy as a corporate citizen: the Deutsche Bank Foundation, Corporate Social Responsibility UK, the Deutsche Bank Americas Foundation, the Deutsche Bank Africa Foundation, and the Deutsche Bank Asia Foundation. In addition, the CSR department includes several globally active groups, for example, the Sustainable Development Group, which, among other things, is responsible for the bank's Sustainability Management System. The bank also has a group-wide policy on donations, memberships, and sponsorships, which is coordinated within CSR.

Acting Sustainably—An Obligation and a Challenge

In May 2005, the "Civil Crisis Prevention" advisory council was established, based on an action plan from the German Federal Government. The 19 council members come from the most diverse areas—including science, security politics, development politics, environment, the church and economics—enabling them to authoritatively represent the main focuses of the action plan. The task of the advisory council, which also includes Deutsche Bank, is to advise and support the work of the "Civil Crisis Prevention" department.

In its contribution to a government report to the German Lower House of Parliament (the Bundestag), Deutsche Bank underlined the importance of sustainability as a maxim for a strong civil commitment. The term "sustainability" means the awareness that economy, environment, and social conditions are inseparably connected and influence each other—at regional level, as well as beyond national and continental borders.

Against this background, it is important to encourage healthy economic and social development for all sections of the worldwide community, and to provide secure living conditions for future generations. In our opinion, acting sustainably is the best way of supporting crisis prevention and peacekeeping work and of combatting terror. We are making our contribution based on the "UNEP Statement by Financial Institutions on the Environment & Sustainable Development" which we helped to draw up in 1992, within the framework of the Agenda 21 in Rio de Janeiro. The consequence: Sustainability was established as a cross-sectional theme in all our business processes and company areas. Alongside the UNEP (United Nations Environment Programme), Deutsche Bank is globally cooperating with competent partners, such as the UN Global Compact, the Global Reporting Initiative, econsense, the German Industry Forum for Sustainable Development, and B.A.U.M., the German Environmental Management Association. Representatives of Deutsche Bank have been voted into leading roles in some of these organisations.

Deutsche Bank's Sustainability Management System

Deutsche Bank was the first large, German financial service provider to establish a comprehensive Sustainability Management System, based on the industry norm DIN EN ISO 14001. Internal policies and standards define the responsibilities of the Management Board, the senior management, and the individual employees regarding economic, ecological, social, and ethical issues. Principles for the actions and decisions of every Deutsche Bank employee can be derived from the Sustainability Management System. All sustainability-related Corporate Centre departments and the PCAM (Private Clients and Asset Management) and CIB (Corporate and Investment Bank) divisions participate in the system. Since 1999, our Sustainability Management System has been audited and certified annually by Det Norske Veritas, in line with DIN EN ISO 14001. Our focus is on continuous improvement.

Sustainability as a Business Case

Acting with sustainability in mind is not just a matter of altruism—it also results in competitive advantages: as production procedures become more efficient and cost-effective, innovative products are developed that may give access to new markets, and companies become more attractive to highly qualified new employees. Taking into account sustainability-related aspects in strategic and operative decisions may give financial institutions an important edge in their core business activities, such as lending, investment, and advisory activities. Using funds in line with sustainability criteria helps to promote future-oriented or particularly advantageous projects and ideas, as well as helping to reduce the risk of either the bank or financial investors losing their capital due to ecological or social dangers, or even suffering damage to their reputation.

Rating agencies are also increasingly using sustainability indicators in their capital market-oriented company assessments. In all evaluated areas of the important "SAM rating" (Sustainable Asset Management), Deutsche Bank scores significantly above the industry average, and is among the top 10 percent. In addition to the positive evaluations, the rating agencies also document a need for us to improve and optimise. We take these suggestions very seriously, and are making every effort to implement the points mentioned.

Based on the results of such sustainability ratings, special sustainability indexes are created at the international stock exchanges, in which only the best in the respective industries are listed. Deutsche Bank has been represented in the most important sustainability indexes from the very beginning, and this is confirmed every year, for example in the:

- Dow Jones Sustainability World Indexes
- Dow Jones STOXX Sustainability Indexes
- FTSE4GOOD Indexes
- Ethical Index Euro
- Ethical Index Global
- ASPI Index

Investors value companies ranging at the top of these indexes. As the comparison between the DJ World Index and the DJ Sustainability World Composite Index shows, the sustainability index always performs better over a 10-year period:

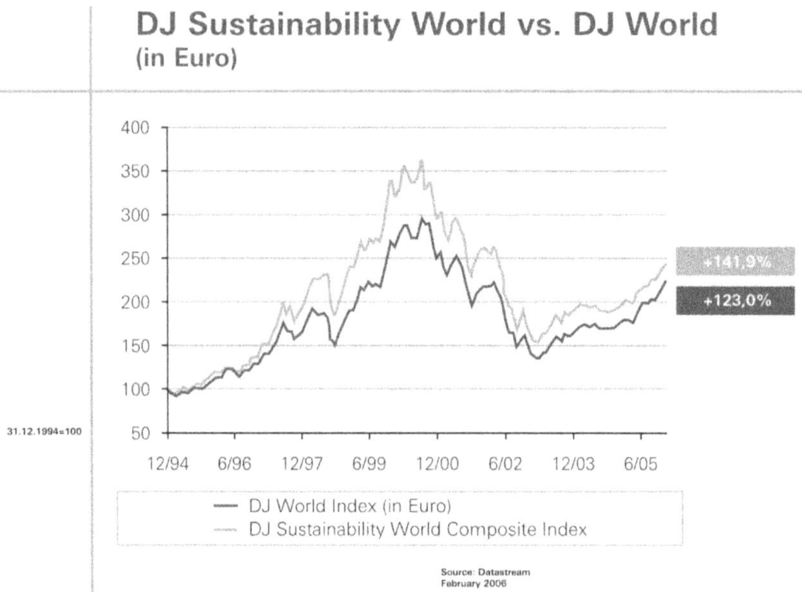

Best Practice I—Microfinancing

Microcredits are a very powerful instrument in the fight against poverty. They provide people who would otherwise never have the opportunity with access to capital and help them to make a living with a small trade. Loan default rates are low, which shows how successfully this concept has been adopted around the world.

We are supporting microcredits with the Deutsche Bank Microcredit Development Fund. The fund was created by our Deutsche Bank Americas Foundation, which also manages sales to investors. It provides microfinance institutions with capital—without amortisation and with very low-interest terms. These institutions use the capital as deposits at local banks, for which they receive double the value in their country's currency. With it they have enough means to offer the population very favourable credits to set up small trades.

Since 1997, over USD 4.2 million has been loaned to 40 microfinance institutes in 25 countries. A total volume of almost USD 55 million has been issued in microcredits.

The "Global Commercial Microfinance Consortium" project, funded at USD 75 million, is another part of our microcredit initiative. Deutsche Bank created the consortium in recognition of the pivotal roles that the

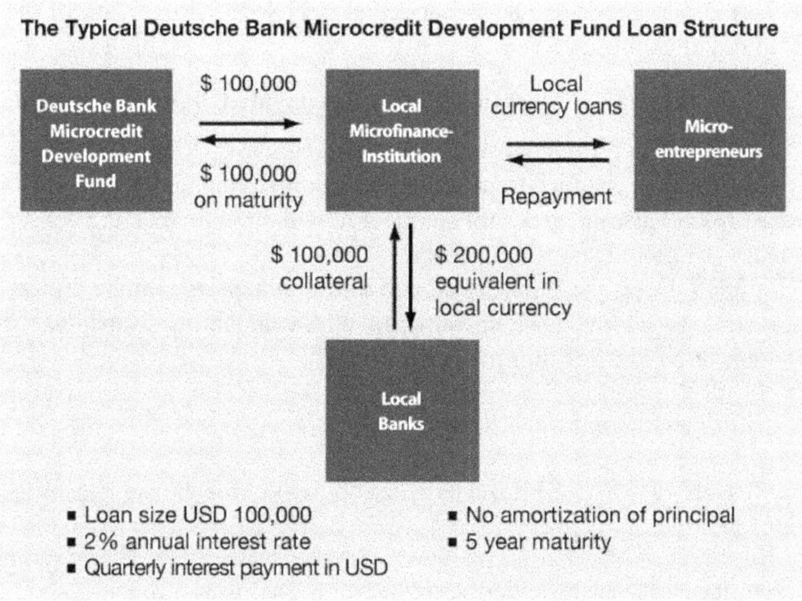

private sector can play in the development arena in partnership with development agencies. The consortium's collaborative model of bringing differently motivated monies under a single umbrella to create synergies, which cannot be achieved by acting separately, is replicable in most areas of development where there is a stream of income that can be financed. The idea of monetizing future flows of revenue and providing capital at scale can be applied to healthcare, education, affordable housing, alternative energy supply, and also to providing financial services to the poor. Deutsche Bank is increasingly convinced of the role it can play in financial intermediations of social capital, and is therefore actively examining ways to use these principles: for example, the creation of the "Eye Fund," in partnership with the International Association for the Prevention of Blindness and Ashoka, to finance eye hospitals in the developing world.

Nobel Prize winner Muhammad Yunus, who first developed the concept of microcredits, underlines the fact that microcredits are not charity, but a viable business scheme. Their long-term success is due not least to the fact that they offer good returns to banks and investors. This is why Yunus says "charity is finite, but business is infinite." The microcredit initiatives are an integral part of Deutsche Bank's CSR activities and a recognised best-practice project in the framework of the UN Global Compact.

Best Practice II—Deutsche Bank's Corporate Climate Strategy

According to former World Bank chief economist Nicholas Stern, it is considerably cheaper from a macroeconomic vantage point to take measures against the greenhouse effect now than to finance the consequences of global warming later on.

In 2005, Deutsche Bank developed a comprehensive climate protection strategy within the framework of its Sustainability Management System. It consists of four main points:

1. Avoiding Greenhouse Gas Emissions

Measures Deutsche Bank has taken to avoid greenhouse gas emissions include:

- Increasing energy efficiency by regularly improving technology
- Reducing energy consumption by changing employee behaviour, for example through energy-saving campaigns such as "Energy fit" (2005)
- Reducing energy consumption by purchasing energy-efficient office equipment
- Requiring employees to conduct video conferences and conference calls in order to reduce travelling
- Supporting public transport by financing jobtickets at numerous branches
- Reducing the number of short flights by issuing BahnCards (railcards) to employees who travel regularly for business
- Reducing the average fuel consumption of company cars by making staff pay for part of the fuel consumption of their car
- Requiring that diesel cars only be purchased if they have a soot particle filter

2. Using and Promoting Renewable Energies

Since January 2006, 20% of the bank's electricity consumption in Germany has come from renewable sources. Moreover, Deutsche Bank's Asset Finance & Leasing department has gained a reputation as a problem solver in this area. A recent example is the construction of an offshore wind power park in the Baltic Sea, which will generate about 300 mega watts per year. The Ventotec Ost 2 plant (total investment: more than EUR 500 m), which is to be installed north of Ruegen by 2008, is one of the first offshore projects in Germany.

Deutsche Bank's commitment to renewable energies started with a wind power fund for sustainability-oriented investors. Via its subsidiary, DWS Investments, Deutsche Bank offers a number of other sustainability-oriented investment opportunities, which combine support for environmentally friendly companies and the promise of attractive returns. In addition, the bank's Private Wealth Management division offers its clients individual asset management, which is oriented towards sustainable and ethical investments.

3. Raising Public Awareness of Climate Change

We know that the challenge of climate change can only be met if there is clear public awareness of the problem. It is against this background that Deutsche Bank Research has been publishing numerous studies on issues such as renewable energies, emission trading, energy policy and the international commodities markets. Moreover, Deutsche Bank is a member of the German Energy Agency (dena) and other working groups and forums dealing with climate change:

Participation in the Carbon Disclosure Project (CDP) is another step toward raising public awareness, albeit with another gist: on behalf of 225 institutional investors, which manage total assets worth more than USD 31 trillion, CDP calls upon companies to disclose their climate protection policies. The goal is to make institutional investors consider the results of these analyses when they make their financial decisions.

4. Neutralising Unavoidable Greenhouse Gas Emissions

As greenhouse gases damage the atmosphere around the world, it is ultimately unimportant for climate protection where exactly these emissions occur and where they are avoided. At the same time, it cannot be denied that some greenhouse gas emissions are unavoidable. On these grounds, two main compensation strategies have been developed:

- emission trading
- neutralisation of emissions

Carbon dioxide emission trading means that certificates are traded, which permit their holder to emit certain volumes of carbon dioxide and other greenhouse gases. The Kyoto Protocol lists a number of mechanisms to support investment in projects to reduce carbon dioxide

The principle of climate-neutrality

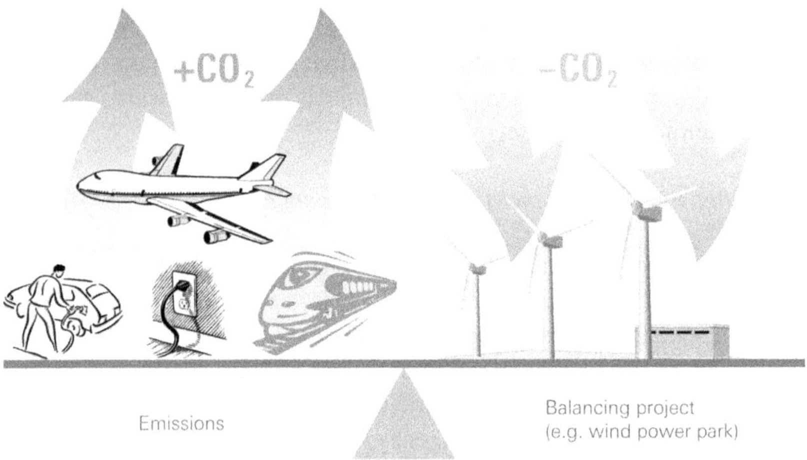

Steps towards achieving climate neutrality*:

- Examination of ways to avoid or reduce emissions
- Calculation of the unavoidable emissions that have to be offset
- Decision on an offsetting project
- Purchase of high-quality emissions reduction certificates
- Annulment of the certificates

* Quality standards, on which the "climate neutral" label of the "Hessische Klima Partner" project (supported by the Hesse Ministry of the Environment) is based, which Deutsche Bank helped develop.

emissions. These investments can be converted into certificates ("carbon credits"), which can be traded just like currencies or derivatives.

As one of only two banks, Deutsche Bank invested USD 5 m in the Prototype Carbon Fund (PCF) in 2000. The fund is the first international carbon fund and was set up by the World Bank. Moreover, it was one of the first banks to start trading in this market and has participated in some of the largest projects and transactions in this area. It is the only bank that participates in the Umbrella Carbon Facility of the largest international public-sector fund, the Umbrella Carbon Fund (UCF), which was also launched by the World Bank. It has invested EUR 30 m in phase 1. Deutsche Bank has not only invested in the private sector's largest CER transaction, but has also taken on its structuring, syndication and wrapping. In 2006, it participated in two of the largest emission reduction transactions ever in China.

With a view to implementing climate-neutral activities, Deutsche Bank participates in the "Deutsche Klimapartner" project. This concept is based on the idea that unavoidable emissions at one location can be offset, and thus "neutralised," by additional climate protection projects at another location. On the grounds of this principle, the climate impact of any product, service, event or even a complete company can be "neutralised." Deutsche Bank has implemented several projects in this field, for example the neutralisation of events such as the "Microfinance Leaders Meeting" (230 t), "Women in European Business" (70 t) and the "Deutsche Bank Invitational Final" (89 t) golf tournament.

In the future Deutsche Bank will continue and, where possible, intensify its sustainability efforts. We are absolutely convinced that acting sustainably will prevail as a "licence to operate" in all important trades and industries.

Trustworthy Products from a Credible Employer

Heike Leitschuh-Fecht

However hard one searches for the fatal flaw, it is only possible to report positively about this company: economically successful, unique ecologically-produced products, an employer with a positive and innovative personnel policy. The 86-year-old history of the Weleda AG, producer of organic body care products and anthroposophic medications, has been a single, uninterrupted success.

Nine o'clock on a typical Wednesday morning. The large hall at the Weleda location in Schwaebisch Gmuend/Baden-Wuerttemberg fills slowly. But the employees are not meeting for a staff meeting. Rather the program set for this early hour is a lecture by a priest, the head of a seminary in Stuttgart, who will address questions related to interpersonal relationships. This is the monthly "worker's hour" to which the company invites its employees in the interest of furthering their consideration of social and philosophical questions. What sort of a company can afford such a "luxury?" A company with a success story that many others can only dream of: An annual increase in turnover of around 10 percent (2007: anticipated to be CHF 330 million, it first reached 100 million in 1989).

The Weleda AG, with its head office in Arlesheim, Switzerland, is one of the worlds leading manufacturers of anthroposophic medications and holistic body care products. The company, founded in 1921 (see box below) by Rudolf Steiner, a natural scientist and philosopher—and founder of anthroposophy—has around 1,700 employees worldwide today, 800 of whom, including part-time staff, work at the German manufacturing location in Schwaebisch Gmuend; it also has operations in France and Switzerland, is represented in 50 countries and offers over 3,500 pharmaceutical products on the world market.

However, the positive figures are not the only reason why Weleda employees are permitted listen to a lecture that doesn't necessarily have anything to do with their job during working hours. The head of company communication, Theo Stepp, goes as far as saying "that such measures are a reason for the company's success."

86 YEARS OF SERVICE TO ANTHROPOSOPHY

The company name Weleda was established in 1924; it was named after 'Veleda', a priestess of the healing arts dating back to the 1st century after Christ. Initially twelve employees worked for the company in Schwaebisch Gmuend. As a subsidiary of a Swiss corporation, the company managed to survive the Nazi era and World II relatively unscathed. Since 1976, Weleda employees have contributed to the homeopathic pharmacopoeia through the German Homeopathic Medicine Commission. In 1997, the company began to develop an environment strategy, subjected itself to the European Union Eco-Audit and was certified according to ISO 14001. In 1999, it published its first sustainability report. In 2002, business magazine and the environment organisation WWF awarded, the at that time board member, Manfred Kohlhase the title of "Ecological Manager of the Year." The distinction of "Top Employer" followed in 2005.

There are Many Reasons for Success

How can the company's sustained good results be explained? Weleda consistently adheres on an environmental policy whereby the products must be viable without any form of synthetic additives or preservatives and the raw materials should successively originate from organic farms—this has been 60 percent successful so far. The company does not see its medicinal products as a substitute for orthodox medicine, but rather as a useful supplement. In all events, it is considered important that they cause absolutely no side effects. This is what enabled the company to become the market leader in the areas of pharmaceuticals for anthroposophic medicine and natural body care products. What is special about anthroposophic medications is that they are applied in a therapy form in which the doctor considers the unique history of the patient's illness and responds with equally specific medicines. This accounts for the great number of different preparations, all of which have different potencies and individual compositions of active substances—compared to homeopathy which always works with a single agent.

"At Weleda, the primary question is not what makes a person ill but what keeps him or her healthy," said Mathieu van den Hoogenband, explaining the company's somewhat different approach. He is Chairman of the Board of Directors or Chairman of the "Group Management" as it is referred to here.

Indeed, those at Weleda frequently use their own special terminology. For example, here the official term for personnel and labour costs, which as in many other companies are marked for reduction, is employee "income" although in fact it is an accrued cost. The cost of new engagements, which is referred to at Weleda as "investment," will prove to be quite high this year (which accounts for why the profit margin, in contrast, isn't as high). This demonstrates the appreciation that the company has for the employees on whose engagement its future relies. Hence, the employees fare better here than in many other companies. "A job with Weleda, that's like a scoring six in Lotto," commented a young man who recently applied for an apprenticeship here.

In fact, the company does a great deal for its employees. In addition to holiday and Christmas pay, they are also entitled to annual participation in the company profit. This is not, as is often the practice, a percentage of their salary but dependent on the actual number of hours worked and so related to the contribution that each individual has made to the company's success. A company kindergarten makes it easier for the employees to combine family and professional live and since recently, there is also a crèche for the little ones—and all the more affordable because it is provided at company subsidised prices. The staff cafeteria offers ecologically-certified meals, a three course meal for only €3.50. This is just to mention the most important initiatives and amenities that can be enjoyed by those who work for this company.

Esteemed and Prized Employer

In fact, Weleda cares not only for the material wellbeing of its employees. That alone would not sufficiently explain why there are hundreds of applicants for every advertised position. "Though we place hardly any ads in the newspaper," comments the Head of Communications Theo Stepp. Weleda mainly publishes its vacancies in Internet. "People seek work that they can identify with, a company that they can be committed to. The salary is not the applicants' primary motivation," explains Stepp. On the one hand, there are the products, which are subject to the company's demand for high quality and of which the employees are proud. They can also respect the company because its words and deeds are consistent and it has never made negative headlines. And you can assume that your job is secure. Large scale dismissals have remained unheard of in the Weleda group. Development stagnated for a time in the 90s, however according to CEO Mr. van den Hoogenband, this has improved continuously since the company learned that it must not only produce good products, but also market these professionally.

True to the anthroposophic principle that all things must be viewed holistically, Weleda strives for a company culture that does not perceive and respond its staff solely in their roles as employees, but rather as individuals with all their abilities, their numerous roles, wishes, worries and difficulties. For this reason, the company promotes not only its employees' professional training but also their social competence and their health.

For example, the employees at the German locations can participate in workshops on eurhythmy, speech development or other health-promoting subjects. The agreement is simple: The employees sacrifice a little free time and the company pays for the courses. "This is a means of promoting our people's holistic development," explains the CEO Mr van den Hoogenband.

When it comes to management style, the dialogue process is given highest priority. The target is: Everyone should have the opportunity to contribute to the evaluation and decision-making processes within their area of work. "The managers at Weleda therefore refer to management through dialogue as support and service," relates Stepp. It is not a matter of hierarchy or control.

Because the company culture at is considered exemplary, Weleda was awarded the title of "Top Job" in 2005, by an initiative that honours companies identified as the best employers in Germany. This includes consideration of the company's vision and management, personnel development, remuneration, the company culture and communication and its family and social orientation.

Work-Life-Balance: Not Just Lip Service

The Weleda AG makes a special effort particularly in the direction of family friendliness. In 2003, the company decided to subject itself to the Hertie Foundation's work & family audit. The initial examination revealed that with its flexible working hours model, children's day care centre and parenting courses, Weleda already has quite a lot to boast, but that's not all. In the meantime a special offer has been developed for parents who, within the context of parental leave, wish to devote themselves intensively to caring for their offspring during their first three years of life but, at the same time, also wish to maintain contact with the company—for example through part-time solutions. A newly developed program ensures that the employees can continue to be involved in personnel development measures or the "worker's hour." As such, the connection to the company is not lost. The head of personnel at Weleda, Roland Sturm sees this as a great advantage for the company: "High quality, specialist know-how is retained within the company and the social competence that is developed during the family phase also benefits the company."

But it doesn't end there: Weleda offers its employees with children and their partners parental training courses and even pays for these. But why? "If the child-rearing goes well," states Roland Sturm, "this benefits both the company and society."

Another initiative that is intended to make it easier to achieve a work-life balance is flexible, self-monitored working hours. A pilot study investigated whether this was a useful alternative to conventional means of recording working hours. Working hours are no longer controlled or documented. For the employee, this means more flexibility and the chance to work according to their own personal rhythm, explained one of the project leaders, Imke Rausch.

In the meantime, several administrative departments have decided in favour of self-regulated working hours; it is up to individual employees to decide whether or not they wish to have their working hours documented.

Weleda employees who are now in retirement also play a role in making the company family friendlier. Within the context of the "Generation Network," they help the workers by providing numerous services such as ironing. This is also a project that benefits both sides: Retired workers can supplement their pensions and maintain contact with the company, and the workers are supported in a manner that eases their load. In 2005, the "Family as Success Factor" competition awarded the company the "Innovation Prize" for the introduction of this project.

A Responsible Relationship to Suppliers

This special attitude towards others doesn't stop at the factory door. Weleda wishes to maintain a "long-term and fair relationship" with its suppliers. This applies particularly to those delivering raw material from poorer countries. For example, the company purchases its wild rose oil from certified ecological farms in the Chilean Andes and Turkey. Within the space the four years Weleda has been able to persuade 300 Turkish farmers to convert to biodynamic agriculture, which in the meantime is practiced on 120 hectares.

They harvest around 400 tons of organic rose petals per annum—this is approximately one fifth of the raw material required for Weleda's total production. A local consultant is financed by Weleda to assist the farmers with this conversion; in this way they are provided with in-depth knowledge of and learn to appreciate the special features of biodynamic agriculture: The company has concluded long-term supplier agreements and agreed to prices that make the business lucrative for these farmers. "In the meantime, the farmers are well aware of the difference that the project makes to their quality of life," states the head of international sourcing, Irena Kalan. Weleda has a similar approach in the Oaxaca Province in southern Mexico, where the company began motivating the farmers to convert to organic sesame eight years ago. Meanwhile, 250 farms are involved. "We convince the farmers through actions, not through promises," explains Kalan. They deliver good quality and we fulfil our side of the agreement. It is already possible for the Weleda Group to cover 180 tons of its total annual requirement of 250 tons of sesame oil in this manner. This offers those at the locations a perspective for remaining in their villages and securing their existence. For the company, this type of supplier relationship is of great significance for its product credibility and for the promise that it makes its customers. We know, from other firms, how quickly this trust is damaged when critical non-government agencies discover inconsistencies here. Aside from this, the quality of the raw materials is a decisive feature through which Weleda differentiates itself from the mass market.

However, there is still s a long way to go to achieve the company's goal of drawing 100 percent of its raw materials from biodynamic farms and fair trade. "In some areas, we still have considerable difficulties in procuring the volume of raw material required by the market in the desired quality," reports the head of communications, Theo Stepp.

Brand Recognition Is Greater than Its Share of the Market

A further factor in the company's success is certainly the intensive communication strategy that it pursues in relation to its customers. Once a year, Weleda invites them to Schwaebisch Gmuend for the "Weleda days." "We want our employees to meet our customers and naturally that the customers experience the company first hand in order to intensify their commitment," says Theo Stepp. Around 25,000 visitors attended this event in 2006 because—in addition to the cultural program—they have the opportunity to participate in a multitude of interesting workshops and seminars.

The *Weleda News,* which is published regularly with a circulation of around 1.2 million copies, is another important element of our communication. It has been published by the company since 1932. Almost every day, groups come from all over Germany to visit the company's herb garden near Schwaebisch Gmuend, which with 18 hectares is the largest in Europe, and to inform themselves on site about the cultivation and use of medicinal herbs.

It is primarily due to these initiatives that the company enjoys such great credibility among its customers and is far better known than its share of the market would suggest: Although Weleda is the market leader in the organic manufacturer's niche; it has a market share of only around one percent of the overall market.

The customers trust this brand whose products are regularly awarded the grade "very good" in independent tests. The company CEO Mr. van den Hoogenband is convinced that "It is our values that appeal to the customers." Because of the high proportion of regular customers, the company can dispense with expensive television and radio advertising; the PR Department in contrast is generously staffed.

Future Challenges

Thanks to the good business figures, the company can look towards the future with confidence. However there is a fundamental problem that must be addressed in coming years: In this company—which was actually established to produce medicines for anthroposophic physicians—the pharmaceuticals division accounts for only around one third of the total turnover and this sector does not yet cover its own costs, which means that it is cross-subsidised. "That's not acceptable in the long term," comments Mr. van den Hoogenband. "We must confront increasingly strong competition. The large companies such as Beiersdorf, L'Oreal and Unilever are also pushing their way into the organic products market but have relatively low raw material costs. We therefore need more funds for research and development in the body care area."

What does that mean in concrete terms? Weleda will work towards increasing this share of overall return from the current third to between 40 and 50 percent. To make this sector profitable, Weleda will stop producing the many small lines using costly industrial procedures (the industrial manufacture of medications is subject to complex legal provisions) and change over to so-called "pharmacy production." This will be developed over the next few years. In addition, the company has set itself the goal of tripling its production volume in the body care sector by 2015 and will expand its capacity appropriately.

Does the capital market also pose a challenge or perhaps a risk for the relatively small joint stock company? If even large companies have to be afraid of hostile take-overs, what dangers lurk here for lightweights like Weleda?

Mathieu van den Hoogenband is unconcerned here: The two largest shareholders, a private Swiss University and a clinic are both of anthroposophic orientation and hold the majority of shares. “We have it in our own hands; we don’t want any anonymous shareholders.”

The shareholders are paid dividends at a level that allows the company to reinvest the majority of its profit. The management of a company that has such owners might also feel like lotto winners.

Everyone a "Social Activist"

Yasuyuki Nambu

Solving Social Problems: A History of Taking on Challenges and Breakthroughs

The inspiration for the founding of the Pasona Group can be found in the employment situation in Japan in 1976. As my university graduation approached and I began my job search, my advising professor gave me a piece of advice. "Nambu," he said, "be sure to talk to the alumni, get them to tell you the details on salary, benefits, retirement bonuses and pensions, and pick a company with a good package."

In Japan at that time there was a huge difference in the way employees were treated depending on the size of the firm. A person who entered a large corporation would have a very different life plan from those who joined small or mid-sized companies. Male graduate were naturally desperate to join any company that was just a little bit bigger.

But as I looked around me I saw people facing an even more difficult situation – female graduates.

The employment situation for women at that time was extremely harsh. Only one in ten women graduating from four-year colleges was able to find a job. Even if they did manage to overcome the barriers and join a company, only the men would receive seniority-based promotions each year, not the women. And should they ever leave the company to raise children or take care of a household, reemployment was an impossible dream in a Japan that at the time defined "to work" as "lifetime employment as a regular employee."

Seeing this, I wanted to create a framework that would allow housewives to work a few hours a day, or a few days per week, while still taking care of their families, and earn a salary commensurate with their skills and experience. A month before graduation I formed a company with several friends, and began a temporary staffing business.

Over the next 32 years the Pasona Group, remaining true to its corporate principle of providing "Solutions to Society's Problems," has helped to create a new kind of "employment infrastructure" to offer opportunities to those with comparatively weak positions in society, including housewives and older workers seeking reemployment, female university graduates and the so called FREETERs, young part-time workers who have difficulties joining a company, and disabled workers who have trouble participating fully in society. We ran up against numerous stereotypes and regulations in our battle to raise social awareness of different types of work styles.

As I look back on the history of the Pasona Group up to now, I see it as the history of taking on challenges and achieving breakthroughs in helping as many people as possible fulfill their desire to work.

The Work of Pasona Group: Realizing People's Potential to the Fullest

When I'm asked what it is that the Pasona Group does, I reply that it's realizing people's full potential. For example, to help older workers who have trouble getting a job, we make an effort to find a position that utilizes their particular abilities and experience. For those with little work experience, we help them bring out their good points and potential. In other words, our job is to create the "infrastructure" and provide the training to allow anyone with a desire to work to do so in a style that best suits them.

After graduating school, graduates have few people to advise them regarding finding employment and work. For these young people Pasona Group offers a "Shigoto (work) College" to give them practical education, training and work experience, and provide opportunities to try doing the work that interests them, or to discover the joy of working. For the music-oriented we offer "MUSIC MATE," a framework that allows aspiring musicians to work while also continuing their musical activities. We also have employment opportunities for aspiring athletes, disabled persons, or anyone that faces difficulty getting on a stable financial footing. We are continually thinking of new ways to realize the potential people possess.

When employment issues for middle-aged and older white-collar workers, as well as NEETs, FREETERs and other young people became social problems following the collapse of the economic bubble, the Pasona Group focused its attention toward agriculture as a career choice. Pasona Group established the "Agriculture Internship Project" as a means of breathing fresh life into Japan's declining agriculture, and to date has accepted approximately 100 trainees. We also provide outplacement support for 16,000 middle-aged and older workers annually displaced by corporate restructuring.

We've all had the experience of standing at a crossroad in life, unsure which way to turn. It is at those times that I hope people will utilize the systems and infrastructure that we offer to find new opportunities, and take on new challenges to discover their potential.

Creating a Society that Links People and Companies in an Equitable Way

I think that the word "employment" will disappear in the near future. The idea of "to hire" or "to be hired" will fade, and "contract" will become the mainstream term. A "company" will become less of a place where people gather, and more a destination where people convene over the internet to work. I feel that the day is coming when people may leave the cities, even engaging in agriculture as they work and live.

Currently in the United States, it's estimated that over 30% of the working population are "telecommuters," utilizing the internet to realize a free working style unconstrained by place or time. I think this will become the norm in the near future.

My goal is an "independent society" in which each worker is a self-sufficient individual not dependent on a company or government, a society in which people and companies are linked in an equitable way. However, this is a society with which the majority of Japanese have little or no experience, and the social foundations not in place to support such a working style. This is why Pasona Group seeks to be a personnel department to Japan's corporate sector, playing a role as the platform that links people and work, and provides support for working people in both public and private matters.

Forging Bonds through One Pasona: The Pasona Family Club

Pasona Group decided to try something new in June this year. The inspiration came from a survey conducted of the temporary staff registered with Pasona Inc.

Many of these staff members live alone, and replied in the survey that their biggest anxiety is falling ill. From this we created the Pasona Family Club (PFC), a fringe benefit program for registered staff, regular employees, and their families. The platform is a web-based virtual community, Pasona Family Town. This "town" has hospitals, with "industrial physicians" who make house calls as necessary. There are people ready to lend their wisdom to others having difficulty with child-rearing or nursing care, as well as those willing to lend an actual hand. Specialists are available to give consultations to those with troubles. Members can also exchange information and chat with others who share their interests, participate in club activities, or enjoy sports or music together.

This new initiative is the basis of "One Pasona," the integration of a range of structures and services provided by Pasona Group companies, such as the employee fringe benefit service of Benefit One Inc., the child-care service of Pasona Foster Inc., and the household chores and care service of Pasona Sparkle Inc. Through this program we hope to provide support across public and private matters for everyone working within the Pasona Group. We hope to nurture the bonds of community that have been gradually lost in the world around us.

Everyone a Social Activist

If you look up the word "company" in the dictionary, you'll find the word "corporation person." This meaning of "company" is the legal entity recognized as similar to a person. I think a company must be more than just a corporation, an entity that merely earns profit and pays taxes. It must also be a consistently good corporate citizen, with a distinct responsibility in society.

People who speak out in society make changes and contribute to society, in order to make it better. They are called "social activists." It is my desire to make the Pasona Group such an assembly of people.

For over three decades, we have worked to realize a society where people can work without disparity in employment systems, corporate scale, industry or region. Over the coming decade, we will strive for a society in which each individual – regardless of age – gender or nationality, is given the opportunity to realize his/her dream. I envision a society in which all people are able to select from a wide range of options the job they like and the work style that suits them best. To realize this goal we will have to face new challenges with passion and a sense of mission, where everyone is a social activist.

Appendix

The Declaration for All Life on Earth

About the Declaration for All Life on Earth

The Declaration for All Life on Earth, launched by The Goi Peace Foundation, promotes a shared vision of a truly peaceful and harmonious world for all life in the 21st century. It sets forth guiding principles to realize this vision and encourages all people to apply them in their individual lives and in their specialized fields of activities. Our collective wisdom and joint efforts are vital to ensure a bright and sustainable future. The Declaration for All Life on Earth is intended to serve as an instrument in bringing together individuals and organizations committed to this common aim.

DECLARATION FOR ALL LIFE ON EARTH

Preamble

The earth is an evolving living entity. Every form of life on earth is an important part of this living entity. Accordingly, we, as individual human beings, must cultivate the awareness that we are all members of a global community of life and that we share a common mission and responsibility for the future of our planet.

Every one of us has a role to play in the evolution of our planet, and to achieve world peace each of us must live up to our responsibilities and obligations. Up to the present time, few people on earth have been fully satisfied with life. We have faced conflicts all over the world in competition for limited resources and land. This has had a devastating effect on the global environment.

As we enter the new millennium, more than anything else, the realization of world peace depends on an awakening of consciousness on the part of each individual member of the human race. Today, it is imperative that every human being bears the responsibility of building peace and harmony in his or her heart. We all have this common mission that we must fulfill. World peace will be achieved when every member of humanity becomes aware of this common mission—when we all join together for our common purpose.

Until now, in terms of power, wealth, fame, knowledge, technology and education,humanity has been divided between individuals, nations and organizations that have possession and those that do not. There have also been distinctions between the givers and the receivers, the helpers and the helped.

We hereby declare our commitment to transcend all these dualities and distinctions with a totally new concept, which will serve as our foundation as we set out to build a peaceful world.

General Principles

In the new era, humanity shall advance toward a world of harmony, that is, a world in which every individual and every nation can freely express their individual qualities, while living in harmony with one another and with all life on earth. To realize this vision, we set forth the following guiding principles:

1. **Reverence for life**
   We shall create a world based on love and harmony in which all forms of life are respected.

2. **Respect for all differences**
   We shall create a world in which all different races, ethnic groups, religions, cultures, traditions and customs are respected. The world must be a place free from discrimination or confrontation, socially, physically and spiritually—a place where diversity is appreciated and enjoyed.

3. **Gratitude for and coexistence with all of nature**
   We shall create a world in which each person is aware that we are enabled to live through the blessings of nature, and lives in harmony with nature, showing gratitude for all animal, plant and other forms of life.

4. **Harmony between the spiritual and material**
   We shall create a world based on the harmonious balance of material and spiritual civilization. We must break away from our overemphasis on the material to allow a healthy spirituality to blossom among humanity. We must build a world where not only material abundance but also spiritual riches are valued.

Practice

We shall put these principles into practice guided by the following:

As individuals:

We must move beyond an era in which authority and responsibility rest in nation states, ethnic groups and religions to one in which the individual is paramount. We envision an "Age of the Individual"—not in the sense of egoism, but an age in which every individual is ready to accept responsibility and to carry out his or her mission as an independent member of the human race.

Each of us shall carry out our greatest mission to bring love, harmony and gratitude into our own heart, and in so doing, bring harmony to the world at large.

In our specialized fields:

We shall build a system of cooperation in which wisdom is gathered together to derive the most from technical knowledge, skills and ability in various fields, such as education, science, culture and the arts, as well as religion, philosophy, politics and economics.

As the young generation:

In the 20th century, parents, teachers and society were the educators of children, and the children were always in the position of being taught. In the 21st century, adults shall learn from the wonderful qualities of children, such as their purity, innocence, radiance, wisdom and intuition, to inspire and uplift one another. The young generation shall play a leading role in the creation of peace for a bright future.

May Peace Prevail on Earth

Contributors

Babos, Paola—is an Associate Expert with the United Nations in the Leadership and Capacity Development Unit of UN-OHRLLS. Focusing on the Least Developed Countries, Ms. Babos works with a range of stakeholders applying whole systems transformation and leadership development to achieve measurable and sustainable change in the domains of peace and development. Prior to joining the United Nations in New York City, Ms. Babos worked in the Balkans and other transition economies. She served in field positions in Serbia and Kosovo, focusing on post-conflict dialogue and reconciliation between Serb, Albanian and Roma communities in the aftermath of the Yugoslav wars. Ms. Babos holds a Bachelor of Science in Government and Economics from the London School of Economics and a Masters in International Relations from the University of Chicago. http://www.un.org/ohrlls

Brown, Lester R.—is Founder and President of the Earth Policy Institute, which purpose is to provide a vision of an environmentally sustainable economy and a roadmap of how to get from here to there. He has also founded the Worldwatch Institute in Washington D.C. in 1974 and launched the State of the World reports in 1984. Dr. Brown is the author or co-author of over 50 books on global environmental issues and his works have been translated into more than forty languages. His most recent book is *Plan B 3.0: Mobilizing to Save Civilization.* The recipient of 40 honorary degrees and a McArthur Fellowship, Dr. Brown has been described by the Washington Post as "one of the world's most influential thinker." Dr. Brown was recently awarded the Presidential Medal of Italy and was appointed an honorary professor at the Chinese Academy of Sciences. Dr. Brown is recipient of The Goi Peace Award 2005. He has an M.S. in agricultural economics from the University of Maryland—and an M.P.A. from Harvard University. Born in 1934, Lester Brown lives in Washington D.C. http://www.earth-policy.org

Dunne, Jacqui—is an Award-Winning Journalist from Ireland and a respected Communications Specialist with 25 years of professional experience. Her areas of expertise include radio and television production, corporate communications and public relations. Ms. Dunne is also Co-Founder and Executive Director of the ACCESS Foundation, an international non-profit organization dedicated to education, implementation, standards and best practices in the domain of complementary currencies. She is also the Founder of Entrepreneurs Without Borders, which mandate consists in improving economic development, especially in developing countries by using a variety of new monetary innovations and duel-currency systems. Ms. Dunne is Executive Editor of two books on money, *Of Human Wealth—New Money* for a *New World* by Bernard Lietaer and Stephen Belgin, and an international cross-discipline report to the Club of Rome entitled, *Money and Sustainability—The Missing Link.* http://www.citerrafilm.com

Faltin, Guenter—is a German Economist and Entrepreneur. He is Professor of Entrepreneurship at Freie Universitaet Berlin, and Founder of "Teekampagne," the largest mail order tea business in Germany. According to the Tea Board of India, "Teekampagne" has been the world's largest single importer of Darjeeling leaf tea since 1998. Noticing many years ago that tea was sold at shockingly high prices, Professor Faltin looked for ways to challenge the traditional tea market. Thus, he created a new business model based on the principle of simplicity, which allows selling the world's best Darjeeling tea at very low prices and therewith making it affordable to many people. Professor Faltin teaches the principle of simplicity in business to students at Freie Universitaet Berlin and encourage them to become entrepreneurs themselves. He has published many papers and books on a culture of innovative entrepreneurship. His latest publication is entitled, *Kopf schlaegt Kapital. Die ganz andere Art, ein Unternehmen zu gruenden. Von der Lust, ein Entrepreneur zu sein* (2008). In 2007, Professor Faltin has received the "Vision Award for Entrepreneurship" at the Vision Summit taking place in Berlin in 2007. http://www.entrepreneurship.de

Ganser, Daniele—Ph.D., is a Swiss Historian who specializes in international relations and international history from 1945 to today. His research interests are peace research, geostrategy, secret warfare, resource wars, globalization and human rights. Dr. Ganser teaches at Swiss universities, including the History Department at Basel University. His current research is focusing on the so called "war on terror" and peak oil (www.peakoil.ch). From 2001 to 2003 Daniele Ganser was a Senior Researcher with the Think Tank Avenir Suisse in Zurich. He was responsible for international relations and led the campaign of the Think Tank, which influenced the national vote that made Switzerland a full member of the United Nations in 2003. Avenir Suisse is funded by 14 largest international companies of Switzerland, including Swiss Re, ABB, Novartis, Roche, UBS, Credit Suisse and Nestlé, and has the general task to prepare Switzerland and its economy for the challenges of the future. From 2003 to 2006 Dr. Ganser was a Senior Researcher at the Center for Security Studies at the Swiss Federal Institute of Technology (EHT) in Zurich. In cooperation with the Swiss Foreign Ministry—the Federal Department of Foreign Affairs (DFA)—he investigated the impact of globalization on war and peace and made researches on how Swiss and international companies support and profit from war, or alternatively, promote peace through corporate social responsibility (CSR). Dr. Ganser speaks four languages. He is married and has two children. Dr. Ganser lives in Basel, Switzerland. http://www.danieleganser.ch/

Gates, Bill—is the Co-Chair of the Bill and Melinda Gates Foundation, which works on global health and education issues. Born in 1955 in Seattle, Wash., USA, Mr. Gates founded Microsoft Corporation in 1975 and led the company to become the worldwide leader in business and personal computer software, services, and solutions. In late June 2008, Bill Gates transitioned out of his day-to-day role at Microsoft to dedicate his full time to his philanthropic work at the Bill and Melinda Gates Foundation. Under the Gateses' leadership, the Foundation's grantmaking is now organized into three programs—Global Development, Global Health and United States. As of 1 April 2009, the Bill and Melinda Gates Foundation has made USD 19,8 billion in total grant commitments since its inception in 1994, and has an endowment of USD 27,5 billion. The Foundation is currently operating in more than 100 countries. Bill Gates is recipient of the Goi Peace Award 2008. http://www.gatesfoundation.org

Gottwald, Franz-Theo—is the Executive Director of the Schweisfurth Foundation in Munich, Germany. He is Honorary Professor for Environmental-, Agrarian- and Nutritional Ethics at Humbold University in Berlin, Guest Professor for Sustainable Value Managements at the Shanghai Academy for Social Sciences, and teaches Political Ecology at the Munich School of Political Science. Prof. Gottwald is also Managing Director of the European Network for Ecological Agriculture, and Curator of various ecological institutions and foundations. He studied social sciences and indology, graduated in catholic theology, and earned his Ph.D. (Dr. phil.) in philosophy. He published various books and reports on corporate leadership and management, philosophy, agrarian culture, awareness-building, and future science. Born in 1955 in Wiesbaden, Germany, Prof. Gottwald is married and has five children. http://www.schweisfurth.de

Henderson, Hazel—Ph.D., is an Independent Futurist, Syndicated Columnist, and Consultant on sustainable development in over thirty countries. She is the Founder of Ethical Markets Media, an independent media company covering the emergence of a sustainable, green, more ethical and just economy worldwide. Her editorial columns are syndicated by InterPress Services worldwide. Dr. Henderson serves on the advisory boards of many organizations, including the Calvert Social Investment Fund, the Cousteau Society, the Council on Economic Priorities, and the Worldwatch Institute. She served on the World Business Council for Sustainable Development Task Force on Eco-Efficiency in Global Capital Markets (Geneva) and is a fellow of the World Business Academy. Dr. Henderson also serves on the Global Commission to Fund the United Nations and co-edited its first report as a special issue of Futures, "The United Nations at Fifty: Policy and Financing Alternatives." Hazel Henderson has authored several books, including *Ethical Markets—Growing the Green Economy* (2007), *Building a Win-Win World* (1996), *Creating Alternative Futures* (1978,1996), *The Politics of the Solar Age* (1981, 1988), and *Paradigms in Progress* (1995). http://www.hazelhenderson.com and http://www.ethicalmarkets.com

Hoelz, Hanns Michael—is Managing Director at the Deutsche Bank AG. As Global Head he is responsible for the fields of corporate citizenship (co-head of Corporate Social Responsibility), sustainable development (group inspector fort he sustainable management system) and sport. Mr. Hoelz is a member of executive boards of a large number of organizations of Deutsche Bank, e.g. the Deutsche Bank Americas Foundation and the Deutsche Bank Africa Foundation. His area of responsibility also covers the representation of Deutsche Bank in national and international committees, including UN Global Compact (member of the former Advisory Council of Kofi Annan), Global Reporting Initiative (member of the executive board) and World Business Council for Sustainable Development (member of the executive board). Furthermore, Mr. Hoelz is a member of the board of trustees of the Stiftung Deutsche Sporthilfe and the German National Anti-Doping Agency. For 15 years now, he has played an important part in shaping the corporate citizenship of Deutsche Bank, and in the past ten years, Mr. Hoelz has placed his focus on promoting the idea of sustainable activities—inside as well as outside the Bank. Mr. Hoelz is committed not only to changing paradigms in thinking in favour of sustainable development, but also to initiating the necessary measures as well as their implementation. Born in 1951, Mr. Hoelz is married and has two children. http://www.deutsche-bank.de

Leitschuh-Fecht, Heike—is Author, Moderator and Consultant for sustainable development. Since 2001, she is Co-Publisher of *Jahrbuch Oekologie,* as well as Publisher of a variety of books, brochures, and articles in journals and German newspapers, such as *Frankfurter Allgemeine Zeitung* (FAZ), *Frankfurter Rundschau, Die Zeit,* and *Oeko-Test.* Ms. Leitschuh-Fecht moderates Local Agenda processes in municipalities. Born in 1958, she has a Master Degree in political science and lives in Frankfurt/Main, Germany. http://www.heike-leitschuh.de and http://www.weleda.com

McFalls, Ricarda—is Managing Director, Development Focus Area, at the World Business Council for Sustainable Development. Previously, Ms. McFalls worked more than 22 years in various international management positions in the global high tech industry, predominantly in business development in transition and emerging economies. While resident in Africa from 1994 to 2007, Ms. McFalls established manufacturing, sales, and service companies in Kenya and Nigeria, built regional distribution networks, and actively engaged with local governments on technology policies. Serving nine years on the board and as elected Chairman of the American Chamber of Commerce in Kenya, she promoted community initiatives to improve the local and regional business environment. Ms. McFalls holds a Masters in Sustainable Development Planning from Stellenbosch University (South Africa), an MBA from the Thunderbird Graduate School of Global Management (USA), and bachelor degrees from the University of California at Santa Barbara. Her recent case study research on inclusive business in South Africa, "Testing the Limits of Inclusive Capitalism" is published by the *Journal of Corporate Citizenship.* http://www.wbcsd.org

Metcalfe, Steve—is Communications Manager at The Prince's Youth Business International (YBI), a network organization for 37 youth business programmes around the world that help young people to start up in business. Mr. Metcalfe is responsible for developing the organization's communication strategy and raising the profile of YBI and the YBI Network. Prior to his assignment at the Prince's Youth Business International, Mr. Metcalfe was the New Media Manager at the International Business Leaders Forum (IBLF) in London, in charge of all digital communications, e-news-letters and media work. Prior to joining IBLF, he was a business journalist on a range of publications—most recently for Mergermarket (now part of the Financial Times Group). Mr. Metcalfe has a degree in English from Leicester University in the United Kingdom. http://www.iblf.org and http://www.youth-business.org

Nambu, Yasuyuki—is the Group CEO of Pasona Group Inc. and President of Pasona Inc. Pasona Inc. is a multinational corporation headquartered in Japan, that provides a variety of staffing services, including temporary staffing, and recruiting in Japan and overseas. Harvesting the potential of the individual is the foundation of Pasona's human resources service. The philosophy and policy of Mr. Nambu and of his company consist in creating a society in which inviduals are able to find work that they like and a career that complements their personal goals, and in which people are free to exercise their talents through an egalitarian relationship between the workplace and the individual, regardless of age or gender. By changing the way people are working in Japan, Mr. Nambu has been named "Entrepreneur of the Year" in 1987, 1988, and 1989. Born in Kobe, Japan in 1952, Mr. Nambu has authored 12 books and numerous articles on business practices and workforce trends. Mr. Nambu revolutionized the way people work in Japan and abroad by giving jobs to many, who without Mr. Nambu's visionary leadership would be unemployed. http://www.pasonagroup.co.jp

Nelson, Deborah—is the Executive Director of Social Venture Network (SVN), a national organization of business leaders, investors and social entrepreneurs who are committed to transforming the way the world does business. Before joining SVN, Deborah Nelson was Marketing Director for Working Assets and Western Region Marketing Director for American Express. Ms. Nelson has a B.A. in English from Northwestern University and an M.B.A. in marketing and management strategy from the Kellogg Graduate School of Management. She co-founded the Social Impact Leadership Coalition (SILC), a network of organizations that promote socially responsible business practices and economic justice initiatives. Deborah Nelson served as a Peace Corps volunteer in Cameroon from 1987 to 1989. When she's not at SVN, Deborah Nelson enjoys exploring the Bay Area with her husband Nick and her two sons Sam and Will. http://www.svn.org

Petit, Patrick U.—is a Mediator (M.M.) and Start-Up-Counsellor. Graduated in political science from the Munich School of Political Science, he is the Representative to the United Nations of The Goi Peace Foundation. In this capacity, Mr. Petit initiated and set up more than thirty peacemaking events worldwide in collaboration with regional and global Intergovernmental Organizations, as well as Parliaments, Parliamentary Assemblies and Civil Society organizations. He produced two commemorative events on United Nations Day in 1999 and the consecutive year, while he has been the Representative to the United Nations of the World Peace Prayer Society in New York. Mr. Petit arranged and moderated the cultural festivities of the Millennium Forum in 2000 at UN Headquarters. He is the initiator and editor of several publications: *Earth Capitalism* (2009), *The People's New Deal* (2009), *Earthrise* (2008) and *Wisdom 21: Shaping the Culture of Peace in a Multilateral World* (2005). Born in 1969 in France, Mr. Petit lives in Munich, Germany. http://www.goipeace.or.jp

Radermacher, Franz Josef—is the Co-Founder and Chairman of the Board of Trustees of the Global Marshall Plan Initiative, and President of the German Federal Association for Economic Development and Foreign Trade (BWA). Prof. Radermacher is also the Director of the Research Institute for Applied Knowledge Processing/n (FAW/n) in Ulm,—which deals with basic issues of globalization and sustainable development –, and is the Academic Chairholder for Information Technology at the University of Ulm. He is the Vice-President of the Eco-Social Forum Europe, and a Member of the Club of Rome since 2002. From 1992–2001, Prof. Radermacher has been a Member of the European Commission's Information Society Forum and has chaired the EC Working Group 4 "Sustainability in an Information Society." Since 2000, he is a Member of the Scientific Council of the German Federal Ministry of Transportation, Civil Engineering and Housing. He is also a Member of the Council for Sustainable Development of the Government of the German State of Baden Wuerttemberg. Prof. Radermacher is the author of more than 300 publications and scientific papers and reports on information society, globalization and sustainability issues, like *Global Impact—Der neue Weg zu globaler Verantwortung* (together with Marianne Obermueller and Peter Spiegel); *Globalisierung Gestalten* and *Welt mit Zukunft—Ueberleben im 21. Jahrhundert* (in collaboration with Bert Beyers). Holder of two PhDs in mathematics (1974) and economics (1976), he earned his postdoctoral Habilitation in mathematics in 1982. Prof. Radermacher is married and has one son. http://www.globalmarshallplan.org and http://www.faw-neu-ulm.de

Roof, Nancy B.—Ph.D., is the Founder and Editor-in-Chief of the integral global journal *Kosmos*, nominated for its excellence and spiritual coverage by the prestigious Utne Independent Press Awards. Kosmos brings leading edge ideas to United Nations Ambassadors, the UN Secretariat, NGOs and the international community of global citizens. Its unique mission is to create a sustainable, compassionate and emerging global civilization through individual, cultural, and systems transformation at all levels of body, mind, and spirit. Dr. Roof is Founding President of Kosmos Associates Inc. She co-founded the Values Caucus at the United Nations in 1994 with the help of Ambassador Somavia of Chile (now Director General of the UN International Labor Organization) and co-founded the Spiritual Caucus at the UN in 2000 for the purpose of bringing contemplation into UN deliberations. Kosmos is a founding partner of the worldwide initiative, 'Creating a New Civilization', launched by The Goi Peace Foundation in Tokyo, November 2005 with the Gorbachev Foundation, Club of Budapest, Club of Rome, Commission on Global Spirituality and Consciousness and World Wisdom Council. She is the first Media Ambassador invited to participate in the World Wisdom Council. Dr. Roof designed, implemented, and pioneered the first training programs in the former Yugoslavia on secondary traumatic stress in war zones. The program trained trainers of 78 organizations, including the United Nations, International Red Cross, governments, Doctors Without Borders, and local groups in three different locations. The program is now being used as a model in other War Zones. She published a widely distributed workbook for further self-training entitled *The Impact of War on Humanitarian Service Providers*. In the early 1970s she co-founded The Mountain School, to teach meditation and interior spiritual practices from a variety of religious traditions. Dr. Roof had a flourishing private practice in individual in-depth psychology based on the psychology she developed combining Western psychology and Eastern spiritual practices. http://www.kosmosjournal.org

Saionji, Hiroo—is the President of The Goi Peace Foundation and its sister organization, The World Peace Prayer Society, a New York based Non-Governmental Organization associated with the Department of Public Information at the United Nations. Mr. Saionji is the great-grandson of Prince Kinmochi Saionji, who was twice Prime Minister of Japan during the Meiji Period. He is President of The Crescent, and a Member of the Alumni Association Board of Directors of Michigan State University, where he earned a Master of Business Administration (MBA). Mr. Saionji is also a Member of the Board of Trustees of Gakushuin University. From 1974–1986, he was a business executive at the International Division of the Nippon Seiko Company. Mr. Saionji conceived the "Creating a New Civilization Initiative," which was launched by The Goi Peace Foundation, in collaboration with thirteen like-minded partner organizations on the occasion of the annual Goi Peace Forum in November 2005 in Tokyo. He travels extensively on speaking tours, and has led peace ceremonies in many countries as well as at the United Nations and other international organizations. Mr. Saionji and his wife, Masami Saionji, have received the Philosopher Shree Dnyaneshwara World Peace Prize, India in 2008. Both live in Tokyo and have three daughters. http://www.goipeace.or.jp and http://www. worldpeace.org

Sharma, Monica—M.D., is the Director, Leadership and Capacity Development, at the United Nations, OHRLLS in New York. Dr. Sharma is responsible for whole systems transformation and leadership development worldwide, with a focus on Least Developed Countries. She is pioneering generative and integral approaches leading to transformation on a global scale. She served in UNICEF in several global, regional and country positions that are meeting the needs of children worldwide. From 2000–2005 Dr. Sharma served as Director of HIV/AIDS for UNDP, generating 4.5 million people directly and influencing another 130 million people. In 2005 she and her team were honoured by UNDP for the best practice area. http://www.un.org/ohrlls

Tasaka, Hiroshi—is the Founder and the President of Think Tank SophiaBank, a global network think tank that fosters social entrepreneurs to change paradigms of social systems. He is also the President of The Japan Social Entrepreneur Forum (JSEF), a networking organization to promote collaborations among social entrepreneurs in Japan. Dr. Tasaka is a Professor at the Graduate School of Tama University in Tokyo, where he teaches the philosophy, vision, policy, strategy and skills of social entrepreneurs to create new social systems. He has worked as a member of the Global Agenda Council of the World Economic Forum since 2008. He has also worked as an advisor for various companies to support them to become social enterprises. Dr. Tasaka is a founding member of The Japan Research Institute. The Institute embraces the vision and strategy of "Industry Incubation," which aims to create new industries with private sector initiatives. As a member of the Board of Directors, he collaborated with over 700 companies to establish 20 consortia from 1990 to 2000. Born in 1951, Dr. Tasaka graduated from the University of Tokyo in 1974. In 1981, he earned a Ph.D. in nuclear engineering from Tokyo University. Dr. Tasaka is the author of more than 50 books, including, *To the Summit—Why Should You Embrace an Ideal in Your Heart; The Five Laws to Foresee the Future; The Age of Living System Paradigm; The Gaia Perspective; What will Happen in the Knowledge Society;* and *Philosophy of Working.* http://www.sophiabank.co.jp or send email to tasaka@sophiabank.co.jp

Wackernagel, Mathis—Ph.D., is a Founder and Executive Director of Global Footprint Network, a charitable research organization with headquarters in California. This organization supports the creation of a sustainable economy by advancing the policy-utility of the Ecological Footprint. The goal is to make ecological limits central to decision-making everywhere. Dr. Wackernagel has lectured at over 100 universities and worked on sustainability issues for organizations on all continents. He has authored or contributed to over fifty peer-reviewed papers, numerous articles and reports, and various books on sustainability that focus on the question of embracing limits and developing metrics for sustainability, including *Our Ecological Footprint: Reducing Human Impact on the Earth, Sharing Nature's Interest,* and WWF International's *Living Planet Report.* After earning a degree in mechanical engineering from the Swiss Federal Institute of Technology, he completed his Ph.D. in community and regional planning at The University of British Columbia in Vancouver, Canada. There he created, as his doctoral dissertation, with Professor William Rees the "Ecological Footprint" concept, now a widely used sustainability measure. Dr. Wackernagel is also an adjunct faculty at SAGE of the University of Wisconsin-Madison, and scientific advisor of the Center for Sustainability Studies in Mexico. http://www.footprintnetwork.org

Warwick, Mal—has distinguished himself through his contributions to the nonprofit sector as one of the world's leading authors, consultants, and public speakers on fundraising for nonprofit organizations and as an advocate for socially and environmentally responsible policies and practices in the private sector. A serial entrepreneur, Mr. Warwick has been active in promoting social and environmental responsibility in the business community nationwide for more than 15 years. Along with Cohen and others, he was a co-founder of Business for Social Responsibility and served on its board during its inaugural year. In 2001, after more than a decade as an active member of Social Venture Network, he was elected to its board and served as Chair (2002–2006). He also was a member of the Founding Advisory Board of the Center for Responsible Business at the Haas School of Business at the University of California, Berkeley, in 2002-2003. Mr. Warwick is the Founder and Chairman of Mal Warwick Associates (Berkeley, Calif., and Washington, D.C.), a fundraising agency specializing in direct marketing. The company has served nonprofit organizations since 1979. He also founded its sister company, Response Management Technologies, Inc., a data processing firm for nonprofit organizations, and was a Co-Founder of the telephone fundraising firm, Share Group, Inc. (Somerville, Mass.). In 1999, he co-founded Donordigital (San Francisco, Calif.), which assists nonprofit organizations with online fundraising, marketing, and advocacy. Mr. Warwick and his associates are responsible for raising at least half a billion dollars—largely in the form of small gifts from individuals. He is also an active member of the Association of Fundraising Professionals (Alexandria, Va.) and served for ten years on the board of the Association of Direct Response Fundraising Counsel (Washington, D.C.), two of those years as President. In 2004, he received the Hank Rosso Award as Outstanding Fundraising Executive from the Association of Fundraising Professionals Golden Gate Chapter and Northern California Grantmakers. In November 2006, Mr. Warwick was awarded the Benjamin Ide Wheeler Medal by the Berkeley Community Fund as "Berkeley's most useful citizen" in recognition of his lifetime contributions to the community. Mal Warwick is the author of *Fundraising When Money Is Tight.* He is the co-author of *Values-Driven Business: How to Change the World, Make Money, and Have Fun* with Ben Cohen, Co-Founder of Ben & Jerry's. http://www.malwarwick.com and http://www.svn.org

For Product Safety Concerns and Information please contact our EU representative GPSR@taylorandfrancis.com
Taylor & Francis Verlag GmbH, Kaufingerstraße 24, 80331 München, Germany

www.ingramcontent.com/pod-product-compliance
Lightning Source LLC
LaVergne TN
LVHW011126300926
849160LV00008B/527

9781412811064

Piano Lesson

Imagine you're holding an egg, like this,
and curve each hand over the keys—take care
to keep it as perfectly egg-shaped as
the notes on the sheet: this fist-sized space where

the promise of music, or something close
to silence is given shape, suspended on
wires strung fine, like held breath, what goes
beyond language or measure, all else gone

but yearning, sheer-winged and lovely, no longer
recognizable as yours and more
your own for it. Even the flat and wrong
notes are precious in your cupped palms—before

you crush them when your father, out of love
for Bach and Mozart, declares: *That's enough.*

Half Moon

A half moon rises instead of the sun.
Of the first winter I remember the rain
falling day after day, the cold seeping through stone,
settling in so it was chillier inside than out.
Hour after hour it came down hard as rocks,
beating pine needles, asphalt, paving stones, skin.
Under layers of wool my unaccustomed bones ached,
rang out like old metal pipes.
We warmed ourselves with the thought of
spring, which everyone promised would be lovely.
Spring came, and it was lovely. Or so we all said:
a frenzy of geraniums, cyclamens, bougainvilleas, fuchsias,
in every hot shade of pink and red, as though contagious.
Inside, the tiles were cool to the touch.
Spring came, then war, then rain again.

In the ashen light of desertion
a half moon rises instead of the sun.
Between the small, uninhabited hours I'd fallen into
an airless, ragged sleep.
I no longer know what color spring is.
This year I am told there is no rain.
Instead, forest fires rage for weeks and
tear gas blooms along the fenced-in desert
like a new perennial, wild.

Dictionary

Of all that went missing
from the boxes I'd packed alone, it is
the broken-spined dictionary that I regret—
of a language I expect never to speak again,
of a life attempted together,
each learning separate vocabularies:
the blare of headlines, on- and off-the-record statements,
rattling lines of cars at checkpoints, the crunch of glass—
every utterance a question; and
January rains singing against stone,
laundry whipping in the wind,
the borrowed music of catcalls and sirens—
every encounter a questioning.
A language in which the verb *to be*
does not exist in the present tense.

Excused, I talk to myself
in half-sentences, all my conjugations
unreliable. Trying not to confuse the present
with the infinitive, I repeat the small consolations of
what I once knew to say, what I might say now
in the conditional past, for the future tense is
always the most difficult.
Yet this, too, is part of the lesson: forgetting
the word for *winter*, mistaking *to decide* for
to begin, is to see that every new venture risks
misinterpretation. Our shared grammar,
both fraught and laughable, is nonetheless
an education in riches, hard-earned, unfurled in
the finely pocked skin of a pomelo fruit,
tea sweetened with cinnamon and sage,
sky-blue tiles against the evil eye.

To Know Where

Considering how those who know
handle you as if breakable, speaking softly,
avoiding the subject altogether, as if
the mere mention could shatter you,
and how those who don't know
ask sunny questions and then stare,
scanning for what they'd missed all these years,
cross-checking you against memory—
you *do* begin to feel as though made of glass:
not brittle but transparent, exposed, like
an X-ray emerging against artificial darkness,
each small bone finely ground to luminescence,
hard, granular points bleached of shadow,
a specimen of clarity.

For perhaps clarity is what is most needed:
to know where the sharp edges are—
fissures, fault lines, what remains
to be broken.
To know where a thing ends and another begins.

But you do not recognize yourself within these
stark lines; what you want to be is
a piece of green sea glass, worn round and smooth,
refracting light at funny angles.

Water

At the temple tourists are setting up their tripods.
In every cemetery the *higan-bana* are in bloom again,
the scarlet spider lilies signaling autumn:
Higan means *equinox*; also *the other side*.

Across the grounds it is hushed at the Jizo-do.
A thousand knee-high Bodhisattva Jizo stand in neat rows
like miniature schoolchildren, watching over the souls of
the stillborn, the miscarried, the aborted.
They are all *mizuko*, meaning *water children*,
washed away, cleansed.
The statues' simple features are identical,
sexless, indifferent in the traditional red bibs
women have dressed some in, leaving gifts of
brightly wrapped sweets and plastic toys—
not chrysanthemums as for the other dead—
seeking to appease them as they would
living children.
Water ripples soundlessly over flat, polished stones,
smoothing them over and over.

There is no forgetting here, only quiet:
We have crossed over to a different region of ourselves,
forever watchful, attentive to the slightest betrayal,
a season without end.

Translation

My Mother's Day card arrives late again this year.
As usual, she sighs long-distance.
I'd miscalculated again, hoping this once
there'd still be time.
I'd chosen a funny card, so unlike either of us:
You drove me all over town and I drove you
up the wall—let's call it even.
For I'd wanted to remind her of how,
checking the rearview mirror, she'd tell me
to lie down if I felt carsick, so that
even now I fall asleep in any moving vehicle.
But she says only:
Next time, a translation.

What flimsy store-bought sentiments,
air-mailed last-minute, translate into is this:
She taught me to spell my name in two alphabets,
gave me *Anne of Green Gables* and later *Jane Eyre*,
drove me to the library and the pool all summer.
And this is how far we have come
apart in different places now.
And into what words can I translate
myself, ask forgiveness for misreading
our trajectories, the time it takes to navigate
bodies of water and deserts unmentioned,
for still expecting her to ferry me across?
For failing the mother tongue of unsaid solaces,
a language in which she's long forgotten
how she'd tell me to close my eyes,
that I'd feel better then, that
we were almost there.

Walking the Ramparts

Do you remember walking the ramparts
of the Old City, the day breezy, a little overcast like
this one, a little raw, the edges green.
There was no one else up there but a skittish cat
the length of the wall from Jaffa Gate, not even soldiers.
From the windows of the boys' school
voices rose and fell in unison, from below
the angry traffic, more distant than expected.
From these windblown heights we could see
the crowded rooftops, clotheslines, satellite dishes,
and into people's courtyards, the lemon trees and potted palms,
electric-hued bougainvillea climbing terraces,
the broken appliances:
what we imagined might or might not be
another's happiness within. Or anyone's.
We'd paid the admission fee
to walk the raised perimeters of what was worth
erecting walls around, stone by stone, even though
they could be knocked down, and will.
Beyond Herod's Gate we stopped to watch three boys
passing a half-deflated ball across a muddy lot,
jaws set, almost grim, as if all the remaining light
depended on it.
It had stopped raining three and a half weeks before,
though the sky hung low over the walls like a shroud.
It was the end of spring.

Taking Your Shoes Off

In Japan, when jumping
off a bridge or tall building, not expecting
to return, it is customary to take off
one's shoes, as when entering any other
private dwelling, a school or shrine, so as
not to track in the dirt you've collected,
carried so far, only no one will bring you
slippers this time. Always point your shoes
in the direction you'll be headed in
when you put them on again, toward
the door but only if you are leaving.
There is no need otherwise
for ghosts here have no feet.
On a sharp cliff off the Pacific known as
the Cape of Grief or of Writhing Feet
pairs of shoes are found each spring
like misshapen crocuses unable to survive
through April. Every time I see
a single worn sneaker limp by the curb or
work boots unclaimed against a lamppost
down Sixth Avenue, I hear doors opening ahead of me
on the sidewalk, on every unlit street and fire escape,
each one an exit accidental or not, these
hundreds of exits opening onto nothing but air.

Foreground

It is not immediately apparent.
You have to look for it past the sun-stippled surface
in the foreground—the shallows so clear
you don't even see the water at first—and in
the slightest variation of light bending:
a tailfin's flicker, an after-shadow.

How cold the water was,
not the damp cold of the campsite, where
our clothes smelled of wood smoke but never dried,
not the chill of tight-lipped stares in roadside diners,
but the cleansing, metallic flash of clarity beneath my skin:
about what we were doing there together,
in unfamiliar greenery, driving across another
lush or blighted summer, following unkept trails—
tourists of our own discontent.
That morning I'd wept at the campsite sink
at the yellowjackets bright in the warped mirror.

Even though I knew we had farther to go,
even though I would ride again in the passenger seat
gripping the door handle, I understood even then,
in the silver angle of the lake widening out
along steep granite rising on either side, that
this was the past, that we were already remembering
ourselves younger, in the foreground,
no longer there.

Les Alyscamps

The light on the Roman burial grounds is the color of
old lace, worn soft, filtered through plane trees, October.
Van Gogh and Gauguin came here to paint,
their hues lively, breathing, like nothing else left.
The grainy quiet of
a crowded Via Aurelia lined with sarcophagi
carries a low hum, or maybe it is only the so-called
canal running hidden alongside.

The chalk white of fine-petaled flowers,
a kind of ringing in the luster of their carved edges,
ricochets off the bleached white shirts of men high up
on scaffolds, washing down the façade of a ruined chapel.
The small stone faces, some sprouting wings,
gape open-mouthed.

Toward the far end, the somewhat orderly procession
dissolves—or rather, assembles—into a tumble of
pocked surfaces, chipped corners, alphabets strewn together
at all fallen angles, overflowing the shaded churchyard
teeming with cats.
The rotting side door opens into a dimness
speckled with dust and the dull roar of a hundred wings:
startled pigeons resettling along a ledge high above.
A round window like an orphan moon
draws a faint sheen of silver over the filthy floor,
as if the light, too, were millennia-old.
No altar, no pews, only three Carolingian tombs and
the arched silence thick as the walls,
lined with mite-filled feathers, yellow claws, eyes.

But already it is a quarter to noon;
the caretaker comes to call out, *Closing time,*
patting centuries of dust off his overalls.
In the doorway, half in, half out, I try to take in
the pale disc of light, its shimmering note.
Just one minute, then I'll be gone.
He says, not unkindly, to come back after lunch,
when there'll be more time. Then
I am ushered out into the now blinding *éclat* of day,
down the path emptying of stragglers,
out of the Alyscamps and into the world of the living,
where lunch must be served on time.
Behind me the heavy iron gate clangs shut.

Corot, in the Evening

1.
I'd hoped to see you alone, maître, in
autumn's early fading light, but instead
already the harsh museum lighting
flattens your tones: green-silver, rose-grey, lead-

blue. I'll wait for the shadows that have fled.
At least these rooms are quiet, just one or
two figures, as in *Ville d'Avray*. You'd said,
One point of luminosity, no more.

I'll sit with *Lady in Blue* like before.
Tell me again about seeing, about
the Roman glass you sent your sweetheart, for
I'm beginning to see the world without,

to *paint the shadows first,* though it's taken
twenty years. Tell me how it arrived broken.

2.
My first visit to the Louvre was such
a contrast: a wide-eyed, heartsick student-
pilgrim, I yearned to get closer, to touch
the realm of great art, to know what it meant.

Jostled by pickpocket crowds, discontent
with books, newspapers, street protests, I sought,
in a world no longer sufficient,
to be transformed into being, to be taught

to live truthfully. In my overwrought
logic, I knew passion because I bled,
hungered for what I couldn't name, thought
only of torn flags, ruins, Medusa's head.

When I recognized your woods, I nearly wept
for a promise never made but kept.

3.

I was ten when I first saw these shades
of cloud and river's edge and birch trees' bone-
white mesmerizing, the poker-faced
cows, the way the unfamiliar light shone

through my first exhibit: What seeds were sown
by one who strove to see *like a child*?
That there's letting go in beauty, that we own
nothing: the water's bruised reflection, wild

grasses, slant of rain-washed walls. Beguiled
by such a wealth of hues, I'd needed no other.
The clarity of what's beyond us. Exiled,
you must have known she'd marry another

while you learned your *métier* in Rome,
then apprenticed yourself to living alone.

Drifts

The first storm of the season blows all day,
dimming the traffic lights, erasing the sky.
Snow comes down, across, in every direction,
drifting wave-shaped up my window screens.
As if to cancel out
the stark silhouettes of branches and fire escapes
serrated against the white afternoon,
now the evening brightens, snowlit, like
a black-and-white photograph overexposed.
I could press all night against the icy glass
as it blots itself out little by little,
listening to the fading hysteria of spinning tires,
the clanging *scrape, scrape* against the sidewalk,
watching my reflected double disappear,
the way even one's own handwriting
becomes illegible in the failing light.

Selected by Robert A. Fink, *Elsewhere* is the twenty-first winner of the Walt McDonald First-Book Competition in Poetry. The competition is supported generously through donated subscriptions from *The American Scholar, The Atlantic Monthly, The Georgia Review, Gulf Coast, The Hudson Review, The Massachusetts Review, Poetry, Shenandoah,* and *The Southern Review.*

About the Author

Kyoko Uchida has published poetry, prose, and translations in *The Georgia Review, The Black Warrior Review, Grand Street, Manoa, New Letters, The Northwest Review, Painted Pride Quarterly, Prairie Schooner, Runes, The Virginia Quarterly Review,* and other literary journals. Her work also has been anthologized in *Stories in the Stepmother Tongue* (White Pine Press, 2000) and *An Ear to the Ground: Presenting Writers from 2 Coasts* (Cune Press, 1997). Born in Hiroshima, she spent her childhood moving back and forth between Japan, the United States, and Canada. She holds an MFA in Poetry from Cornell University, lives in Brooklyn, New York, and works for a nonprofit organization.